BARGAINING WITH A RISING INDIA

Bargaining with a Rising India

Lessons from the Mahabharata

BY
AMRITA NARLIKAR
ARUNA NARLIKAR

OXFORD
UNIVERSITY PRESS

Great Clarendon Street, Oxford, OX2 6DP,
United Kingdom

Oxford University Press is a department of the University of Oxford.
It furthers the University's objective of excellence in research, scholarship,
and education by publishing worldwide. Oxford is a registered trade mark of
Oxford University Press in the UK and in certain other countries

© Amrita Narlikar and Aruna Narlikar 2014

The moral rights of the authors have been asserted

First Edition published in 2014

Impression: 1

Published in the United States of America by Oxford University Press
198 Madison Avenue, New York, NY 10016, United States of America

British Library Cataloguing in Publication Data
Data available

Library of Congress Control Number: 2013957002

ISBN 978–0–19–969838–7

Printed in Great Britain by
Clays Ltd, St Ives plc

To
Durga and Mahadeva
in respectful gratitude

Acknowledgements

Working on this book has been extremely enriching for us, intellectually and emotionally. To bring together our expertise in modern International Relations and classical Sanskrit sources was intellectually a delightfully stimulating task. Emotionally too, this book holds a special value for us because many of the stories that we discuss here are amongst the most loved stories of our childhoods.

Aruna began her intellectual journey into the Mahabharata with her mother, Dr Vanamala Bhawalkar, who was a scholar of Sanskrit and a published author on many subjects, including the Mahabharata. She is grateful to both her parents, Vanamala and Professor D. R. Bhawalkar for the many spirited conversations on Indian philosophy, and a lively intellectual environment at home.

Amrita thanks many of her colleagues for useful conversations on this exciting and unusual project. She is particularly grateful to Martin Daunton, Rosemary Foot, Andrew Hurrell, Charles Jones, Miles Kahler, Donna Lee, and Brendan Simms for stimulating questions and valuable suggestions. She thanks the Master, Fellows, and staff of Darwin College for providing such a happy and supportive environment to work in, and is especially grateful to Geoffrey Lloyd, Leo Howe, and Alan Blackwell for many helpful discussions. Jagdish Bhagwati, Willy Brown, Desmond King, and Robert Stern have always been a source of inspiration, encouragement, and support. She is indebted to Markus Gehring, Adrian Kent, and Jocelyn Probert for their unwavering friendship.

We are both grateful to Oxford University Press for the opportunity to work on this project, and especially to Dominic Byatt for his enthusiastic support and constructive suggestions throughout. We also thank the production team at OUP, particularly Carla Hodge and Elizabeth Suffling, for their splendid cooperation.

We owe our greatest debt to Professor Anant Narlikar. His active involvement significantly improved the project. His staunch support and spirited encouragement kept us going. And his wonderful and unique storytelling skills made working on this project all the more enjoyable.

Contents

1

Playing Hardball?

India in International Negotiations

Effective bargaining holds the key to dealing successfully with any rising power. Politicians who seek alliances, business entrepreneurs who seek market access, or indeed international bureaucrats who wish to secure greater cooperation on international agreements must engage the new power through persuasive negotiation. While the diplomatic cultures and styles of most cultures show some national peculiarities,[1] the new powers of today present additional challenges. The so-called BRICs[2]—Brazil, Russia, India, and China—have fundamentally different political structures from the core, and their visions of global order have presented a challenge to those espoused by the liberal West.[3] Understanding the roots of their negotiating cultures presents the first step towards bargaining successfully with them. This book deals with the 'I' in the BRICs, namely India, and focuses particularly on analysing India's negotiating traditions through the lens of a classical Sanskrit text, the Mahabharata.

Why does India's negotiation behaviour need explaining? To begin with, India has never been an easy negotiating partner for the West. Stephen Cohen, for instance, writes that India 'seems to relish getting to no'; further, the West has long been 'irritated' and 'frustrated' by India's negotiation style.[4] Experimental studies further confirm that Indians are tough negotiators, showing reluctance to compromise along with a readiness to reject offers.[5] There are many plausible explanations as to why India has proved to be a difficult negotiating partner, including its relatively recent colonial past, particular configurations of domestic interests, and bureaucratic politics in domestic institutions. But a few studies argue that consistencies across issue areas and continuities over time in India's negotiation behaviour suggest that this

---

[1] Druckman et al. 1976; R. Cohen 2004; Salacuse 2004.   [2] O'Neill 2001.
[3] Hurrell 2006; Narlikar 2010.   [4] S. Cohen 2001.   [5] Druckman et al. 1976.

behaviour might have deeper and more local roots. To come to grips with these, a better understanding of cultural variables is necessary.[6] And while there is a great variety of means that can be used to access national traditions, we chose to focus on a major literary source in the form of one of the two great epics that have informed Indian politics and morality for centuries: the Mahabharata.

A study that brings together scholarship on modern-day negotiation behaviour and classical readings may appear to be unusual at first glance. In fact, the engagement between classical theories and current problems is well rooted in an established repertoire of writings, such as works that apply the tenets of Clausewitz, Machiavelli, and Sun Tzu to understanding concerns of modern statehood, statecraft, war, and bargaining. What is surprising, though, is that Indian classical theories have been put to only limited use with reference to today's problems; bar a few stray applications of Kautilya's Arthashastra with regard to understanding or recommending foreign policy strategies, the rich classical India scholarship that refers directly or indirectly to bargaining remains sparingly utilized. We aim to address this gap.

In this introductory chapter, we present the intellectual puzzle that underlies our book: to what extent does India's bargaining behaviour, as a rising power, reflect cultural continuities? In Section 1.1, we start off by highlighting the importance of cultural variables as a route to understanding bargaining and negotiation, and further explain the logic that underlies our choice of the Mahabharata as a lens into India's bargaining traditions, norms, and beliefs. In Section 1.2, we offer a conceptualization of negotiation behaviour. The concepts introduced in this section are used throughout the book. We also draw on secondary sources to highlight the characteristics that have come to be associated with India's negotiation style. Section 1.3 situates the bargaining characteristics identified in the previous section within a debate on India's foreign policy and negotiation behaviour today that has perplexed and divided analysts. While both sides broadly agree that India's dealings with the outside world—for the almost half-century following India's independence—were fraught and marked by a 'prickly' negotiation style that conformed with the characteristics outlined in Section 1.2, they diverge significantly on their assessment of the bargaining behaviour of a rising India. In Section 1.4, we provide the outline of the book. The fifth and concluding section discusses the contribution that this book makes to the existing literature, competing books, and the readership to which it will directly appeal.

---

[6] R. Cohen 2004; Kumar 2004; Hurrell and Narlikar 2006; Narlikar 2010.

1.1. CULTURE AND NEGOTIATION

The importance of culture in negotiation is recognized, and research on this subject has been flourishing. Negotiation analysts have for some time now been alerting us to the influence of cultural differences on diplomatic and business negotiations.[7] Culture for the negotiation analyst is defined by 'a group's relatively homogenous evaluations of multiple, interrelated phenomena'.[8] Raymond Cohen, in his landmark study on the subject of culture and international negotiation, identifies three distinctive features of culture: 'that it is a quality, not of individuals but of the society of which individuals are a part; that it is acquired—through acculturation or socialisation—by individuals from their societies; and that each culture is a unique complex of attributes subsuming every area of social life'.[9] Negotiation analysis also gives us theoretical insights and useful categorizations of how culture has been conceptualized. Robert Janosik, for example, identifies four ways in which practitioners and scholars think about culture—culture as learned behaviour, culture as shared value, culture as dialectic, and culture in context—and further provides an assessment of the costs and benefits of these different approaches.[10] Benefiting from rich interdisciplinary insights, scholars have investigated the psychological processes (ranging from cognition, bias, emotion, and motivation) that underpin negotiation, as well as social processes (such as communication) and context-specific variables (that include third-party intervention, the role of justice considerations, and the impact of technology).[11]

Specifically on the role of culture in Western societies, a useful and original instance of such work is Avner Offer's study of the 'scripts of honour' that tipped the world into the First World War.[12] The historians of the Annales school were also accustomed to studying 'the enduring physical, material, and eventually *mental* structures'[13] (our emphasis) that set the boundaries of human behaviour (individual and collective) as they came to grapple with the idea of *mentalité*.[14] Among the challenges that remain, however, is the need to go beyond Western intellectual traditions and incorporate a diversity of cultural perspectives in negotiation studies.[15]

---

[7] E.g. Druckman et al. 1976; Faure and Zartman 1993; R. Cohen 2004; Gelfand and Brett 2004; Salacuse 2004.

[8] Drake 2001, p. 320.   [9] R. Cohen 2004, p. 11.   [10] Janosik 1987.

[11] Gelfand and Brett 2004.   [12] Offer 1995.   [13] Lucas 1999, pp. 231–2.

[14] We thank Martin Daunton for bringing some of these historical sources to our attention.

[15] Recent scholarship has emphasized the need for such research. Henrich 2010 et al. have argued that many broad claims on human psychology are based on narrow samples from Western societies. Findings that rely primarily on sample groups of people that they refer to as 'Western, Educated, Industrialized, Rich, and Democratic (WEIRD) societies' provide more the outlier than the norm or standard for generalization. They urge caution on generalizations about human nature from this group, and that understanding human psychology will require broader subject pools.

A few such studies, which examine the role and relevance of indigenous concepts in modern society, have been in the offing. Myron Weiner recognizes and eloquently explains the links between ancient Indian political thought and contemporary Indian politics:

> Having been so deeply rooted in the realities of India's hierarchical and social structure and the country's system of religious belief—both of which continue to exist—it would be surprising if these ideas were totally at variance with contemporary beliefs and behaviour. This is not to say that there is a direct causal continuity between past and present. The presence of similarities, however, is enough to make us consider the possibility of similar underlying premises (to use Eisenstadt's terms) derived from deeper, fundamental assumptions concerning the nature of man—assumptions that mark one culture from another, such that contemporary Indians are more akin to their ancestors in some respect than they are to other contemporaries.[16]

Other examples in the non-Western traditions include the work of psychologists Pande and Naidu, who analyse the health benefits of the concept of non-attachment or Anasakti that is advanced in the Bhagwad Gita.[17] A small subset of works in this genre deals with the influence of such concepts on international negotiations. Examples here include works that analyse the relevance of the Chinese concept of *guanxi* in negotiations involving the Chinese,[18] or *amae* in negotiating with the Japanese.[19] Our book contributes to this set of writings. There are several routes that one could take to access indigenous negotiating traditions, including experiments, surveys, and also anthropological studies specific to particular organizations. We, however, chose to take the literary route, and explore negotiating concepts in the Mahabharata and also investigate their relevance today.

The Mahabharata and the Ramayana are India's two great epics.[20] While the Ramayana deals much more with the ideal, the Mahabharata's depiction of human fallibility makes it intrinsically more political. Just how deeply the Mahabharata is embedded in the popular imagination is evident not only in the plethora of commentaries and translations that continue to be published, but also in its dramatization in cinema, television, and theatre. Its heroes are still idolized, its gods are still worshipped, and references to it recur in everyday conversation amongst India's Oxbridge-educated elite and the illiterate masses alike. There is indeed, as Gurcharan Das writes, 'a rich menu of *Mahabharatas* on order'.[21]

---

[16] Weiner 1984, p. 113.   [17] Pande and Naidu 1992.

[18] Kumar and Worm 2004. Also see Faure 1998.

[19] E.g. Doi 1973; Blaker 1977; Berton 1998.

[20] Note, however, that the Mahabharata is more encompassing than the Ramayana in many different ways, including the fact that a brief version of the Ramayana appears in the Mahabharata.

[21] Das 2009, p. 303.

The importance of the Mahabharata in the Indian psyche is nicely captured by V. S. Sukthankar: 'Is it not passing strange that, notwithstanding the repeated and dogged attempts of Western savants to demonstrate that our Mahabharata is but an unintelligible conglomerate of disjointed pieces, without any meaning as a whole, the epic should always have occupied in Indian antiquity an eminent position and uniformly enjoyed the highest reputation? . . . What is more remarkable still is that this epic . . . is still living and throbbing in the lives of the Indian people . . . Even Oldenberg, who had pronounced the epic to be a chaos, felt—and rightly—that "in the Mahabharata breathe the united soul of India and the individual souls of her people." It is a high claim, and yet the Mahabharata may be said to be more even than that.'[22] Sukthankar further goes on to describe the work as a 'dateless and deathless poem . . . which forms the strongest link between India old and new'.[23] Sukthankar's commentary serves as a useful background as to why the Mahabharata, to us, was the most straightforward choice in our search for the roots of Indian negotiating traditions.[24]

The epic, which comprises 18 volumes, is broadly a story of the great and terrible war of succession that was fought between two factions in one family—the Pandavas and the Kauravas—who were first cousins and all descendants of the King Bharata (for those new to the Mahabharata, please refer to the Appendix for a very short summary of the core plot).[25] So close is the association of this text with the concept of war that in popular parlance the

---

[22] Sukthankar 1957, pp. 29–30.   [23] Sukthankar 1957, p. 32.

[24] This is not to say that a study of India's numerous secular and religious traditions would have no relevance for understanding India's negotiations today. We may indeed be interested in conducting such a study ourselves at a future date. Amongst the various texts that we considered addressing to answer our puzzle, the ones on our shortlist were the Arthashastra and the Panchatantra. While both these deal with political questions—the former is a manual in statecraft while the latter comprises fables that were designed to teach statecraft to princes—negotiation and bargaining are not central to either volume (though they do appear somewhat selectively in some of the stories and prescriptions). Even more importantly for our purposes, neither has captured the popular imagination as the epics have: only a small and specialized readership is aware of the tenets of the Arthashastra; the Panchantra, while more popular than the Arthashastra, is seen today more as fables for children that appear in comic books rather than a treatise of morality or political action or negotiation. The Mahabharata, in contrast, occupies a very important place in the Indian mindset, and in choosing this as our primary source we use the same strategy as scholars who have focused on Confucius in understanding Chinese negotiation behaviour, or others who have focused on the impact that political philosophers such as Hobbes, or Rousseau, or Machiavelli have had on the making of Western polities.

[25] We consulted several versions of the text, and have relied mainly on the critical edition by the Bhandarkar Institute for the original Sanskrit verses. However, on occasion we have also used the Gita Press edition, and in these instances we specify the use of this version of the Mahabharata and give the Gita Press numbering for the shlokas. In both instances, we provide our own translations. For those wishing to gain a more accessible and shorter account of the story than the 18 volumes of the critical edition, there are several abridged translations to choose from. We recommend the one edited by Smith 2009.

word 'Mahabharata' has become synonymous with 'war'. What is overlooked in most descriptions and analyses, however, is that the Mahabharata is fundamentally at least as much a story of negotiation as it is of war. In fact, only five of the 18 volumes deal with the war itself, whereas the theme of negotiation appears across the entire set: the bargaining over succession, the failure of that negotiation and associated mediation efforts which lead to the 18-day war of cataclysmic proportion, negotiation on the Pandava side on the morality of the war itself (embodied in the Bhagwad Gita) and actions taken in the war, and finally negotiation in the aftermath of the war. Embedded within the main story is also a multitude of other stories—histories and mythologies of characters and places—many of which bear further lessons for the conduct of war and negotiation of peace. Particularly striking throughout the text is the inclination of the characters to not just philosophize, moralize, and debate, as per Amartya Sen's 'Argumentative Indian',[26] but to constantly engage in bargaining and negotiation.[27] A study of the Mahabharata thus provides us potentially new and exciting insights into the extent to which India's negotiating behaviour is ingrained in its classical traditions.[28]

1.2. CONCEPTUALIZING NEGOTIATION

Negotiation behaviour can be conceptualized along several lines. Building further on some of our recent work, we break down the concept of negotiation behaviour into four aspects: negotiation strategy, framing, coalitions, and timing. On all four aspects, Indians negotiating in different forums reveals several characteristic features—almost a distinctive world view—and all of these characteristics together point to Indians being tough negotiators. These

---

[26] Sen 2005.

[27] The Mahabharata is known to have grown via an oral tradition. But a much-loved and popular legend of the Mahabharata illustrates how even the process of its writing was the subject of a negotiation between the god of creativity, Ganesha—the remover of all obstacles and the first to be worshipped—and the sage Ved Vyasa. Vyasa, the composer of the epic, asked Ganesha for his assistance in writing the text. Ganesha agreed to be his scribe, but placed a condition: Vyasa would have to continue the dictation of the text without any pauses or breaks. Vyasa then placed his own condition: the dictation would continue without any breaks, but Ganesha had to understand everything he was writing. And with the terms of the arrangement thus negotiated and agreed upon, the writing of the Mahabharata began, with the mighty elephant-headed Ganesha breaking off his own right tusk to use as a pen. And as the dictation and writing progressed, Vyasa wove some complex and convoluted verses into his great epic poem. To understand these, even the supremely intelligent Ganesha needed some time, which allowed Vyasa some well-earned breaks!

[28] In fact, as one of our anonymous referees rightly pointed out, the Mahabharata has oddly attracted very limited interest as a 'deep cultural artefact that impacts India', say in contrast to the Ramayana where at least some such works exist, e.g. Rajagopalan 2006.

characteristics are discussed briefly below. Our task in this book is to investigate how deep-rooted these characteristics are, and we do so by studying the extent to which they find echoes in the Mahabharata. It is also our task to analyse the extent to which these bargaining traits remain pervasive in India's diplomacy, and especially India's bargaining as a rising power.

The first variable along which negotiation behaviour can be conceptualized is negotiation strategy. Negotiation strategies vary across a spectrum from distributive to integrative. Distributive strategies include tactics such as refusing to make any concessions, threatening to hold others' issues hostage, issuing threats and penalties, and worsening the other party's best alternative to negotiated agreement (BATNA). Integrative strategies comprise attempts to widen the issue space and explore common solutions, that is, 'strategies designed to expand rather than split the pie'.[29]

Several analysts have argued that India's negotiation behaviour involves strategies that cluster at the distributive end of the spectrum. Stephen Cohen captures this in his classic work *India: Emerging Power*, in which the chapter on India's foreign policy is titled 'The India that can't say yes'.[30] Moreover, Cohen is not alone in his conclusions. In their comparative study focusing on Argentina, India, and the US, Druckman et al. found that Indian bargainers tended to be 'less compromising', 'more win-lose oriented', and also placed a great emphasis on 'need'. The authors argued, 'The emphasis on *both* competitiveness and need suggests a view of the world as containing limited resources.'[31] This is a classic example of a world view that is zero-sum, and is thus driven by attempts to split (rather than expand) the pie. It is our purpose to understand how far this is grounded in India's negotiating culture and also whether it thrives amidst India's rising power.

The second variable that allows us to usefully conceptualize negotiation behaviour is framing. Tversky and Kahneman developed this concept to refer to 'decision-maker's conception of the acts, outcomes, and contingencies associated with a particular choice. The Frame that a decision-maker adopts is controlled partly by the formulation of the problem and partly by the norms, habits, and personal characteristics of the decision-maker.'[32] Negotiation analysts have applied this concept to their own subject matter.[33] Specifically of relevance to us are the two distinctive ways that seem to characterize the manner in which Indians frame their demands. First, Indians are verbose, in marked contrast to the Chinese. As Amartya Sen puts in, 'Prolixity is not alien to us in India . . . We do like to speak.'[34] The second is the Indian tendency to moralize. Lucian Pye, for instance, writes that 'Foreigners have often been

---

[29] Odell 2000.   [30] S. Cohen 2001.   [31] Druckman et al. 1976.
[32] Tversky and Kahneman 1981.
[33] For a particularly effective application see Odell and Sell 2006.
[34] Sen 2005, p. 3.

baffled by the moralizing of Indian politicians. In most cultures there is an element of aggression in moralizing which is usually seen as provocation...and therefore foreigners infer an element of hostile intent behind Indian moralizing. In fact, much of the moralizing by Indian power holders is a form of narcissism, of self-congratulation for being so apparently virtuous.'[35] Raymond Cohen concurs with Pye in his analysis of India's negotiations with the US: 'India...is never loath to attack supposed American moral shortcomings. American negotiators tend to be intensely irritated by Indian moralism, the assumption that India is somehow the repository of righteousness and objective truth in the world.'[36] To what extent this type of prolix and moralistic framing is a defence mechanism of the weak can be learnt at least partially by studying the traditions of framing negotiating demands in India's classical texts, and further whether this framing style is changing as India acquires greater power.

The third variable of negotiation behaviour is coalitions. The reason why coalitions are a vital aspect of negotiation behaviour is because they provide us with an important indication of the reliance of the individual or state on allies versus the preference and ability to go it alone. Coalitions can increase the actor's ability to withstand pressure but they can also tie the actor's hands, thereby rendering concessions difficult to make and agreements more elusive.[37]

Surprisingly, the coalitions variable is somewhat under-theorized in general negotiation analysis,[38] although we do find empirical examples offered by negotiation analysts of how India behaves with allies. In particular, we have several insightful commentaries on India's leadership of and participation in the Non-Aligned Movement, and its close relationship with the Soviet Union and the Eastern bloc.[39] Raymond Cohen writes: 'The policy of nonalignment, defined as India's right to determine its foreign policy orientation freely and without duress, became sacrosanct. After all, Indian forces had fought and died in two world wars without even being consulted on the decision to go to war. Not only was alignment in the Cold War rejected, but fierce opposition was consistently expressed to anything that smacked of limiting Indian sovereignty.'[40] The trend that emerges most powerfully is that of an India that has traditionally been reluctant to bandwagon with the hegemon, and more likely to balance. Further, while it has been suspicious of formal alliances that might curtail its sovereignty in any way, its participation in coalitions (especially those involving other developing countries) has been energetic. Cohen rightly points out that India maintained close links with many countries in the

---

[35] Pye 1985, pp. 142–3.   [36] R. Cohen 2004, p. 95.   [37] Narlikar 2009.
[38] Recent exceptions are Narlikar 2003; Odell 2006; Narlikar 2009.
[39] E.g. S. Kux 1993; S. Cohen 2001; Malone 2011.
[40] R. Cohen 2004, p. 57.

developing world in the era of the Cold War because of its commitment to anti-imperialism and decolonization; importantly, it continued to maintain these links into the post-Cold War era too.[41] The extent to which a rising India still adheres to the trend of balancing rather than bandwagoning, resisting formal alliances with powerful players, and maintaining coalitions that adhere to some level of Third Worldist solidarity forms a part of the investigation taken on in this book.

Finally, the notion of time varies from one culture to another. Raymond Cohen offers us an interesting generalization in his study that compares the US negotiation style with other cultures. He writes: 'Americans . . . are mostly concerned with addressing immediate issues and moving on to new challenges, and they display little interest in (and sometimes little knowledge of) history . . . In marked contrast, the representatives of more antique societies possess a pervasive sense of the past, of the long run . . .'[42] Extrapolating from Cohen's work, the variable of time translates effectively into at least two parameters: a) how deep historical memories run and b) how far negotiators are from the particular culture willing to accept delays or whether they are strongly committed to set deadlines.

On both counts, India reveals distinctive characteristics. First, the sense of history—or at least an interpretation of history—is overwhelmingly present in Indian negotiators. Stephen Cohen, for instance, observes that 'Indian officials believe they are representing not just a state but a civilization. Few state-civilizations are India's equal . . . Indians believe that India-as-civilization has something to offer the rest of the world.' And hence the seriousness with which it takes its 'global mission'.[43] The same deep-rooted sense of history pervades the institutional memories of Indian bureaucracies, and contributes at least partly to 'a defensive arrogance and acute sensitivity to real and perceived slights'.[44] Second, several scholars have pointed out through empirical and experimental investigations that Indian negotiators are seldom in a hurry to reach agreement. Raymond Cohen in fact refers to 'India's "geologic sense of time" and ready acceptance of delay'.[45] This may seem odd in a democracy where politicians are accountable to their electorate and are usually required to show deliverable results within defined time frames. But bureaucratic and political cultures point to different imperatives at work in India, where ease and speed in reaching international agreement are likely to be interpreted as 'unseemly haste' and failure to take public interest into account.[46] This reinforces the Indian reluctance to make concessions and the readiness to reject deals. Both characteristics of the Indian negotiator's approach to time lead us to pose the following question: as a rising India acquires

[41] S. Cohen 2001.   [42] R. Cohen 2004, pp. 35–6.   [43] S. Cohen 2001, p. 52.
[44] S. Cohen 2001, p. 86.   [45] R. Cohen 2004, p. 180.   [46] Salacuse 2004.

positions of influence in Great Power clubs and as its economy continues
along the trajectory of dramatic modernization, does the evidence point to
friendlier interpretations of past and recent interactions with the West and
also a more 'monochronic' interpretation of time that is dominated by the
more modern pressures of meeting deadlines?[47]

All four aspects of its negotiation have earned Indian negotiators the
reputation of being avid, courageous, sometimes even noble, naysayers, and
not without some cost. Usually, not even a hegemon can afford persistent
recalcitrance. For a rising power, the costs of such defensive naysaying may be
higher still. Most immediately, they include the risk of deadlock, unrealized
gains from a failed or delayed negotiation, and penalties from negotiation
partners in the form of negative linkages across issue areas.[48] In addition, there
are reputational costs. With a reputation (well deserved or not) of consistently
saying no, persisting in a form of international trade unionism, and challenging the system, the new power risks getting branded as a disruptive influence
and troublemaker. The constant use of such strategies can be interpreted as a
signal that the new power is unappeasable, and is thus also more likely to
attract containment rather than engagement strategies from the established
powers. It is our purpose to investigate how far the bargaining traits highlighted in this section do, in fact, translate into the negotiation behaviours and
practices of India as a rising power. As other studies have shown, moreover,
the roots of this negotiation behaviour run deep—deeper than conventional
explanations of negotiation behaviour such as institutional lags or interest
group pressures would suggest.[49] The Mahabharata, particularly what it has to
say about bargaining and negotiation, offers us a new lens into these cultural
roots and associations of the different characteristics of India's bargaining
behaviour.[50] It also has the potential to take us a few steps further: it can shed
new light on how seemingly recalcitrant or irresponsible behaviour from the
perspective of the dominant (Western) powers in the system may hold
elements of heroism and idealism from the perspective of a rising power
that is also (along with its competitor and counterpart, China) an ancient
civilization.

---

[47] R. Cohen 2004, p. 36, describes monochronism in the American context as follows: 'In
American society, with its calendars and timetables, the business of government is a regimented
affair. Monochronism—one thing at a time—reigns supreme.'

[48] Narlikar 2006.

[49] S. Cohen 2001; Kumar 2004; Sen 2004a; Narlikar and Hurrell 2006; Narlikar 2010.

[50] Besides offering us potentially novel insights into the deep roots of India's bargaining
behaviour, a study of this vital and vibrant text further helps us flesh out and bring to the fore
some of the bigger ideas and visions that underpin India's negotiating positions, but which
remain underspecified in the current day as they have become so deeply embedded, so 'hardwired', into the Indian negotiating mindset.

1.3. THE PUZZLE OF INDIA'S NEGOTIATION BEHAVIOUR AS A RISING POWER

While the previous section discussed some of the characteristic traits associated with India's negotiating culture, here we ask whether or not they translate into India's foreign policy, historically and today. The debate between foreign policy analysts, negotiation analysts, and indeed practitioners, is polarized and the verdict is still out. In this section we discuss the main points of contention in this debate.

The debate has a common starting point, with agreement on two important issues. First, both sides agree that modern India's bargaining with the outside world, through the first half-century of its independence or so, illustrates several of the characteristics that we discussed in the previous section. Its prickly, ideological, and inflexible toughness made it a difficult negotiation partner for many different countries. Stephen Cohen sums this up nicely:

> Western diplomats were for many years put off by India's flexible nonalignment, which for a time was a pretext for a close relationship with the Soviet Union. They were also irritated by the style of Indian diplomats. While professional and competent, they seemed compelled to lecture their British or American counterparts on the evils of the cold war, the moral superiority of India's policies, or the greatness of its civilization . . . As for Beijing, the 1987 question of one Chinese official, asked half in jest, half seriously, 'Why are the Indians so inscrutable?' reflected his puzzlement with what is seen as an unrealistic combination of arrogance and poverty. Only Moscow seems to have gotten along well with New Delhi.[51]

Second, both sides agree that India's negotiation style and content have acquired unprecedented importance today. A recalcitrant, naysaying India, bound by the 'Hindu rate of growth' and limited military wherewithal, was in general little more than a minor irritant in the conduct of international affairs and the preservation of global order and stability. Today, the stakes are much higher. The Goldman Sachs study of 2003 predicted that India, in just 30 years, would be the third largest economy in the world, and could have potentially the fastest growth for the next 30 and 50 years.[52] At $43.1 billion in 2010, its military spending was high, and India ranked ninth in the list of top ten military spenders. Not only is it a nuclear weapons state (having declared its nuclear status through Pokhran II in 1998), but it was also the largest recipient of major conventional military weapons between 2006 and 2010.[53] Further, the international community is taking India more seriously than ever before. This is reflected in the bilateral and regional deals that the

---

[51] S. Cohen 2001, p. 66.   [52] Wilson and Purushothaman 2003.
[53] SIPRI Yearbook 2011.

established powers have signed with it (and especially the US–India nuclear deal) or are negotiating over. Just as important is India's inclusion at the several high tables of global governance. India is, for instance, a member of the Leaders' Level G20; it is invited to and participates in all small-group consensus-based decision-making meetings of the World Trade Organization (WTO); and while it has still not succeeded in securing a permanent seat in the UN Security Council, it was elected for the seventh time to serve the two-year term of non-permanent members from January 2011. As scholars, practitioners, and pundits recognize, how this rising India negotiates is no longer a question of academic interest or amusement alone. Any international agreement is likely to have little meaning or value if India were to veto it or walk away from it, and India's market and military prowess are large enough to allow it considerable disruptive potential.[54] Analysts on both sides of the debate thus acknowledge that the world needs India to play ball, lending some urgency to the question of how India negotiates and might best be negotiated with. But having agreed on these two issues, the two sides then diverge dramatically.

The controversy over India's negotiations stems from a divide in opinion and analysis regarding how the country's negotiation behaviour has changed (or will change) as its power increases. On the one hand are scholars who argue that, as India rises, its growing integration in the world economy and accompanying recognition of its international standing will decrease its tendency to play the role of the tough and defensive negotiator. Driven by a convergence of interests with other major powers, or through greater socialization via greater norm convergence, and perhaps both, India will become a more flexible and pragmatic negotiating partner. On the other hand are scholars who argue that there is little evidence to believe that India (or other rising powers) will, by dint of interest convergence or norm convergence, play ball as its power increases. Rather, the evidence suggests that it will use its standard bargaining tactics with even greater vehemence, and reassert the vision that underpins these bargaining behaviours. Effectively, this is really a debate about how deeply entrenched India's negotiation habits, norms, and beliefs actually are. We elaborate each side of the debate below.

The first view, which emphasizes socialization and increasing regime conformity as an accompaniment of rising power, has a well-established base in scholarship and has been applied to different country cases.[55] C. Raja Mohan is a strong proponent of this view, specifically in the Indian context:

If a single image captured India's national strategic style, it was that of a porcupine—vegetarian, slow-footed and prickly. The famous defensiveness of

---

[54] In other words, even though India does not yet enjoy the 'agenda-setting' prowess that characterizes Great Powers, its 'veto-player' status as a rising power does give the power to walk away and thereby impose considerable costs on other negotiators. See Narlikar 2007 for details.
[55] E.g. Legro 2007; Ikenberry 2008.

the porcupine became the hallmark of India's approach to the world ... India's engagement with the world since the early 1990s posits a fundamental change in course and a reconstitution of its core premises. Whether it was the de-emphasis of non-alignment or the new embrace of the US, or the attempts to rethink regionalism in the subcontinent and its environs, a radically different foreign policy orientation emerged by the turn of the millennium.[56]

In a subsequent article Mohan offers a somewhat more qualified analysis, recognizing that India is constrained 'by an unresolved tension between the inertia of its policy positions framed during the early years of building the post-colonial state and the logic of its emerging major power status'.[57] But his overall assessment is still sanguine:

Given India's past record on global issues, and its strong preferences for the third world, many in the United States might wonder if New Delhi is really ready to play a leading role in shaping the global commons in partnership with other countries, especially the United States ... Change might be on the way as India begins to adapt, *even if incrementally*, to its increased weight in the international system and the responsibilities that come with it.[58]

While recognizing the tension in India's bargaining position that the debate represents, Mohan is unambiguous in his verdict regarding the type of strategy that will win out. First, he argues that in the diverging pull between autonomy versus responsibility, India is showing a 'nuanced' shift towards the latter. Second, he asserts that India is giving up its 'universal multilateralism' in favour of 'selective coalitions' that lead it away from its allies of the Third World. And third, he posits that as it has had to adapt to the 'logic of major power status, India has been compelled to discard some of its past baggage about equity and justice in the construction of global regimes', thereby resulting in a switch in its championing of the cause of global equity to global order. But there is an alternative view, which represents the polar opposite to the one espoused by Mohan.

Even in an account that is rather sympathetic towards India, David Malone makes the following observation, which suggests at least strong remnants of India's 'prickliness' even as its power rises:

A noted denizen of India's Ministry of External Affairs, a keen bilateralist at that, when asked what India does best internationally replied without a moment's hesitation 'multilateral diplomacy'. And yet queries about Indian performance at the UN and elsewhere in the multilateral sphere hardly validate that judgement: 'arrogant', 'moralistic', and 'confrontational' are terms more invoked by developing and industrialized counterparts, despite recognition that Indian negotiators are rarely less than 'impressive' and often 'brilliant'.[59]

---

[56] Mohan 2003, pp. 261–4. [57] Mohan 2003, p. 139.
[58] Mohan 2010, p. 138; emphasis added. [59] Malone 2011, p. 270.

Malone's observation will not come as a surprise to those who recognize that rising India's preoccupation with autonomy concerns remains serious. The occasions where it has abandoned old friends from the Third World are few; these rare instances are further a product of highly unusual circumstances. And in further stark contrast to Raja Mohan's view, India's interpretation of its responsibilities is limited, and rather different from what the West expects of it. Examples of India's willingness to take on the responsibilities of upholding global order are rare. Cases of continued Indian recalcitrance in international negotiations still abound across institutions and issue areas. George Perkovich's analysis provides several examples to support the view that India's rising power has not reformed its bargaining behaviour: 'In the November 2001 WTO negotiations at Doha, India appeared the primary impediment to a stronger international consensus favoring liberalization. Fairly or not, the richer countries, particularly the United States felt that the Indian chief negotiator, Musaroli Maran, typified an old, unwelcome, and counterproductive India style of moralism and doggedness... India's long position as a moralistic and contrarian loner in the international community has not excited others about working with India at the apex of the UN system.'[60]

This polarized debate about how a rising India negotiates, and will negotiate as its power increases, derives fundamentally from differing interpretations on how deep-rooted its bargaining behaviour actually is. A study of India's classical texts offers us a vital route into investigating this systematically, and thereby ascertaining the readiness with which this bargaining behaviour can be altered (through India's growing prowess as well as incentives created by outside parties). A study such as ours can provide us with an indication of the 'baggage' that India brings with it to the negotiating table, particularly historical beliefs and cultural norms that condition its expectations of rights and responsibilities negotiated. Especially if the analysis of bargaining continuities is conducted with an eye on changes, variations in the pattern, and exceptions to the rule, important insights may be gained on the endogenous and exogenous factors that may persuade India to emerge as a more cooperative and responsible negotiating partner. And hence this book.

1.4. STRUCTURE OF THE BOOK

The purpose of this book is to explore the cultural roots of India's negotiation behaviour and explore the extent to which they help to explain the bargaining behaviour of a rising India. The following chapters are organized according to

[60] Perkovich 2003.

each feature of the negotiation behaviour that was discussed in Section 1.2, that is, strategy, framing, coalitions, and timing, with an analysis of the insights of the Mahabharata into each of these aspects, and also their applications to the negotiation behaviour of India as it rises. The treasure trove of the Mahabharata is too vast to allow us to examine each and every story for its relevance to the intellectual puzzle. But to ensure consistency, we choose ten negotiation episodes from the Mahabharata for each chapter. The first set covers three stories taken from the pre-war part of the epic. The stories involve the central protagonists—the Kauravas and the Pandavas—cousins whose relations gradually deteriorate and ultimately lead up to the 18-day war, and also their teachers, elders, and allies whose lives are irretrievably entwined in the politics of bargaining and war. The second set of three stories is drawn from the period of the graphic 18-day war, when protagonists debate and negotiate over the strategies of war, and also bargain with their opponents in attempting to trigger defection and weaken the other side. The third set of stories brings together three episodes drawing either from a) one of the many related stories, not immediately about the key protagonists who fought the war, but nonetheless interlinked with the main story either as its history or told as one of the many myths and legends surrounding it, or b) the post-war period, when negotiations continued between survivors of the war on the legitimacy of war actions, managing the consequences of the war, and when seeking salvation. Importantly, to allow variance on the dependent variable, we have a fourth category comprising a) deviations from the norm and exceptions seen in the previous nine stories covered in each chapter and b) one new story that shows a clear variation from the dominant trend (e.g. show willingness to make concessions, use pragmatic rather than moralistic terms of framing, form bandwagons rather than balancing coalitions, or work with time frames that are short and have tight deadlines). Studying the exceptions in each of the chapters is important for understanding the conditions under which deviation from the norm takes place. At the end of each chapter is a table which summarizes the successes and failures of bargaining behaviour in the ten stories. The relevance of insights drawn from all four sets of episodes, in each chapter, is investigated through an examination of India's modern-day negotiations.

We focus primarily on examples from a rising India when analysing modern-day negotiations, but inevitably must also turn to its recent historical past to illustrate continuities and changes. Note that our focus is primarily on India's negotiations in multilateral regimes rather than in regional and bilateral negotiations. This choice was driven by the fact that the debate referred to in the previous section revolves primarily around the kind of power India will become internationally (as opposed to regionally) and also the extent to which it will be willing to assume global responsibilities as a rising power with Great Power aspirations. Finally, it is worth mentioning that while we will draw on examples of India's negotiation behaviour in different regimes, we focus specifically and systematically on its changing participation in the multilateral trade and nuclear non-proliferation regimes. Such a focus allows us more comparability across the chapters. Additionally, a focus on the trade and non-proliferation cases allows us insights into the areas of 'low politics' and 'high politics' respectively. Further, to the extent that both regimes have incorporated important changes to accommodate India into a position of influence, they represent 'easy' test cases for an alteration of India's negotiation behaviour: if we find that India's behaviour retains many of the old 'prickly' qualities even in these two regimes, then it is unlikely that India will become more accommodating in other issue areas.

In this first chapter, our main purpose has been to introduce the puzzle of the cultural roots of India's negotiation behaviour as a rising power, and further explain why we believe the Mahabharata offers particularly useful insights into understanding India's negotiation culture. We have also developed the four variables that are used in the rest of this book—negotiation, framing, coalitions, and timing. A brief outline of the following chapters, structured around these four variables, follows below.

Chapter 2: India's Negotiation Strategy: The Heroism of Hard Bargainings

India's Negotiation Strategy: 'No land shall we surrender to the Pandavas, not even the amount of land on which the point of a needle stands' (Mahabharata, V.125.26).

Chapter 2 begins with a theoretical overview of negotiation strategies as given by the literature on bargaining and negotiation, and outlines the dominant trends in the negotiation strategies used by India since independence and more recently as a rising power. The greater part of the chapter examines ten episodes (pre-war, war, post-war and related stories, and exceptions) from the Mahabharata to examine how far classical traditions espouse conciliatory diplomacy. Interestingly, as analysis of the text reveals, both the 'goodies' and the 'baddies', the winners and the losers, in times of peace and war and indeed after, find it difficult to make concessions. The Mahabharata also specifies the limited conditions under which concessions should be made, which we explore with reference to both the text and also modern-day negotiations.

Chapter 3: Framing from a Moral High Horse

Framing from a Moral High Horse: 'Even if the world were to be destroyed, even if I were to acquire immortality, even if I were granted kingship of all three worlds, I cannot break my vow' (Mahabharata, I.103.19).

The 'moralizing by Indian power holders' has long 'baffled' foreigners.[61] In keeping with the format of the four other chapters focusing on the variables of negotiation behaviour, we first analyse the particular frames that Indian negotiators have used on the international stage. Bar a few exceptions, we demonstrate the general tendency of Indian negotiators to frame demands in terms of moral principles rather than strategic imperatives (even though the latter are real and present). Nor is such framing purely rhetorical; Indian negotiators have adhered to their principles even when there are costs.

The reliance on moralizing when framing one's demands, and the adherence to certain principles in spite of the costs, becomes less 'baffling' through the study of the Mahabharata. The Mahabharata, at its core, is a story about 'the victory of righteousness (*Dharma*)'.[62] It is verbose, and brimming over with moralizing and appeal to principle. In this chapter we examine four sets of stories in the Mahabharata to analyse the frames that its protagonists use. One of the fascinating findings from a textual analysis of the epic is that the purpose of moralization is not simply to win legitimacy for one's actions; even in the absence of an audience, protagonists go through elaborate rituals to justify their own actions to themselves. We also use the four sets of cases in the chapter to examine the extent to which moral principles are referred to during bargaining in the Mahabharata, and then discuss the extent to which they continue to be reflected in India's negotiations today.

Chapter 4: Coalitions: Choosing Allies, Sustaining Friendships

Coalitions: 'Just and wise kings come to the assistance of those who ask them first' (Mahabharata, V.4.9).

In the course of its rise to power, India shows a fair degree of consistency in taking on the leadership of coalitions, particularly those involving other developing countries.[63] In the past, alliances with the South took the shape of the Non-Aligned Movement, the G77, and Third Worldist solidarity. Today, we see at least some vital continuities in India's negotiation behaviour, at least in that many of its coalition allies remain developing countries, even though the discourse used to justify and explain these alliances has changed. After a brief overview of India's history of alliances in multilateral forums, we use four episodes of the Mahabharata to investigate the importance accorded to coalition formation, strategy of choosing one's allies and preserving alliances, how considerations of coalition loyalty are balanced out against the potential gains to be had from defection, and if there are any conditions specified

---

[61] Pye 1985.   [62] Bhawalkar 1999.
[63] Narlikar 2003 for a categorization of coalitions.

for bandwagoning with the strong rather than attempting to balance against them by allying with the weak. Some attention is also paid to investigating whether formal or informal coalitions are preferred.

Chapter 5: Time: The Long Shadow of the Past and the Future

Time: 'One day for Brahma is the equivalent of one thousand yugas, as is one night. Those enlightened beings who know this truth also understand the meaning of time' (Mahabharata, VI.32.17; Bhagwad Gita, VIII.17).

The Indian readiness to engage in prolonged negotiation derives at least partly from its bureaucratic and political culture, described by Stephen Cohen as 'agreement averse',[64] which allows Indian negotiators to stand firm and hold out rather than secure an agreement. Interestingly, the willingness of Indian negotiators to bide their time in international bargaining predates India's rise to power. Also, India's interpretation of avoiding 'unseemly haste' differs from China's (e.g. Deng Xiaoping's dictum was: 'Observe developments soberly, maintain our position, meet challenges calmly, hide our capacities and bide our time, remain free of ambition, never claim leadership').[65] In the Chinese case, the emphasis appears more to be in gaining a carefully calculated, strategic advantage with time; in the Indian case, the strategic dimension is at best only one amongst several considerations, and where speed is often regarded as haste and associated with a failure to follow due process. Both the existence of this long shadow of the future and the particular ways in which it is conceptualized and translated into the negotiation process need explaining. In this chapter, we investigate how negotiators (in the Mahabharata and the present day) interpret the culture-specific notion of time, focusing particularly on the extent to which references to the past are used and allowed to influence negotiations, and further the responsiveness of negotiators to time pressures and deadlines.

Chapter 6: Conclusion

Conclusion: How to negotiate with a rising India?

   While difficulties in negotiating with India are not new, the need to negotiate effectively with it is, and only growing as its power rises. Understanding the rich negotiating culture wherein India's bargaining behaviour is embedded forms a crucial step to facilitate this process. This last chapter sums up the findings of the book, and their implications for the emergence of India as a

---

[64] S. Cohen 2001.   [65] Narlikar 2010.

responsible Great Power and with potential for international leadership. It also suggests specific ways in which knowledge of India's negotiating culture can help outside parties bargain more effectively with India for mutual advantage and systemic stability.

1.5. CONTRIBUTION TO THE LITERATURE

This book sits first and foremost in the study of Politics, and more specifically International Relations and Negotiation Analysis. The interdisciplinary nature of this work, however, also means that it fits naturally into a second set of scholarship, based particularly in the fields of Literature and Philosophy, which focuses on the Mahabharata. Our book draws on both sets of scholarship. Its aim is to contribute primarily to the first set of writings, but we hope that the book will be of interest and relevance for scholars of the Mahabharata, irrespective of the academic discipline in which they are based.

In the literature on international negotiation, experimental studies point to specific behavioural characteristics of Indian negotiators.[66] Empirical analyses confirm these findings, and suggest that the sources of India's negotiation behaviour are deep-rooted and culture-specific, going beyond what standard explanations of interest group politics, partisan politics, or institutional politics would suggest.[67] But there are very few works that trace these sources. Extensive sociological, anthropological, and comparative political studies remain confined to their own fields, and do not develop their implications for Indian foreign policy or negotiation. And to the best of our knowledge—both in English and in the vernacular Indian languages—there seem to be no works that attempt to unpack the 'negotiating culture' variable using literary sources. Our book aims to fill both these gaps.

This book is also to be distinguished from most other works that deal with the Mahabharata. In numerous writings, the philosophy and meaning of the Mahabharata have been subject to rich intellectual discussion, its characters subject to detailed literary analysis, and its relevance examined in relation to modern-day dilemmas.[68] While these provide useful backgrounders for us, our book differs from the great majority of these works in two respects. First, the central purpose of our book is *analytic*: to examine how far the traditions of the Mahabharata are translated into the negotiation of Indian foreign policy today. The text does not give us causal explanations of India's negotiations

---

[66] Druckman et al. 1976; Salacuse 2004.
[67] S. Cohen 2001; Hurrell and Narlikar 2006; Narlikar 2010.
[68] A nice recent example of this is Das 2009; classics include Sukthankar 1957; Karve 1991; Chaitanya 1993; Ramanujan 1999; Matilal 2002.

today, but it is *illustrative* of the roots of Indian diplomacy. This stands in sharp contrast to the *normative* content of most modern works on the Mahabharata that keep an eye on the present, whose aim is usually to solve modern-day moral and political dilemmas by drawing on the universal and generalizable lessons of the epic. As far as we are aware, moreover, no scholarly or academic analysis has been conducted regarding the relevance of the Mahabharata for understanding the specific subject of India's negotiations abroad.

The core readership for the book is academic: graduate students and scholars of Foreign Policy, Indian Politics, International Relations Theory, and International Negotiation, and also others in related fields such as Business Negotiation. Practitioners of foreign policy and business who have faced the difficulties and joys of dealing with India are likely to be equally interested. The surge, however, in popular interest in India, as part of the BRICs phenomenon, allows us to hope that the book will also appeal to a broader audience—the same audience that has enjoyed and appreciated books on applications of Sun Tzu to current negotiations and works such as Roger Fisher and William Ury's *Getting to Yes*. We believe that while the intellectual need for a book such as ours is a long-standing one, and the widespread interest in negotiating with one of the world's leading growth markets creates an unprecedented practical urgency for writings along the lines that we propose.

One caveat is in order. The purpose of this book is to understand and analyse India's negotiating positions from a cultural (and specifically, literary) perspective. This means that to offer advice on how India *should* negotiate is not its primary purpose. Rather, analysing India's negotiation behaviour in international forums today, our book explains the chief features of this behaviour in terms of India's cultural traditions. We believe that such an understanding is important so that Indian negotiators are more aware of their intellectual roots, but it is crucial for outsiders who seek to improve their bargaining relations with India. India's status in the world today presents a remarkable opportunity to the world as well as challenges. Successful bargaining with India will result in the creation of a more multipolar, pluralistic, and stable world. Failures in negotiation, however, will not only lead to greater recalcitrance from India but, by failing to produce buy-in from the world's largest democracy, will also risk producing increased systemic instability. Knowing how India negotiates can help us harness the opportunities and mitigate the risks.

REFERENCES

Berton, Peter. 1998. How Unique is Japanese Negotiating Behaviour? *Japan Review*, 10, 151–61.
Bhawalkar, Vanamala. 1999. *Woman in the Mahabharata*. New Delhi: Sharada.

Blaker, Michael. 1977. *Japanese International Negotiating Style*. New York: Columbia University Press.

Chaitanya, Krishna. 1993. *The Mahabharata: A Literary Study*. New Delhi: Clarion Books.

Cohen, Raymond. 2004. *Negotiating across Cultures: International Communication in an Interdependent World*. Washington DC: United States Institute of Peace Press (2nd revised edition).

Cohen, Stephen. 2001. *India: Emerging Power*. Washington DC: Brookings Institution.

Das, Gurcharan. 2009. *The Difficulty of Being Good: On the Subtle Art of Dharma*. Delhi: Penguin India.

Dasgupta, Chandrasekhar. 2011. Sweet Surrender: Jairam Ramesh has Turned India's Climate Policy on its Head. *The Telegraph*. 17 January. Accessed at <http://www. telegraphindia.com/1110117/jsp/opinion/story_13451487.jsp> on 16 August 2013.

Drake, L. E. 2001. The Culture-Negotiation Link: Integrative and Distributive Bargaining through an Intercultural Communication Lens. *Human Communication Research*, 27:3, 317–49.

Druckman Daniel, Alan Benton, Faizunisa Ali, and Susan Bagur. 1976. Cultural Differences in Bargaining Behaviour: India, Argentina and the United States. *Journal of Conflict Resolution*, 20:3, 413–52.

Faure, Guy Olivier. 1998. Negotiation: The Chinese Concept. *The Negotiation Journal*, 14:2, 137–48.

Faure, Guy Olivier and William Zartman eds. 1993. *Culture and Negotiation: The Resolution of Water Disputes*. Thousand Oaks, CA: Sage Publications.

Fisher, Roger and William Ury. 1981. *Getting to Yes: Negotiating Agreement without Giving In*. London: Random House.

Gelfand, Michele and Jeanne Brett eds. 2004. *The Handbook of Negotiation and Culture*. Stanford: Stanford University Press.

Henrich, Joseph, Stephen Heine, and Ara Norenzayan. 2010. The Weirdest People in the World? *Journal of Behavioural and Brain Science*, 33:2–3, June, 61–83.

Hurrell, Andrew. 2006. Hegemony, Liberalism, and Global Order. *International Affairs*, 82:1, January, 1–19.

Hurrell, Andrew and Amrita Narlikar. 2006. The New Politics of Confrontation: Developing Countries at Cancun and Beyond. *Global Society*, 20:4, 415–33.

Ikenberry, John. 2008. The Rise of China and the Future of the West. *Foreign Affairs*, 27:1, January–February, 23–57.

Janosik, Robert. 1987. Re-thinking the Culture Negotiation Link. *Negotiation Journal*, 3:4, 385–95.

Karve, Iravati. 1991. *Yuganta: The End of an Epoch*. Hyderabad: Disha Books/Orient Longman.

Kumar, Rajesh. 2004. Brahmanical Idealism, Anarchical Individualism, and the Dynamics of Indian Negotiating Behaviour. *International Journal of Cross Cultural Management*, 4:1, April, 39–58.

Kumar, Rajesh and Verner Worm. 2004. Institutional Dynamics and the Negotiation Process: Comparing India and China. *International Journal of Conflict Management*, 15:3, 304–34.

Kux, Dennis. 1993. *India and the United States: Estranged Democracies (1941–91)*. Diane Publishing Co.: Pennsylvania.

Legro, Jeffrey. 2007. What China Will Want. The Future Intentions of a Rising Power. *Perspectives on Politics*, 5:3, September, 515–34.

Lucas, Colin. 1999. In Stuart Clark ed., *The Annales School: Critical Assessments*. London: Routledge.

Malone, David. 2011. *Does the Elephant Dance?* Oxford: Oxford University Press.

Matilal, Bimal K. 2002. *Collected Essays of Bimal Krishna Matilal: Ethics and Epics*, ed. Jonardon Ganeri. Delhi: Oxford University Press.

Mohan, C. Raja. 2003. *Crossing the Rubicon: The Shaping of India's Foreign Policy*. Delhi: Viking.

Mohan, C. Raja. 2010. Rising India: Partner in Shaping the Global Commons? *Washington Quarterly*, 33:3, 133–48.

Narlikar, Amrita. 2003. *International Trade and Developing Countries: Bargaining Coalitions in the GATT and WTO*. London: Routledge.

Narlikar, Amrita. 2006. Strategic Calculation or Peculiar Chauvinism: The Negotiation Behaviour of a Rising India. *International Affairs*, 82:1, January, 59–76.

Narlikar, Amrita. 2007. All that Glitters is not Gold: India's Rise to Power. *Third World Quarterly*, 28:5, 983–96.

Narlikar, Amrita. 2009. A Theory of Bargaining Coalitions. In Amrita Narlikar and Brendan Vickers eds. *Leadership and Change in the Multilateral Trading System*. Leiden: Martinus Nijhoff.

Narlikar, Amrita. 2010. *New Powers: How to Become One and How to Manage Them*. New York: Columbia University Press, London: Hurst.

O'Neill, Jim. 2001. *Building Better Global Economic BRICs*. Goldman Sachs, Global Economics, 66, 30 November.

Odell, John. 2000. *Negotiating the World Economy*. Ithaca: Cornell University Press.

Odell, John. 2006. *Negotiating Trade: Developing Countries in the WTO and NAFTA*. Cambridge: Cambridge University Press.

Odell, John and Sell, Susan. 2006. Framing the Issue: TRIPs and the Public Health Declaration. In John Odell ed., *Negotiating Trade: Developing Countries in the WTO and NAFTA*. Cambridge: Cambridge University Press.

Offer, Avner. 1995. Going to War in 1914: A Matter of Honour? *Politics and Society*, 23:2, 213–41.

Perkovich, George. 2003. Is India a Major Power? *Washington Quarterly*, 27:1, 129–44.

Rajagopalan, Swarna. 2006. Security Ideas in the Valmiki Ramayana. In Swarna Rajagopalan ed., *Security and South Asia: Ideas, Institutions and Initiatives*. London: Routledge.

Ramanujan, A. K. 1999. *The Collected Essays of A.K. Ramanujan*, ed. Vinay Dharwadker. Oxford: Oxford University Press.

Salacuse, Jeswald. 2004. The Top Ten Ways in which Culture can affect your Negotiation. *Ivey Business Journal*, September–October, 1–6.

Sen, Amartya. 2005. *The Argumentative Indian: Writings on Indian Culture, History, and Identity*. London: Penguin.

Sen, Julius. 2004a. Negotiating Trade Agreements with India. *SAIIA Trade Policy Briefing*. no. 8, November.

Smith, John D. 2009. (Abridged and translated) *The Mahabharata*. London: Penguin Classics.

Sukthankar, V. S. 1957. *On the Meaning of the Mahabharata*. Bombay: Asiatic Society.

Takeo, Doi. 1973. *The Anatomy of Dependence*. Tokyo: Kubansha.

Tversky, Amos and Daniel Kahneman. 1981. The Framing of Decisions and the Psychology of Choice. *Science*, 211:4481, January, 453–58.

Weiner, Myron. 1984. Ancient Indian Political Theory and Contemporary Indian Politics. In S. Eisenstadt, Reuven Kahane, and David Shulman eds., *Orthodoxy, Heterodoxy and Dissent in India*. New York: Mouton Publishers.

2

India's Negotiation Strategy

The Heroism of Hard Bargaining?

One's choice of negotiation strategy depends on several conditions specific to the particular bargaining situation: whom one is negotiating with, what is at stake, what one's goals are, and so forth. But endogenous factors can be just as important as exogenous ones in determining the choice and implementation of negotiation strategy. In the case of individuals, personality and psychology traits impact upon both the use and success of hard versus soft bargaining tactics.[1] In the case of states, negotiating culture can play a crucial role in determining the dominant negotiating strategy of their politicians and diplomats with the outside world.[2] In this chapter, we investigate whether there is a pattern in the negotiating strategies of the characters of the Mahabharata to suggest dominance of one type, and, further, the extent to which a similar pattern of dominance persists in India's negotiation strategies today as part of its foreign policy behaviour.

The chapter proceeds in seven sections. First, we provide an overview of the standard categorization of negotiation strategies, and also briefly outline the dominant trend in the negotiation strategies of India since independence and as a rising power. Sections 2.2 to 2.6 discuss insights into negotiation strategies as offered by the Mahabharata, drawing on stories from the pre-war parts of the epic (Section 2.2), bargaining strategies in the course of the war (Section 2.3), negotiation strategies in the post-conflict period and also in the related stories and legends (Section 2.4), and the exceptions to the dominant trends (Section 2.5). Each section summarizes the insights offered by the stories. These insights are then brought together in Section 2.6, where we conduct an analysis of India's dominant trends in bargaining behaviour as well as deviations from the norm. We further investigate how far the classical insights remain applicable in modern-day negotiations, focusing particularly on

---

[1] Barry and Friedman 1998. [2] R. Cohen 2004; Salacuse 2004.

India's negotiations in multilateral trade and the nuclear non-proliferation regime. Section 2.7 concludes.

2.1. NEGOTIATION STRATEGY: THEORY AND PRACTICE

Analysts classify negotiating strategies into two categories representing the two ends of a bargaining spectrum: distributive and integrative (also sometimes referred to as value-claiming and value-creating respectively). Distributive strategies are employed to claim value from others and to defend against such claiming. Negotiators engaged in distributive bargaining must usually 'start high, concede slowly, exaggerate the value of concessions, minimize the benefits of the other's concessions, conceal information, argue forcefully on behalf of principles that imply favourable settlements, make commitments to accept only highly favourable agreements, and be willing to outwait the other fellow'.[3] Other tactics in the same genre include refusal to make any concessions, exaggerating one's minimum needs and priorities, manipulating information to disadvantage the other party, worsening the other party's BATNA (best alternative to negotiated agreement), issuing threats and imposing penalties. At the other end of the continuum lie integrative strategies, which target the attainment of goals that are not in fundamental conflict with each other, and thus can be integrated to mutual gain. Integrative bargaining usually involves attempts to exchange information relatively freely, understanding the other party's real needs and objectives, emphasizing commonalities and shared interests, searching for mutually beneficial solutions, even reframing the issue space itself, and a variety of other actions that John Odell sums up nicely as 'designed to expand rather than split the pie'.[4]

While no state consistently and constantly applies the same bargaining strategy across different issue areas and with different international actors, it is not difficult to identify a dominant strategy for most states. Influenced in good measure by the particular negotiating culture—conceptualized as 'a single shared value, a commonly-held cluster of values, or an ideology'— countries tend to exhibit a 'typical bargaining style'.[5] Post-independence India's negotiation strategies showed a clustering of negotiation strategies towards the distributive end, so much so that Stephen Cohen branded India's positioning as 'Just say no'. Contrary to expectations within the country and outside, many of the characteristic traits of India's distributive bargaining persisted even as India's power rose: Cohen, in his book *India: Emerging*

---

[3] Lax and Sebenius 1992, p. 50.
[4] Odell 2000; Lewicki et al. 2009; also see Hopmann 1995 and Odell 2006.
[5] Janosik 1987, p. 389.

Power, labels India's foreign policy chapter as 'the India that can't say yes'.[6]
Particular cases are discussed later in this chapter, but a brief overview follows.

After independence and the trauma of partition, India's position was not
one of overwhelming absolute power, or indeed relative power in relation to
most Western counterparts. Nonetheless, it showed itself to be a proud and
intrepid exponent of the distributive strategy. On international trade, from as
early as the 1950s, India led other developing countries in seeking exceptions
to the foundational principle of the GATT (General Agreement on Tariffs and
Trade), that is, the principle of Most Favoured Nation status, and instead
demanded Special and Differential Treatment for developing countries. The
resistance to engage in reciprocal concessions in the GATT was distributive
bargaining at its most fundamental. This trend continued: for example, in the
Uruguay Round of trade negotiations, India took the lead—and was the last to
eventually back down only when completely isolated—in refusing to make any
concessions until its demands were met. India was an active and leading
member of the United Nations Conference on Trade and Development
(UNCTAD), which was established in 1964, in good measure as an alternative
institution to the GATT on terms significantly more favourable to developing
countries. The creation of the UNCTAD was a distributive move on the part of
the developing world, of which India was a leading player. The distributive
trends in bargaining continued in other economic issues as well. India, for
example, was a leading proponent of the call for a New International Economic Order—a call for economic global justice that was explicitly distributive
in demanding a transfer of resources from the developed to the developing
world (discussed in greater detail in Chapter 4 on framing). On climate change
mitigation, India as part of the G77-plus-China, and alone, traditionally
adopted a firm stance on the diminished and differentiated responsibilities
of developing countries. On nuclear weapons and disarmament, its position
was largely unwavering: until universal disarmament was achieved, there was
no question of India giving up its nuclear option. Its opposition to the use of
nuclear weapons was framed in strongly moralistic tones, but its refusal to sign
the Comprehensive Test Ban Treaty (CTBT) or the nuclear Non-Proliferation
Treaty (NPT) sent clear signals to the 'nuclear-haves' that India was not going
to make concessions on this area until 'nuclear apartheid' ended. Across issue
areas, therefore, India's dominant negotiating strategy was distributive, even
when it bargained from a position of relative weakness in the global hierarchy.[6]

There were a few exceptions to this norm of distributive bargaining. Let us
consider two. First, Nehru invited the involvement of the UN over Kashmir in
1948, thereby internationalizing its dispute with Pakistan. At first glance, this
may well appear as a move towards integrative bargaining: after all, what could

---

[6] S. Cohen 2001.

be a better way of securing mutually beneficially solutions than seeking the help of an impartial international arbiter? In actuality, this was not the case. While India maintained a sensible strategic caution against escalating the situation to a full-blown war in haste, its appeal to the Security Council was not for mediation but to order Pakistan to withdraw its troops. In other words, this was not behaviour towards reconciliation or exploration of a joint international solution, but towards the legitimization of its non-negotiable claims (and the delegitimization of the Pakistani infiltration into and invasion of Kashmir) to the international community. This was effectively still distributive behaviour—diplomatically framed, and perhaps less overt than some of the actions highlighted above, but distributive nonetheless. Importantly, this slightly more subtle distributive behaviour did not go down well with a large section of the Indian policy community, especially because of the outcome that it generated; that is, the UN's failure to condemn the Pakistani action and instead intervene in the dispute through the creation of the UN Commission on India and Pakistan and the UN Military Observer Group for India and Pakistan. Having been burnt by this attempt at relatively less hard bargaining, India came to espouse the discourse of state sovereignty, autonomy, and non-intervention with even greater vigour for decades afterwards.[7] And Nehru's decision to involve the UN remains the subject of considerable criticism in the policy community even today.[8]

The second issue, which we could possibly interpret as integrative behaviour, is India's leadership of the Non-Aligned Movement (NAM). Some effort was made towards framing the NAM, and India's participation in it, as an illustration of the refusal of India and its Third World allies to get drawn into the Cold War and choose sides. Nehru's framing of non-alignment was skilled and smart, and at least suggestive of integrative bargaining in its attempt to view each international situation on its own merit rather than bind the country into a firm and inflexible position. In his own words, non-alignment was a 'summary description' of the policy of 'friendship towards all nations, uncompromised by adherence to any military pacts. This was not due to any indifference to issues that arose, but rather to a desire to judge them for ourselves, in full freedom and without any preconceived partisan bias. It implied, basically, a conviction . . . that if we were to join one military group than the other it was liable to increase and not diminish the risk of a major clash between them.'[9] This is a strong and persuasive defence of non-alignment,

---

[7] India's willingness to sign the Partial Test Ban Treaty (PTBT) in 1963 can be viewed in a similar light. Nehru attracted domestic criticism on this; the limited payoffs that this regime compliance generated (i.e. no security guarantees from the major powers) and the actual costs (i.e. the emergence of a nuclear China next door in 1964, which was not a signatory to the PTBT) may have contributed to a hardening of the Indian stance on future multilateral initiatives on non-proliferation. See Moshaver 1991; Narlikar 2006.

[8] Swamy 2001.   [9] Nehru 1963.

especially as it came in the aftermath of India's disastrous war with China in 1962. But two caveats must be borne in mind. First, non-alignment did not win India many friends in the First World, where it was seen as 'neutralism' at best (repeated and eloquent denials by India on this notwithstanding),[10] and a cloak for its alignment with the Socialist bloc at worst.[11] Nehru himself recognized in the same article that India's non-alignment policy had 'no doubt . . . displeased some people to begin with . . .'. Second, there is a real question as to how 'non-aligned' India really was. In a statistical study of voting behaviour by the non-aligned countries, Shay finds that until October 1962 India's voting behaviour in the UN General Assembly was strongly pro-Soviet: on positive votes, India sided with the West only 11 per cent of the time, while its positive votes cast with the Soviet Union amounted to 89 per cent. After the Chinese invasion, however, India's voting behaviour swung dramatically. Writing in 1968, Shay records that India's votes with the West reached 82 per cent, while its votes with the Soviet Union were 18 per cent. No other country shows a comparable switch in its voting patterns in this period. The implications of this are discussed in Chapter 4 on coalitions; suffice it to note, however, at this point that a) India's non-alignment was not seen as integrative bargaining from the outside, and India largely adhered to it even while recognizing that its opponents saw it as an offensive distributive strategy, and b) at least in the period until 1962, for all practical purposes India's non-alignment did end up displaying pro-Soviet inclinations, which effectively translated into distributive bargaining tactics from the viewpoint of the West.

What then of India as a rising power? One might expect that as it came to bargain from a position of strength and especially if it were welcomed into the Great Power clubs, some of its 'famous defensiveness' and 'prickliness' might decline,[12] and it might be more willing to use integrative negotiation strategies.[13] In practice, however, we find this is not the case. India, in most issue areas, has continued to use the distributive negotiation strategy even after it has acquired increasing stakes in the system. Detailed examples of India's negotiation strategy as a rising power follow in the rest of this chapter. At this point, however, note that as its power rises, India's distributive strategy has potentially much higher impact (in contrast with its use of similar distributive

---

[10] Krishna Menon thus asserted in 1960, for instance, 'We are not a neutral country. We refuse to accept responsibility for the appellation "neutralism" . . . We are not neutral or neutralist, positive or otherwise. We would take part, we would participate, we would express our views. Even that expression positive neutrality is a contradiction in terms. There can be no more be positive neutrality than there can be a vegetarian tiger.' Cited in Shay 1968, p. 228.

[11] E.g. S. Cohen 2001; Zins and Boquérat (eds.) 2004.   [12] Mohan 2003.

[13] For examples of the argument of increasing buy-in from rising powers, see Johnston 2003; Kang 2007; Ikenberry 2008.

strategies as a lesser power). Insofar as Schelling identified 'the power to hurt' as 'bargaining power', India certainly enjoys veto power in multilateral institutions today.[14] Hence, for example, it has successfully demonstrated its ability to hold up the multilateral trade negotiations process at the World Trade Organization (WTO), mainly as a result of its refusal to make concessions on agriculture; on climate change too, one of the reasons why a meaningful and binding agreement has been difficult to reach is because India (along with its allies from the developing world) has refused to take on binding commitments. This is not to say that India's negotiation position is invariant and unchanging across all issues. For some, India's willingness to take on voluntary controls on emissions reflects a softening of its former hard-line stance. And even more importantly, the India that had traditionally enjoyed at best a cool relationship with the US is now the India that is hailed as a 'natural ally' by the US, and has come to enjoy a unique and privileged position in the NPT regime through its bilateral deal with the US. In return, India too has made some concessions—surely a sign of integrative bargaining? These cases provide us valuable illustrations of the extent to which and also the conditions under which India engages in integrative bargaining, and will be discussed at length in Section 2.6.

2.2. NEGOTIATION STRATEGIES OF THE MAIN PROTAGONISTS, PRE-WAR

Prior to the war, we have a host of stories to draw from, which are detailed in the first five books that constitute the Mahabharata. We offer three below in this section, all of which deal with central protagonists in the main story.

2.2.1. Bargaining over the future—the fisherman and Bhishma

Bhishma—a central and heroic figure in the story of the Mahabharata, and referred to as 'Bhishma Pitamah' or grandsire of the Kauravas and Pandavas— was formerly known as Devavrata. He was the son of King Shantanu, but no ordinary mortal was he: his mother was the holy river Ganga, and he himself was one of the eight 'vasus' (gods) who had been reborn as a man.[15] His

---

[14] Schelling 1966.
[15] The story of Ganga and Shantanu is also one where negotiation is an important theme. Ganga agreed to marry Shantanu on the condition that he would never question her past, nor would he question any of her actions or reprimand her for them. Shantanu agreed. He subsequently witnessed and abhorred the shocking and repetitive acts of his wife: the consecutive

mother Ganga had ensured that he received his education from the most supreme peers in the fields of weaponry ('astravidya' from the hermit Parashurama, son of Jamadagni), statecraft and statesmanship ('rajadharma' and 'arthashastra'), the Vedas (from the sage Vashishtha), law and justice (the 'Neetishastra' from Shukracharya, the teacher of the Asuras), and was also embodied with the knowledge propounded by Brihaspati (Guru, the teacher of the devas). When Devavrata arrived in the city of Hastinapur with his father, Shantanu, he was installed as heir apparent.

Some years later, King Shantanu went into the woods and was enamoured with the daughter of a fisherman, Satyavati, and wished to marry her. Satyavati's father, the chief of the fishermen (Dasharaja), drove a hard bargain, however: he would permit such a marriage if and only if King Shantanu pledged that Satyavati's future son would be the heir to his throne and his entire kingdom:

अस्यां जायेत यः पुत्रः स राजा पृथिवीपतिः
त्वदूर्ध्वमभिषेक्तव्यो नान्यः कश्चन पार्थिव
I.94.51

The son resulting from this marriage would be crowned king, and none other.

Having already installed his son Devavrata as his heir apparent, Shantanu could not make such a promise. But his heart was heavy as this also meant that he would not be able to obtain the beautiful Satyavati as his wife.

Devavrata, on learning of the real cause of his father's grief, went in person to negotiate with Dasharaja, accompanied by an entourage of distinguished Kshatriya elders. Dasharaja's position was firm and unchanging: while recognizing the merit of such a marriage and signalling his commitment to this alliance by highlighting that many other worthy suitors had been turned down, he reiterated his demand.

---

drowning of their seven sons soon after birth. On the birth of their eighth son, he could no longer contain himself and demanded an explanation for her 'sinful' actions. At this point, Ganga reminded him of their agreement, and her resolve to leave him forever upon being thus questioned. But she also revealed her divine identity to him, and explained that their eight sons were in fact the eight vasus (gods) who had been cursed to take birth as mortals. Ganga had been entrusted with the duty of putting them out of their human misery immediately after birth, and thereby also liberating them from their curse. But the eighth son, named Devavrata, Ganga agreed, would be a gift to Shantanu from her. She would look after him until he was accomplished in all the expertise in arms and all other warfare techniques, studied the Vedas, learnt the Dharma of a king and that of a good human being, and then she would bring him back to his father. She kept her promise, and after a few years Ganga-putra Devavrata, the prince, strong like a bull and bright like the sun, was brought back to his father, King Shantanu. The story is indicative of both the hard bargain that was initially struck between Shantanu and Ganga, and also the firmness/inflexibility with which it was adhered to, such that not even many years of a loving marriage would deter Ganga's resolve to forsake her husband upon being questioned.

Devavrata responded with grace, and promised, 'I will do as you demand. Only the son of Satyavati shall be our king.' In acting thus, Devavrata had abdicated, willingly, his claim to the throne. But even this generous offer did not suffice. Dasharaja stated:

यत्त्वया सत्यवत्यर्थे सत्यधर्मपरायण
राजमध्ये प्रतिज्ञातमनुरुपं तवैव तत्
नान्यथा तन्महाबाहो संशयोस्मत्र न कश्चन
तवापत्यं भवेद्यत्तु तत्र नः संशयो महान्
I.94. 83, 84

Oh Follower of the truth and Dharma, this pledge that you have made amidst these Kshatriya kings is a fitting tribute to your greatness. I do not have the slightest doubt of your word. But I have grave doubts about your future sons, who may not adhere to your promise.

Dasharaja, not satisfied with Devavrata's generous and selfless pledge, was now effectively asking the rightful heir apparent to sign away the rights even of his future descendants. Devavrata complied by taking a vow of celibacy, which would have significant consequences for the history of the kingdom. We discuss Devavrata's vow in detail in the next chapter on framing. But note at this point that when Devavrata took his vow, the gods, sages, and other enchanted beings (apsaras) showered flowers from the heavens and cried out in admiration, 'The prince to take this terrible and awe-inspiring vow will be known as Bhishma!'[16]

Dasharaja's negotiation strategy was distributive bargaining at its most obvious: he had started out with high opening demands, had shown no flexibility in his position with either King Shantanu or his son Devavrata, had highlighted strong BATNAs by referring to alternative suitors who had been turned down, and had subsequently only increased his demands. Interestingly, he is no villain in the huge drama of the great war epic we have at hand, nor is he presented as such at any point; he is only trying to secure the future of his daughter. Just as relevant is the ease with which Bhishma—one of the supreme heroes of the text—caves in to the demands of Dasharaja. He does not, for instance, try to come up with creative, integrative solutions that could satisfy all parties (such as a division of the kingdom, or specified periods of rule for the potential heirs of Satyavati and his own). Bhishma is no weakling: his willingness to concede stems from his duty and loyalty towards his father. He goes on to adopt strictly distributive negotiation tactics in different parts of the epic and in the face of massive costs. Importantly, he resists entreaties by many (including Satyavati herself) and attempts at coercion (by the powerful

---

[16] The precise translation of 'bhishma' is difficult, but the word connotes a mixture of the qualities of terrible, difficult, awe inspiring, and great. The sacrifice inherent in Devavrata's vow won him this title.

sage Parashurama) to forsake his vow—his big concession to Dasharaja– that
threatens the future of the entire clan of the Kurus and lays the roots of the
great conflict between the cousins. Bhishma's terrible vow—his one-off concessionary tactic in the first instance—from the perspective of the Mahabharata, generates costly and unfortunate consequences for all its protagonists
including future generations of Bhishma's family (even though it secures
Bhishma the admiration of the gods and the boon from his father that
Death could only approach him when Bhishma commanded him to do so).
The costs for the family include difficulties in ensuring that a male heir is born
to continue the royal lineage. Bhishma is entreated several times to renounce
his vow, including by Satyavati (his stepmother) to help ensure the family line,
but he stands firmly by his word.

2.2.2. Arjuna, Dronacharya, and Ekalavya

The sage Drona was the renowned and distinguished guru of both the
Kauravas and the Pandavas. It was Drona who trained the Kshatriya cousins
in the use of weaponry, both celestial and earthly, and is referred to frequently
in the text as Dronacharya ('acharya' translating into teacher). Arjuna was his
favourite and most accomplished student, and so great was Arjuna's devotion
to learning and Drona's commitment to teaching him that Drona made his
protégé a promise:

प्रयतिष्ये तथा कर्तुं यथा नान्यो धनुर्धरः
त्वत्समो भविता लोके सत्यमेतद् ब्रवीमि ते
I.131.27 (Gita Press edition)

I speak the truth: I will try to ensure that there is no other archer in the world who
would be equal to you.

And having made this promise, Dronacharya gave Arjuna his special attention
to teach him the diverse techniques of weaponry that could be employed in
many difficult and diverse situations.

As Drona's fame as a teacher of military arts spread, students flocked to him
for learning. Among these was the prince Ekalavya, the son of an Indian
aboriginal tribal king (Nishadaraja), Hiranyadhanusha. Drona turned him
away on grounds of his low caste, but behind Drona's stated reason was his
fear that were Ekalavya to receive the appropriate training, he might outperform all of Drona's Kshatriya pupils. Still respectful towards Dronacharya and
unwavering in his quest to learn from the supreme teacher, Ekalavya went into
the forest, built a clay statue resembling Dronacharya, and began to practise
archery before it as one would before a teacher. With great devotion and effort,
this self-taught archer acquired skills that were equal to none but Arjuna
himself. One day, when the Kauravas and Pandavas were out on a hunting

expedition in the jungle, they came across Ekalavya performing a remarkable feat of archery. When asked to identify himself, Ekalavya responded courteously not only by referring to his tribal lineage but also by stating that he was a pupil of Drona. On returning to the city, the Kaurava and Pandava princes narrated to their teacher the skilled archery they had witnessed; and in private, Arjuna complained to Dronacharya: 'You had told me with great affection that none of your students would be equal to me. Then how is it that one of your students, the courageous son of the Nishadaraja, is mightier than I am?'

Dronacharya could not have his word, nor that of his favourite pupil, come under such challenge. Accompanied by Arjuna, he went to the forest to find Ekalavya. Ekalavya greeted Drona with the respect one accords to one's teacher, upon which Drona demanded his due fee, that is, Gurudakshina, from the one who claimed to be his pupil. Ekalavya promised him anything he wished for, and Drona demanded—and duly received—a very high price: the thumb of Ekalavya's right hand.

एकलव्यस्ततश्रुत्वा वचो द्रोणस्य दारुणम्
प्रतिज्ञामात्मनो रक्षन् सत्ये च नियतः सदा
तथैव हृष्टवदनस्तथैवादीनमानसः
छित्त्वाविचार्य तं प्रादाद् द्रोणायागुंष्ठमात्मनः
I.131.57, 58 (Gita Press Edition)

Hearing the heart-rending words of Dronacharya, always true to his word and determined to keep his promise, Ekalavya remained cheerful and generous-spirited as ever; without giving the matter a second thought, he cut off the thumb of his right hand and gave it to his teacher.

Dronacharya, having accepted the Gurudakshina, was impressed with Ekalavya's sacrifice, and indicated to him how he might still be able to fire arrows without the use of his thumb. With this handicap, however, Ekalavya's skill as an archer was much reduced and his arrows were no longer as swift as they used to be. Arjuna once again became the archer of supreme and matchless skill.[17]

In this episode, we see that Ekalavya's sacrifice is graceful and considerable; this low-caste prince with his matted hair and dark skin is the one who makes the prompt and unquestioned concession. We also see the use of a highly distributive strategy adopted by a major protagonist of the epic—one who is respected equally by the Kauravas and the Pandavas, and who occupies the particularly venerated position of the guru or teacher. In the use of this strategy, Dronacharya has in mind the interests of, and is supported by, one of the most heroic figures of the epic—Arjuna—the courageous and noble Pandava prince who is a great favourite with the god Krishna.

---

[17] Arjuna is reported to have been gladdened by this event, and his worries disappeared. Dronacharya also now has the satisfaction of knowing that he has fulfilled his promise to Arjuna.

Ekalavya pays a prohibitively high price for his learning, which he has acquired by an unconventional route (after having been turned away from the more straightforward route by Dronacharya). He is no enemy of Drona's or Arjuna's; he poses no direct threat to the kingdom; his fault is to have acquired his skill in spite of Dronacharya's resistance and to have thereby emerged as a potential competitor to Arjuna, thus posing a challenge to Drona's promise to Arjuna.

The story offers several insights. First, it reveals the ties of teacher–pupil loyalty. But it also reveals that a very high price can be demanded, without any reproach, when negotiating with an 'outsider'. Second, the story points to the possible underestimation in the literature of the concept of 'face' in the Indian context, which has been applied extensively to East Asian negotiation: we might hypothesize, in the light of the Drona–Arjuna–Ekalavya episode, that the likelihood of highly distributive bargaining increases when saving one's face is at stake. Third, the only time we see the slightest indication of a small integrative move is when Ekalavya, having complied fully and unquestioningly with Drona's demand, is effectively given recognition as a student of Dronacharya by the guru having accepted the Gurudakshina. With the transaction thus completed, and Ekalavya having paid the price of becoming an 'insider', Drona instructs him on how he might still be able to use the bow and arrow skilfully despite his missing thumb. This is a very small concession on Drona's part, and it comes only after Ekalavya has complied fully, with a big sacrifice, to alleviate Arjuna's insecurity regarding his prowess as a matchless archer and to assure Dronacharya that his promise to Arjuna will not be broken.

2.2.3. The Pandavas and the Yaksha

A famous story in the Mahabharata is about the encounter between the eldest Pandava Yudhishthira and a magical being of the lake, a Yaksha. The prelude to this story is of particular relevance to us in this chapter, and we recount it below.

The Pandavas were sent into exile by the Kauravas after having lost their possessions in a rigged gambling match. Their travails and adventures are covered in Book 3 of the Mahabharata, the Vana Parva. As they neared the end of their 13-year exile, the five Pandava brothers found themselves on a mission to assist a sage: a deer had run off with the sage's firewood and staff, which were essential for the performance of a fire sacrifice (agnihotra) that he was conducting. The brothers gave chase to the deer, but the fleet-footed creature vanished. Weary, disheartened, and thirsty, the brothers sat under the shade of a banyan tree. On being instructed by the eldest, one of the brothers climbed a tree and spotted the signs of a lake, which could perhaps alleviate their thirst.

Thus Nakula, the fourth brother, was sent out to the lake to return with water for the group.

Nakula arrived at the lake, which appeared to be made of crystal and was inhabited by cranes. As Nakula reached out to drink the water, he heard a voice from the heavens:

मा तात साहसं काषीर्मम पूर्वेपरिग्रहः
प्रश्नानुक्त्वा तु मादेय ततः पिब हरस्व च
III.296.12

Child, do not presume to drink from this lake, on which I already have a rightful possession. First answer my questions, oh son of Madri, and then you may drink the water and also take some with you.

Nakula, however, was very thirsty; he disregarded the voice and its claim to the lake, drank the cool water from it, and died. When Nakula failed to arrive, Sahadeva was sent out to search for him. Sahadeva saw the lifeless body of his brother, and heard the same warning. Disregarding the claim to the lake that the voice stated, he nonetheless drank from the waters, and paid with his life.

When both Nakula and Sahadeva did not return, the other three Pandava brothers were deeply concerned. Courageous Arjuna was sent out as the rescue party, and he left armed and prepared with his bow and arrows, and also an unsheathed sword. Aggrieved and agitated on seeing the bodies of his two brothers, he looked around for the perpetrator of these crimes, but found none. With his bow still drawn, as he went towards the water for a drink, once again the same warning was heard. Hearing the words thus uttered, Arjuna reciprocated with a fierce threat:

वारितस्त्वब्रवीत्पार्थो तृष्यमानो निवारय
यावद्बाणैर्विनिर्भिन्नः पुनर्नैवं वदिष्यसि
III.296.27

Show yourself and try to stop me, and when my arrows shoot you to smithereens, you will not dare to speak in such a manner again.

And immediately after responding to the claim on the lake by the nameless voice, Arjuna fired enchanted arrows around the lake, and further unleashed a ferocious volley of magical weapons at his invisible foe. Once again, the voice spoke: 'What is the point of inflicting such violence, O Partha? . . . If you partake of the waters of this lake before answering my questions, then you will meet your instant death.' Ambidextrous Arjuna, alert with bow and arrow at the ready, now drank from the lake, and also fell to the ground, lifeless.

Yudhishthira, after having waited in vain, then sent out the strong and powerful Bhima to find the missing Pandavas. Bhima saw the bodies of his three brothers, and, assuming that he would have to fight a battle that day, decided to prepare himself by satiating his thirst. Consistent with the previous encounters, the voice once again offered the same warning to the fourth Pandava to arrive on the scene. Bhima too, like his brothers before him, ignored the warning, drank the waters of the enchanted lake, and met his death.

Anxious for the safety of all his brothers, now Yudhishthira set out in search of them himself. On reaching the lake, he was the first and the only Pandava brother to consider (admittedly after emotional lamentations and anger) whether his brothers may have caused offence to some mighty being of the forest. He was also the brother to whom the voice admitted to having slain his brothers, and further admitted to being a Yaksha. And finally, he was the only brother who, upon receiving the same warning as his brothers that the Yaksha had the prior claim to the lake, stated:

नैवाहं कामये यक्ष तव पूर्वपरिग्रहम् . . .
III.297.24
यथाप्रज्ञं तु ते प्रश्नान्प्रतिवक्ष्यामि पृच्छ माम्
III.297.25

I have no wish to claim possession on what is already yours . . . I will try to answer your questions to the best of my abilities without making any grand claims about my own intelligence.

True to his promise, Yudhishthira offered answers laden in wisdom to the Yaksha, and having thus satisfied him not only acquired the right to drink the water from the lake but also was able to get the Yaksha to restore the life of all four brothers.

In this story, four of the five Pandava brothers failed the test of the Yaksha. The failure arose from the use of a strict distributive strategy that was tantamount to a refusal to negotiate. The first two brothers who ventured on the quest simply ignored the disembodied voice that claimed a right to the lake. This was arrogant enough in its own right, but even more so coming from Sahadeva, who also saw the dead body of his brother lying by the lakeside. Bhima's strategy was very similar to that of Nakula and Sahadeva. And, surprisingly, the usually reasonable Arjuna's strategy was even more distributive than that of the other three: his response to the warning, rather than an attempt to reason with the voice, was to first issue a threat, and then to carry out the threat by unleashing his arrows without even waiting for the foe to reveal himself. The use of distributive tactics did not work to the advantage of any of the four brothers in this instance.

Yudhishthira, in contrast, was the last brother to arrive on the scene, and used integrative tactics. He accepted the claim of the Yaksha to the lake, and reassured him by word and deed that he had no intention of challenging this claim. The reward came first in the form of his right to drink the water; then, further, the opportunity to revive any one of his four brothers; and finally, having impressed the Yaksha with his profound sense of justice, his rescue of all four brothers from death itself.

This story indicates first and foremost that the distributive negotiation tactic is the norm, even for the Pandava princes who represent the side of truth and virtue in this epic. Despite the evidence that confronts them in the shape of the lifeless bodies of their brothers, Sahadeva, Arjuna, and Bhima disregard the Yaksha's warning. Second, amongst the four brothers there is some variation in strategy, but all cluster at the distributive end. Nakula and Sahadeva's strategy is simply to ignore the warning, effectively an attempt to avoid negotiation, and continue on their intended course without taking in new information. Bhima assumes the likelihood of battle after seeing the bodies of his brothers, thereby revealing greater responsiveness to new evidence than Nakula and Sahadeva. But his response is to prepare himself for battle by drinking from the lake, paying no attention to the warning voice, and thus generating the same outcome. Arjuna's negotiating strategy is the most distributive: while the other three brothers chose to ignore the Yaksha, Arjuna challenges the voice to battle and signals his intentions by firing off a volley of arrows. Third, Yudhishthira, the eldest Pandava who is also known as Dharmaraja, is the only one of the brothers to use integrative bargaining. He is the exception to the norm. He acknowledges the claim of the Yaksha respectfully, and answers his questions on his own terms. Further, as we discuss in Chapter 3, his attention to the issue of morality and justice wins him the admiration of the Yaksha, who as a reward revives all the Pandava brothers and brings them back to life.

2.2.4. Insights for Negotiation

The three stories above indicate the use (with differing degrees of success) of distributive strategies by characters who are no villains in the epic. As we go on to illustrate later in the chapter, the Kauravas are just as familiar and adept at distributive strategies. But importantly, the first insight offered by all three stories is that distributive bargaining in the Mahabharata is not the domain solely of villains but also of heroes (even Arjuna, the son of the god Indra himself).

Second, two stories of the three also illustrate the costs of integrative strategies. In Bhishma's case, we find not only Bhishma himself stuck with a 'terrible' vow, but also his entire clan and future generations of his clan that pay the price in the form of a vicious war of succession, which came to be known as the Mahabharata. In Ekalavya's case, we find the use of the integrative strategy extremely costly: this brave tribal prince has been deprived of the supremacy of his skill in archery by having behaved in a concessionary manner. In contrast, the third story offers us the costs—the extreme penalty of death—that accrue to the four Pandava brothers for using distributive tactics with the Yaksha, whereas Yudhishthira is rewarded for his strategy of conciliatory bargaining. But the integrative bargaining comes from the right-eous, duty-bound, and ever truthful Yudhishthira—the son of Dharma himself—who is presented throughout the epic as an exception to the norm (so much so that in the battle of Kurukshetra, the wheels of Yudhishthira's chariot float above the ground, until the point he tells his only 'half-truth' and the wheels sink to the ground). In the fifth section, we discuss this case further to investigate the extent to which Yudhishthira's integrative bargaining forms one of the few exceptions that prove the 'rule' of distributive bargaining as the dominant negotiation strategy.

Third, the integrative bargaining by both Bhishma and Yudhishthira takes the shape of concessions—arguably complete capitulation in fact—rather than a willingness to jointly explore and recreate the negotiating space and find solutions in favour of all parties. Bhishma does not even suggest alternative solutions as a counter to the escalatory demands of Satyavati's father. Yud-hishthira not only accepts the terms of the Yaksha without any attempt at negotiation, but achieves favourable outcomes (such as the revival of his brothers) by impressing the Yaksha with his answers rather than bargaining with him. These are strategies aimed not at expanding the pie but giving away one's own share of it, and hence at best an odd form of integrative bargaining.

Fourth, the stories begin to hint that the use of distributive strategies is conditioned by the target: Bhishma is not a particularly pliable personality and very seldom engages in integrative bargaining in the rest of the epic, but he complies entirely with the demands of Dasharaja out of his love, loyalty, and duty to his father. Dronacharya has no hesitation in demanding the terrible sacrifice from Ekalavya, partly to ensure that his own promise is not broken but equally to ensure that Arjuna is not challenged by the tribal upstart. Securing the sacrifice of an outsider to alleviate Arjuna's insecurity is accept-able to Dronacharya; to have his word or his favourite student challenged by an outsider is not. Moreover, Dronacharya is not the sole repository of blame in this story: so is the usually moral Arjuna, whose complaints prompt Drona to take the actions that he does, and who accompanies Drona into the forest for the demand of the Gurudakshina.

Finally, common to all the three stories are at least two distributive tactics: high opening demands and a refusal to make concessions. This was true in the case of the four Pandava brothers in their dealings with the Yaksha, and it was also true in the case of Dronacharya's bargain with Ekalavya and in the negotiation between Shantanu and Bhishma versus Dasharaja on the marriage of Satyavati. In Dasharaja's case, we saw him escalate his demands after Bhishma had met the initial one, and we saw ready compliance from the hero Bhishma resulting in a one-sided agreement on terms entirely favourable to Dasharaja and his daughter. In the other two stories, we see immediate compliance from Ekalavya in response to Drona's demands, and a complete rejection of the Yaksha's demands by four of the five Pandava brothers.

The interesting common feature that binds the high opening demands and refusal to make concessions is the take-it-or-leave-it approach adopted by most parties.

2.3. WARTIME NEGOTIATION STRATEGIES

The great and disastrous war that is the central theme of the Mahabharata lasts only 18 days. But the devastation caused in these 18 days is overwhelming, and we have five books within the epic that recount the strategies of war that were used, and also the thought, debate, and bargaining that went into their making. We discuss three cases of negotiation that were vital in the progress of this great war, and continue to occupy a place of considerable importance in the Indian imagination even today.

2.3.1. Karna's solitary battle in full distributive mode

Karna was the eldest Pandava brother, who had been abandoned by his mother Kunti soon after his birth, and was brought up as the adopted son of a charioteer. He became a loyal ally of Duryodhana and fought bravely by his side at Kurukshetra. Karna is the tragic hero of the epic: denied his claim to his royal lineage, subject to mockery and ridicule as an overambitious social climber, charismatic and glorious in personality like his father Surya (the sun god), of noble courage and matched in skill only by Arjuna as a warrior, generous to a fault, loyal unto death, and on the wrong side of history. In this section, we explore the negotiation strategy of this solitary hero in battle.

Karna entered the battle of Kurukshetra only on the 11th day, when Bhishma ceased to serve as the Kauravas' commander-in-chief.[18] The morale of the Kauravas had been badly damaged by Bhishma's exit, which was caused by severe injuries inflicted by Arjuna, and it improved with the arrival of Karna on centre stage. Karna took charge of the Kaurava side on the 16th day of the war as commander-in-chief, and his main combatant and target was Arjuna. On the 17th day, having received a battering by Arjuna's arrows, Karna decided to finally make use of the arrow that he had worshipped and preserved with great care specifically for Arjuna as his mark. This

---

[18] Dronacharya had proposed a leading role for Karna in the Kaurava military formation; but Bhishma, the chief commander, denied him this role on the grounds of Karna's many misdemeanours. Karna retaliated by stating that he would not serve in battle at all under Bhishma. The lack of integrative bargaining amongst themselves thus deprived the Kaurava side of one of their most valorous warriors for more than the first half of the war.

arrow—Nagaastra—was shaped at the mouth as a Naga (cobra), and was endowed with great powers of destruction that were in large measure a result of Karna's devotion, worship, and single-minded cause. Unknown to Karna, a brave snake of princely blood—Ashwasena—had first climbed into his quiver and then into the Nagaastra to assist Karna. Ashwasena had long harboured enmity towards Arjuna who had, when in exile, killed Ashwasena's mother when burning down the Khandava forest. The presence of this courageous, determined, and justice-seeking snake on Karna's arrow further enhanced the strength of this already deadly weapon. Karna took aim. The heavens rang with the cries of the gods; and the thousand-eyed Indra himself feared for his son Arjuna's life on observing the snake hidden in Karna's arrow.

Just as Karna was about to shoot his powerful arrow, his charioteer, Shalya, warned him, 'Your arrow will not pierce the neck of your enemy. Reconsider your aim and realign your arrow to decapitate your opponent.' This sensible advice, however, provoked the wrath of Karna. Eyes burning red in anger, he responded:

अथाब्रवीत् क्रोधसंरक्तनेत्रो मद्राधिपं सूतपुत्रस्तरस्वी
न संधत्ते द्विः शरं शल्य कर्णो न माद्रृशा जिह्मयुध्दा भवन्ति
VIII.90.26 (Gita Press edition)

Shalya, Karna never aims his arrow twice. Warriors like me do not engage in such devious practices.

And Karna then released his arrow. As Shalya had anticipated, Krishna—Arjuna's charioteer—lowered the wheels of the chariot into the earth, and the white steeds drawing the chariot knelt down. Karna's arrow, with the assistance of Ashwasena, knocked off Arjuna's precious and radiant crown (gifted to him by Indra), but failed to meet its objective. Arjuna still lived.

The snake Ashwasena now returned to Karna, and spoke:

मुक्तस्त्वयाहं त्वसमीक्ष्य कर्णे शिरो हृतं यन्न मयार्जुनस्य
समीक्ष्य मां मुञ्च रणे त्वमाशु हन्तासि शत्रुं तव चात्मनश्च
VIII.90.45 (Gita Press edition)

You did not think through your aim (as you were not aware of my presence on your arrow), and so I was unable to slay Arjuna. Release me again on your arrow after taking all into careful consideration, and I will destroy your foe and mine . . . Even if Indra himself came to the rescue of Arjuna today, Arjuna would still have to descend the netherworld.

Karna responded to Ashwasena: 'Naga, Karna does not wish to claim victory in this battlefield on the strength of anyone else's support. I would not fire the same arrow twice, even if I had to slay a hundred Arjunas.[19] I have another

---

[19] And having Ashwasena on another arrow would have meant a second use of the same weapon; Ashwasena could not be used for a second time according to Karna's principles, even though Karna had not been aware of Ashwasena's presence the first time.

snake-mouthed arrow, I am making optimal effort, and I have great anger towards Arjuna. I will destroy Arjuna. Rest assured and make your way.'

Hurt and angered by Karna's refusal of his help, the terrifying Ashwasena, unaided and alone, attacked Arjuna. His attack failed, and he was brutally killed by Arjuna's arrows. The duel between Arjuna and Karna continued with heavy fire; at the end of the day, Karna would be mercilessly killed (discussed in detail in Chapter 3).

In this story, the revenge-bound Ashwasena's strategy towards Karna was integrative: he wished to join forces with Karna to allow both Karna and himself the joint gain of Arjuna's death. Karna's strategy, in contrast, was highly distributive. First, he refused to change his aim, even though his charioteer had anticipated Krishna's actions and had asked him to realign his arrow. Rather than respond to this new information and act accordingly, Karna simply reiterated his commitment to never changing the aim of an arrow that he had already affixed and targeted. Instead, he went on to argue that realigning one's aim was dishonourable conduct for a warrior. The result of this inflexibility was that his long-cherished and empowered arrow missed its aim. Second, Karna also turned down Ashwasena's offer of having his arrow re-strengthened and re-fired through his help. He appealed to the same principle in turning down this offer that could have led to mutual gain. His argument that he did not wish to win the battle with the strength of another was effectively also an argument of refusal to share success and glory (without which integrative moves are naturally very difficult). The result of Karna's distributive bargaining was an outcome fatally detrimental to both Ashwasena and Karna.

2.3.2. The resort to explicit threat even by Krishna

Arjuna was disturbed and extremely reluctant to fight a war that would involve the destruction of his own kin: Lord Krishna persuaded him of the morality and justness of this war through his sermon which constitutes the Bhagwad Gita. This is one of the greatest of the many inspiring philosophies that form a part of Hinduism, and we discuss a few small negotiation-focused aspects of the Gita in Chapter 3 on framing. At this point, however, we refer to an episode in the Bhishma Parva when Arjuna's hesitations returned, this time to the great annoyance and provocation of the usually patient, gentle, and good-humoured Krishna.

Bhishma Pitamah, son of Shantanu, was regarded as the grandsire of both the Kauravas and Pandavas. Despite recognizing the merit of the Pandava cause, he fought on the side of the Kauravas, on the grounds that his duty lay towards the kingdom rather than any one party. As a warrior he was formidable and nearly invincible: recall the boon that he had been granted by his father in return for his 'terrible vow', which allowed him to choose the hour of his death. Under Bhishma's leadership as commander-in-chief, for the first ten days of the war the Kauravas enjoyed considerable advantage.

On the third day of the war, Bhishma's onslaught on the Pandava army was acute and relentless, and the losses to the Pandava side innumerable and severe. Krishna reminded Arjuna of his promise to take on all his Kaurava opponents including Dronacharya, Bhishma, and others. And thus Krishna urged Arjuna, 'Give credence to your word. Remind yourself of the duty of the Kshatriya, free yourself of unnecessary apprehensions, and fight.' Arjuna reluctantly agreed. But as Bhishma's annihilation of the Pandava army continued, it became evident to Krishna that Arjuna was holding himself back from unleashing the full force of his retaliation on the much respected and loved grandsire.

No longer able to bear the devastation wreaked by Bhishma on the Pandavas, which was due to Arjuna's moral qualms and hesitation, Krishna was enraged. He leapt out of Arjuna's chariot, and rushed forth towards Bhishma. Roaring like a lion, resplendent in his glory, his eyes glowing a fiery red, the Lord of the Universe stormed towards Bhishma. All who witnessed the weaponless Krishna move with such fierce determination to slay Bhishma uttered in horror 'Bhishma is slain', and fled from Krishna's path.

Seeing Krishna intent upon destroying Bhishma by his own hand, strong-armed Arjuna rushed after him and attempted to restrain him. With great difficulty and using all his strength, he was able to hold on to his feet and stop the god at his tenth step. And holding on to his feet thus, Arjuna pleaded with Krishna to turn around, saying the following:

निवर्तस्व महाबाहो नानृतं कर्तुमर्हसि
यत्त्वया कथितं पूर्वं न योत्स्यामीति केशव
मिथ्यावादीति लोकस्त्वां कथयिष्यति माधव
ममैष भारः सर्वो हि हनिष्यामि यतव्रतम्
VI.102.66, 67

Keshava, you had given your word that you would not fight in the war. Do not break your pledge. If you do, people will call you a liar.
The burden to fight Bhishma is mine alone, and I will slay the grandsire. This I do swear by my weapons, truth, and by my good Karma.

Krishna returned to the chariot, still furious and in silence. And then Arjuna, true to his promise, began to fight Bhishma in earnest and wholeheartedly, while Bhishma's arrows continued to rain on the Pandavas.

This story reveals the importance of using distributive strategies, particularly threats, in negotiations, even between allies and friends. The entire exposition of the Bhagwad Gita, and the many highly persuasive arguments within it, did not prove sufficient to persuade Arjuna that it was his duty to fight and slay Bhishma. His hesitation jeopardized the Pandava position in the war. Only a clear demonstration by Krishna—the Lord of the Universe, avatar of Vishnu, and also Arjuna's closest ally and friend—that he himself would fight Bhishma, in contravention of his pledge that he would not fight in the war, finally catalysed Arjuna into action. Effectively, only the distributive strategy by Krishna managed to generate the response from Arjuna that the Pandavas needed if they were to avoid complete annihilation at Bhishma's hand.

2.3.3. Kripacharya advises Duryodhana to make peace with the Pandavas

By the 17th day of the war, the Kaurava army had lost their mightiest generals and warriors (including Bhishma, Drona, and Karna). As the Pandavas wreaked havoc upon their largely decimated army, the surviving Kauravas were weary, and Duryodhana was grief stricken and distraught at the loss of his many kinsmen, friends, and soldiers in the war. Then, Kripacharya—one of the great teachers who had fought on the Kaurava side—advised Duryodhana to make peace. The resulting debate is illustrative of the importance attached to the distributive strategy even when bargaining from a position of great weakness.

Kripacharya made at least five arguments as he advanced the cause of peace to Duryodhana. First, he pointed out, with accuracy, that the Kauravas had been unable to defeat the Pandavas even with such illustrious and seemingly invincible heroes fighting on their side: what chance did the Kauravas have now that many of these great warriors had been destroyed? Second, he pointed to the formidable strength of the Pandavas that derived not only from their own merit, particularly brave Arjuna's, but also the support and strength that they drew from having Lord Krishna on their side. Krishna, he said, 'cannot be defeated by the gods themselves'. The Pandava strength effectively made them invincible. Third, he reminded Duryodhana of the many injustices and provocations that the Kauravas' actions had inflicted on the Pandavas. In other words, justice and morality were not on the side of the Kauravas—another very good reason to end this unjust war. Fourth, he urged Duryodhana, whose losses were multiple and great, to consider self-preservation. He cited the wisdom of Brihaspati on war and peace: 'When one's strength is reduced to becoming an equal of or lesser than the enemy, one should make peace; one should make war only when one is decidedly stronger than the enemy.' There was ample evidence that the Kauravas were greatly weakened, and should therefore seek peace with the Pandavas. Finally, he pointed to the generosity and wisdom of the Pandavas: were Duryodhana to make peace now, the likelihood that he might be reinstalled as king was high. 'If, by yielding to the Pandavas, we can still retain our kingdom, then that would be a better outcome for us, rather than foolishly pursuing this war and our defeat.'

Kripacharya's advice was sensible, and covered both moral and strategic grounds: rather than seek complete annihilation by persisting with the war from a weakened position, making peace with the Pandavas would offer the Kauravas better terms. Duryodhana's response, however, was to continue with the war, albeit he showed considerably more recognition and penitence of the Kauravas' wrongdoings than he was wont to do.

Described at this point in the text as 'the noble-spirited son of Dhritarash-tra' ('*mahamana*'), Duryodhana saluted Kripacharya for his selfless contributions to the war effort and also for offering him the advice that only a true friend would. But Kripa's words, Duryodhana said, did not please him, 'just as a dying man is ill-amused by medicine'. He recounted the many offences that the Kauravas had committed against the Pandavas, and argued that there was little chance of obtaining forgiveness from them after such great and such long-standing provocation. Further, and perhaps even more importantly, even if peace were obtained on relatively favourable terms, Duryodhana strongly argued that he could not live on the charity of the Pandavas:

उपर्युपरि राज्ञां वै ज्वलितो भास्करो यथा
युधिष्ठिरं कथं पश्चादनुयास्यामि दासवत्
कथं भुक्त्वा स्वयं भोगान्दत्त्वा दायांश्च पुष्कलान्
कृपणं वर्तयिष्यामि कृपणैः सह जीविकाम्
IX.4.22, 23

As the sun shines in the heavens, I shone above all other monarchs. How can I now walk behind Yudhishthira as his chattel?
I have enjoyed many material luxuries, and have also shared them generously in many acts of charity and giving. How can I now lead a life of penury, and share it with other destitute folk?

But it is not just the prospect of humiliation and dishonour, of having to live under the generosity and charity of the Pandavas, that deters Duryodhana. He reminded Kripa of the Kshatriya code of honour that regarded death away from the battlefield and in the comfort of one's bed as an ignominy and a sin, and also that he had a debt that he intended to repay:

ये मदर्थे हताः शूरास्तेषाम् कृतमनुस्मरन्
ऋणं तत्प्रतिमुंचानो न राज्ये मन आदधे
IX.4.42
सुयुध्देन ततः स्वर्गम् प्राप्स्यामि न तदन्यथा
IX.4.45

Remembering those brave men who laid down their lives for me, I now wish to repay the great debt that I owe them, rather than covet the kingdom . . . I will attain heaven by fighting the honourable fight, and do not desire anything else.

And thus, oft-times villain and occasional hero Duryodhana rejected the pathway of peace.

The story offers us three useful insights. First, and most minimally, the story reveals the persistent inflexibility of Duryodhana's negotiation strategy, even under severely altered conditions: he has at least partly recognized the error of his ways in his dealings with the Pandavas in the past, and his strategic advantage and hopes of a victory are now all but gone. Nonetheless, he refuses to change the course that he has embarked on. Second, the story takes us a step further in showing us the importance of the concept of face or honour. This was also discussed particularly in the context of the story of Drona and Ekalavya. Drona was willing to destroy the future of an extremely promising warrior to keep his word to Arjuna; Duryodhana now is willing to destroy himself (and the remainder of his troops) to preserve his independence and honour rather than live under the reign of the Pandavas (even as a king, were they to return him to his position as part of the peace treaty). We will see a similar and even stronger reference to the honour code in the case of Karna, discussed in Section 5 on cases of integrative bargaining. Third, the case provides us a powerful illustration here of a disregard of considerations of power in favour of principle: the overwhelming power of the Pandavas acts as no deterrent; choosing honour over self-preservation, Duryodhana decides to—and does—fight unto death.

2.3.4. Insights for negotiation

The above three episodes are a good illustration of how characters of the Mahabharata negotiate when the going gets really tough. Five themes stand out.

First, the tendency towards the use of the distributive strategy, by heroes and villains alike, persists. In wartime, this tendency is typified by the tendency of negotiators to (literally) stick to their guns, and therefore their inability/ unwillingness to make concessions. Karna is thus unwilling to realign his arrow, even after being duly warned that it will miss its target, and is again unwilling to reload and reuse it despite the high probability of victory resulting from Ashwasena's help. Duryodhana, despite staring defeat in the eye, similarly refuses to make concessions to save himself and his dwindling troops.

Second, recall that Section 2 of this chapter discussed the ready use of distributive tactics against outsiders, in contrast with conciliatory diplomacy towards one's friends and allies. The story of Krishna and Arjuna in Section 3, however, shows that under extreme conditions, when all attempts at persuasion fail, even close friends may have to resort to the use of threats and direct action to bring allies into line.

Third, akin to the lessons drawn from the pre-war set of stories, negotiation options almost always assume the tones of black and white, and the middle ground or the grey areas of integrative bargaining, finding creative solutions, and expanding the pie all remain elusive. Kripacharya attempts to show Duryodhana a path that will save him from the complete ignominy of defeat. By admitting to the wrongs he has committed and surrendering even at the late stage of the war, he can secure himself a future perhaps even as a king. But Duryodhana rejects this solution, seeing victory and defeat as the only two meaningful and polarized choices, and compromise as a dishonourable and unacceptable proposition. Arjuna's half-hearted battle against Bhishma provokes the divine rage of Krishna: a powerful foe such as Bhishma demands unwavering resolve, and Arjuna has been remiss in his duty by pulling his punches. Ashwasena's innovative proposal to Karna of reloading his powerful Nagaastra, and reinforcing it with Ashwasena's strength, is similarly rejected: Karna insists that he will fight his battles alone, rejecting the counsel of both his charioteer and the prince of snakes. Effectively, this refusal to settle for a middle ground, while indicative of a refusal to make concessions, is also suggestive of a noble commitment to ideals where no half-measures will suffice.

Fourth, reinforcing a theme that appeared in Section 2.2, we find that the notions of honour and face appear as powerful motifs in wartime negotiations. Karna berates his charioteer for suggesting that he reconsider his aim by appealing to the warrior code. On similar grounds, he declines the assistance of Ashwasena that could have ensured the certain defeat of his arch-enemy and nemesis Arjuna, and perhaps even ensured the victory of the Kaurava side. In the second story in this section, we find that Arjuna, whose affection for Bhishma has thus far been immune to persuasion by Lord Krishna, finally embraces his assigned role when he realizes that his failure to commit wholeheartedly to the war will result in Krishna having to take up arms himself. Arjuna's moral fibre is appalled at this prospect because of the loss of face this would involve for Krishna, in the light of his vow not to fight in the war: the fact that everyone would call Krishna a 'liar' is a bigger factor in getting Arjuna to fulfil his 'duty' than all other forms of persuasion by Krishna himself. And even Duryodhana, seldom portrayed as a hero in the epic, appears tragically heroic when he declines Kripacharya's advice by reminding him of the Kshatriyas' honour to die in the battlefield. Other studies of international negotiation have demonstrated that an excessive adherence to principles and positions, rather than interests, will make it difficult to reach agreement. The overwhelming commitment of all the protagonists to an honour code in wartime results in inflexible negotiating positions; a climbdown, in the face of such high principle, is nearly impossible under the circumstances.

Fifth, while coalitions are extremely important in the Mahabharata, and remain vital in India's emergence as a potential Great Power, the stories of both Karna and Duryodhana are important illustrations of the willingness to go it alone. That said, they do not present the norm, and both Karna and Duryodhana pay with their lives for their isolationism. As Chapter 4 illustrates, coalitions are seen as a vital part of politics in the Mahabharata, and in modern times isolationism is rare and never a winning strategy, and defection is rarer still.

2.4. NEGOTIATION STRATEGY IN THE AFTERMATH OF WAR AND IN THE RELATED STORIES

The richness of the Mahabharata encompasses stories of negotiation among the main characters, post-war, and an especially plentiful trove of myths, fables, and legends that gives context and body to the main story. We now turn to these, offering one story from the post-war negotiation and two of the side stories.

2.4.1. Ashwatthama and his jewel

Soon after the main 18-day war was over and the Pandavas had won, the near-invincible Duryodhana took refuge in the waters of a lake. He was finally caught and defeated by Bhima by a foul and deceitful swoop of the mace. Drona too had been brought to his knees by trickery on the part of the Pandavas in the war. Ashwatthama—the son of Drona and fierce ally of Duryodhana—along with Kripacharya and Kritavarma constituted the small group of weary survivors of the Kaurava army. Grief stricken by the death of his kinsmen and friends, and enraged by the tactics that the Pandavas had used in the war, Ashwatthama sought permission from the dying Duryodhana to slay the Pandavas. He was duly named the commander of the largely decimated Kaurava army. And on that night, whilst Kripa and Kritavarma rested and when the endgame seemed to have been played out, he pondered on his plan. He observed that a fierce owl, using his advantage of night vision, was successfully able to kill a flock of crows asleep in a banyan tree. Inspired by this, Ashwatthama resolved to use the stealth of the night to wreak havoc and death on the camp of the sleeping Pandavas. He was advised that an attack at night violated the most fundamental rules of war. Disregarding this, Ashwatthama invoked the power of Shiva, and inflicted horrific carnage on the Pandava camp. When Ashwatthama left the camp at dawn, he and his two companions rejoiced that all the Pandava clan and their allies were slain. In fact, however, the five Pandava brothers, their wives, and Krishna survived.

Learning about the slaughter of her brothers and sons, Draupadi was overcome by grief and anger. Taunting Yudhishthira, she raised the cry for justice and punishment. She threatened that were Ashwatthama not punished for his dreadful deeds, together with his companions, she would fast unto death. Yudhishthira attempted (unsurprisingly, given the extreme circumstances, in vain) to pacify her by reassuring her that their kinsmen had attained the kingdom of god by pursuing the path of righteousness. He further pointed out that Ashwatthama was already far away, and she had no way of ensuring his fall.

Draupadi's response to this was firm. She demanded the following:

द्रोणपुत्रस्य सहजो मणि: शिरसि मे श्रुत:
निहत्य संख्ये तं पापं पश्येयं मणिमाहृतम्
राजश्चिरसि ते कृत्वा जीवेयमिति मे मति:
X.11.20

I have heard that Drona's son was born with a jewel on his forehead. If this sinner is killed and the jewel is brought before me, I will don that jewel on my own head and only then will I embrace life. This is my firm determination.

And she turned to Bhima, reminding him of his many feats of bravery, and entreated him to slay the son of Dronacharya. Bhima, ever courageous, flew in hot pursuit of Ashwatthama. At this point, Krishna reminded the Pandava brothers that Ashwatthama was dangerous: on an earlier occasion, too, he had indicated a readiness to acquire and an intention to use powerful weapons, and he was equipped with the mighty Brahmaastra (whose use had been granted to him, upon his insistence, by his father Drona). Ashwatthama would not be averse to using this Brahmaastra against Bhima, and so together Krishna, Yudhishthira, and Arjuna hastened after Bhima to assist him.

True to Krishna's prediction, Ashwatthama, fearing for his life from Bhima's wrath and capability, released the Brahmaastra with the Pandavas as its target. Arjuna was the only warrior who had the knowledge, control, and possession of a retaliatory weapon of equal strength to match the weapon of Brahma himself, and duly unleashed his celestial weapon to neutralize Ashwatthama's advancing missile. The meeting of these supreme and celestial missiles would have ensured the destruction of the world. A nuclear deterrence, of sorts, was breaking down into mutually assured destruction. The sages Narada and Vyasa arrived on the scene to berate both warriors for their irresponsible unleashing of such weapons of terrible power, and urged Arjuna and Ashwatthama to recall their missiles. While Arjuna complied, Ashwatthama possessed only the partial knowledge of releasing the weapon and did not know how to recall it. He admitted this to the two sages, and was then instructed to deflect the weapon (which he did on the unborn children of the Pandavas—a deflection that Krishna was subsequently able to remedy by bestowing life on the stillborn Parikshita).

The result of the intervention by the sages was that Ashwatthama—and the Kaurava side that he represented—were now well and truly defeated. But additionally, the sages also insisted that Ashwatthama surrender his gem to the Pandavas—the same gem of power that had adorned his forehead, and which Draupadi had demanded as proof of his destruction. In return, Ashwatthama would be spared his life.

At first glance, this might appear to be an integrative solution: rather than carry out Draupadi's instructions to the fullest, the Pandavas had spared Ashwatthama his life and taken his jewel. Draupadi too, on being given the jewel and on being told that Ashwatthama had been deprived of his jewel and his weapons, did not object to his life being spared. She accepted the 'compromise' and stated, 'The son of our teacher is akin to our teacher himself, and worthy of our respect. I only wished to avenge the excesses that we have been subject to.'

On closer inspection, however, the costs imposed on Ashwatthama were extremely high. His life was spared, but this was in fact not an integrative solution at all: he was one of the eight immortals who could never die, so the bargain offered to him of his life in exchange for his jewel was redundant. The gem, on the other hand, was priceless to him: it gave the wearer protection from weapons, disease, hunger, and also from the gods, demons, nagas, and thieves. He nonetheless surrendered his jewel out of respect for the sages' instructions. This was a major loss. But even greater than the loss of this powerful jewel was the infliction of a dreadful curse upon Ashwatthama by Krishna, as retribution for his multiple sins:

त्रीणि वर्षसहस्राणि चरिष्यसि महीमिमाम्
अप्राणुवन्क्वचित्कांचित्संविदं जातु केनचित्
X.16.10

You must now reap the fruits of your ill deeds. For 3,000 years, you will wander the earth alone, without the joy of companionship or conversation.

The curse goes further than that, though: not only is Ashwatthama condemned to a lonely existence for 3,000 years, but he is further cursed that he will reek of pus and blood, will be unwelcome in any lands of civilization and habitation, and will carry the burden of all existing diseases. Many in India believe that to this day, the loyal son of Drona wanders the earth, defenceless and friendless, always on the outskirts of society, afflicted by wounds that never heal and diseases that can never be cured, and unable to free himself from his accursed life. Even in the face of the reprehensible and extreme atrocities that he had committed, this was a high price to pay to the victors.

The story of Ashwatthama is an important illustration of how far even the most virtuous heroes of the Mahabharata will go in their refusal to make concessions. Ashwatthama's actions are abhorrent, but it is important to bear in mind that he stands in the company of the great and the good who also resorted to devious methods and deception.[20] Even the heroes of the Mahabharata are not reluctant to use distributive strategies. Draupadi would prefer to embrace death rather than allow Ashwatthama to get away with his war crimes. The actions of the Pandava brothers are not far removed from Draupadi's position: there is neither forgiveness nor forgetting. Ashwatthama, at the end of the encounter, is weaponless and defeated, but this is not enough: his jewel of magical protective powers must be seized and a dreadful curse inflicted. The negotiating dynamic is predominantly tough and escalatory, and the escalation does not stop even when the victory of the Pandavas is complete.

2.4.2. Indra and the sage Chyavana

The two Ashwins—twins of exceeding beauty who were the physicians of the gods—had restored the aged sage Chyavana to his youthful form, and also bestowed on him a most handsome appearance. Their reasons for acting thus were far from selfless: they sought the beautiful and young wife of the sage, Sukanya. But in the spirit of fair competition and also to pose a challenge to

---

[20] We see a particularly heart-rending account of the misdemeanours of the Pandavas from Duryodhana as he lies dying and reminds Krishna of his many stratagems and trickery. The list is a long one: Duryodhana himself was defeated by an unfair and illegal blow of the mace; Bhishma was killed by placing Shikhandin in the firing line; Drona was deliberately misinformed by the Pandavas that his son had been killed, thereby destroying his spirit and will to fight; Karna's death was a product of many unfair and dishonest strategies, which included the diversion of his most powerful weapon on Ghatotkacha, by diverting Ashwasena and the Nagaastra, and by shooting at him when the wheel of his carriage was stuck. All these actions were unfair and broke the laws of war. And thus Duryodhana accuses Krishna: 'Had you fought the battle in a fair manner and without the use of guile . . . you would never have won this war. But you took the path of deceit, and got us and other Dharma-abiding princes slain.'

Krishna, in turn, reminds Duryodhana of the appalling wickedness pursued by him and his brethren even before the war began. The vile acts of the Kauravas are numerous, as Krishna recounts them to the dying Duryodhana. They include the Kaurava refusal to allow the Pandavas their legitimate half of the kingdom, the repeated cheating at the game of dice, the attempt to poison Bhima, the attempt to burn all the Pandavas in the house of lac, the many shameful attempts to dishonour the blameless Draupadi, and the killing of Abhimanyu—a child and battling alone—through trickery and deceit.

her, they offered to transform her husband to a complete likeness of themselves in youth and beauty. Sukanya would then be faced with the choice of any one of the three men. Sukanya agreed to the game upon the sage's urging, and was also able to distinguish her husband from the Ashwins and choose him. The sage, now delighted with the deal that he had secured—exceedingly attractive appearance and youth, and also his wife—promised the Ashwins a drink of Soma-rasa, the drink of the gods that granted immortality.

Subsequently, at a sacrificial ceremony, Chyavana kept his promise and duly brought the Soma-rasa to offer it to the Ashwins. Indra—the king of the gods—however, was present at the sacrifice and forbade the offering. The Ashwins were physicians of the gods, not gods themselves, argued Indra, and thus were not entitled to the drink of immortality. Debate then ensued between Indra and Chyavana. Chyavana insisted that the Ashwins, with their healing powers, noble purpose, and handsome appearance, were akin to the gods themselves and hence worthy of the celestial drink. On finding his arguments ignored, the god Indra issued a clear threat:

अभ्यामर्थाय सोमं त्वं ग्रहीष्यसि यदि स्वयम्
वज्रं ते प्रहरिष्यामि घोररूपमनुत्तमम्
III.124.15

If you take this Soma-rasa for the Ashwins, I will attack you with my most powerful and fearsome weapon, the thunderbolt.

The sage Chyavana remained unalarmed. Seeing him advance smilingly towards the Ashwins with the Soma-rasa, Indra picked up his terrible weapon. But just as he was about to hurl his thunderbolt, Indra found himself bound by Chyavana's spell and unable to move his arm. And from Chyavana's prayers, incantations, and offerings to the sacrificial fire, a monstrous and dreadful demon, Mada, emerged to destroy Indra. So frightful was his appearance that neither the gods nor the demons could describe him. His eyes gleamed like the sun and the moon, his mouth seemed aflame with the fire that would bring the universe to its end.

स भक्षयिष्यन्संक्रुद्धः शतक्रतुमुपाद्रवत्
महता घोररूपेण लोकाञ्शब्देन नादयन्
III.124.24

His furious roars engulfed the entire earth, and he ran towards Indra to consume him.

Indra was possessed by fear at the sight of this powerful demon so rapidly advancing towards him. Entreating Chyavana for mercy, he not only abandoned his injunctions against the consumption of the Soma-rasa by the Ashwins, but further tried to justify his previous resistance as intended only to stimulate the sage into a demonstration of his tremendous prowess. In other words, the display of force produced the intended effect, and more, that is, explanations and justifications that bordered on the side of an apology. Having secured the outcome that he had desired all along from Indra, Chyavana released him from his spell and also destroyed the demon. And thereafter he made his promised offering to the Ashwins, which they gladly accepted.

The story has a happy ending, but it is important from a negotiations perspective in its demonstration of the importance of a distributive strategy. Chyavana's initial attempts at reasoned argument and persuasion failed to convince Indra, and in fact prompted the threat of reprisals. In contrast, the demonstration of unsurpassable power produced the intended effect.

2.4.3. Shukracharya, Kacha, and Devyani

The gods and the demons—the devas and the asuras/danavas/rakshasas—had long battled for mastery of all three worlds. There was a time in this war when the demons enjoyed a strategic advantage over the gods: their teacher, Shukracharya, possessed the secret knowledge of Sanjeevani, and was thus able to bring slain demons back to life. Constantly renewed and revived, the demonic forces seemed unstoppable.

The only solution to this problem was that the gods also acquired the knowledge of Sanjeevani. To this end, they sent Kacha—the son of Brihaspati, the guru of the gods—on a mission of espionage. They asked Kacha to present himself as a disciple of Shukracharya and win him over with his devotion and worship, and also endear himself to Shukra's daughter Devyani, to acquire the priceless knowledge and skill of Sanjeevani.

Kacha was accepted as a disciple of Shukra. In keeping with the plan, he also charmed Devyani with countless attentions, which were well received. As time passed, the demons discovered Kacha's intentions. To protect the vital knowledge of Sanjeevani and also driven by their hatred of Brihaspati, they killed Kacha. But Devyani implored her father to restore Kacha's life; Shukra duly employed the Sanjeevani to revive his pupil. The same pattern of events recurred. The third time, however, the demons came up with a more devious plan. They killed Kacha, burnt his body, and then mixed his remains in Shukracharya's wine. Revival from such a state would be nearly impossible.

Devyani once again pleaded with her father to revive the man she loved, and threatened to fast and follow Kacha into the kingdom of death were he not brought back to life. Shukracharya, infuriated by the repeated and murderous acts of the demons and again unable to deny the pleas of his grieving daughter, attempted to recall Kacha back to life. Kacha then responded from Shukra's stomach, explaining what had become of him, and how only his ascetic virtues had allowed him to endure the pain of death, cremation, and consumption. To now be revived, Kacha would have to rip open his teacher's stomach, which would kill Shukra. The only way in which the lives of both could be preserved was for Shukra to teach the Sanjeevani to Kacha, who would emerge from his teacher's body; while the process of Kacha's revival would kill his teacher, he would then use the knowledge of Sanjeevani to restore Shukra to life. This plan was indeed carried out, but it meant that the demons, by killing and disposing of Kacha in the manner that they had done, also ended up making him the recipient of the coveted and secret knowledge that they had sought to protect from him.

Having fulfilled his duties as a pupil and having accomplished his mission of acquiring the Sanjeevani for the gods, Kacha prepared to return home. Devyani, however, expected marriage with the man whose life she had saved so many times through entreaties to her father, and who had certainly been encouraged to think along these lines by Kacha through his many attentions to her. Kacha refused to marry her on the grounds that as he had re-emerged from Shukracharya's body, their relationship was that of a brother and sister and could not be a conjugal one. Devyani did not react well to being thus scorned, and put a curse on Kacha:

यदि मां धर्मकामार्थे प्रत्याख्यास्यसि चोदितः
ततः कच न ते विद्या सिध्दिमेषा गमिष्यति
I.72.16

I seek marriage with you in keeping with the precepts of Dharma. If you refuse to take me as your wife, the knowledge you have acquired will not be of any service to you.

Kacha would not accept this curse passively. He pointed out that Devyani's curse was driven not by Dharma but by lust. And so he retaliated with a counter curse:

तस्माद्भवत्या यः कामो न तथा स भविष्यति
ऋषिपुत्रो न ते कश्चिज्जातु पाणिं ग्रहीष्यति
I.72.19
फलिष्यति न ते विद्या यत्त्वं मामात्थ तत्तथा
अध्यापयिष्यामि तु यं तस्य विद्या फलिष्यति
I.72.20

Your heart's desire will remain unfulfilled. No son of a sage will ever marry you. You have said that my knowledge will not be fruitful for me. So be it. But this knowledge will be successfully used by those to whom I choose to teach it.

The story is illustrative of some interesting negotiation behaviour. First, Kacha's entry into the story is one based on a deception: there is, for instance, no attempt to persuade Shukracharya either to refrain from using the Sanjeevani on the asuras or to share his knowledge with the devas to level the playing field. We discuss the role of deception in the Mahabharata later in this section, and also in other places in the book. Second, we see an integrative move on the part of Shukracharya: recognizing that his daughter would be distraught if either Kacha or her father dies, he proposes and implements the creative solution of saving Kacha through his own death and also ensuring his own revival by teaching Kacha the Sanjeevani. But this integrative bargaining behaviour generates a big cost—Kacha returns to the devas at the end of his Brahmacharya, and by teaching them the Sanjeevani destroys the strategic advantage that Shukracharya's side had enjoyed for thousands of years. Third, the dominant bargaining behaviour remains distributive: Devyani demands from Kacha that he does the honourable thing and marries her, and when he refuses, curses him. Kacha, far from the code of chivalry, not only refuses to marry her, but retaliates by cursing her in return. Both offer justifications and attempt to persuade each other before resorting to these distributive tactics. But the justifications and persuasions are framed from a high moral ground on either side—a characteristic feature of bargaining in the Mahabharata that we discuss in detail in Chapter 3.

2.4.4. Insights for negotiation

The stories in this section reinforce three important lessons about negotiation behaviour in the Mahabharata.

First, even though magnanimity in victory is advised in the text, in practice we do not see this. Instead, we see the persistence of an escalatory and strongly distributive dynamic even after goals have been achieved and conflict has ended. This is most patently obvious in Ashwatthama's case. His misplaced sentiments of revenge and loyalty lead him to violate one of the most fundamental norms of war, that is, to refrain from attacking a sleeping foe. But the price that Draupadi demands of him for his crimes, and the concessions that Krishna, the sages, and the Pandava brothers extract from him are very high. Ashwatthama, deprived of his weapons and bereft of all his allies, with the Kaurava defeat complete, poses no threat to the Pandavas. His jewel of power is taken away, and worse, Krishna curses him with an unbearable existence that will last 3,000 years. This escalatory dynamic appears even in the Kacha–Devyani story, when love and friendship are replaced by curses and counter curses. The curse that Kacha places on Devyani seems especially harsh, given that he has been through his clever deceptions of Shukra and his daughter, and he has succeeded in his mission of procuring the secret and precious knowledge of Sanjeevani.

Second, the use of distributive moves is usually justified by an appeal to some moral principle. We discuss this in greater detail in Chapter 3. But suffice it to note at this point that the appeal to principle remains high, rather than an appeal to pragmatism, when justifying the use of distributive bargaining behaviours. Hence, for example, Ashwatthama is given a clear indictment of his sins, while Kacha and Devyani both offer moral justifications for their use of spells and curses.

Third, and very importantly, the use of integrative strategies and conciliatory behaviours is shown to produce negative results. This is most obvious in the story of Indra and the sage Chyavana. Chyavana's use of reason, persuasion, and argumentation only prompts Indra to resort to force. In contrast, the explicit demonstration of force by Chyavana produces compliance and contrition. Shukracharya—one of the few characters to use a truly creative and integrative strategy—finds himself burdened with a high cost. Not only does he have to part with the vital knowledge of Sanjeevani that undermines the power of the asuras (i.e. his side), but he also ends up with his beloved daughter heartbroken (and to preserve whose happiness he has sacrificed the Sanjeevani).

2.5. INTEGRATIVE BARGAINING: CONDITIONS FOR AND RESULTS OF EXCEPTIONS?

In the cases from the Mahabharata examined thus far, and also from the foreign policy insights into a rising India, the dominant negotiation strategy appears to be distributive. But what is the shape of integrative bargaining in India's negotiating culture? In this section, we recap the insights that the above cases offer us regarding the exceptions to the norm of distributive bargaining, and also offer a detailed case study regarding the results that derive from genuine integrative bargaining.

2.5.1. Evidence of conciliatory behaviour, Sections 2.2–2.4

We have already come across examples of some concessionary tactics, but most of these differ from the genre of behaviours that characterizes integrative bargaining. The conciliatory diplomacy that we witness in the Mahabharata shares three features. First, the negotiating dynamic remains largely black and white, with choices presented and accepted as take it or leave it; the grey area of give and take that constitutes integrative bargaining is largely absent even in concessionary moments. Second, concessions are most common when dealing with one's own allies, or one's 'moral superiors' or elders. Third, in situations when concessions are made towards an outside party with whom one does not share a familial or moral bond, then they usually come only after the demonstration of great force and after one's credibility as a powerful negotiating partner is undermined. Concessions made from a weakened bargaining position are naturally extreme, again leaving little scope for finding creative solutions that might be of mutual benefit.

Examples of the first characteristic appear in most of the stories where we see any concessions voluntarily offered: Bhishma concedes to all the demands made of him by the Dasharaja, without attempting to find a compromise solution; Yudhishthira accepts all of the Yaksha's demands; Dronacharya, when reminded of his promise to Arjuna of his matchless supremacy in archery, does not even attempt to find a negotiating space that could accommodate the unfortunate Ekalavya and have both archers share the accolades.

Second, in the stories discussed in the previous sections, concessions are willingly made based on a sense of either personal attachment to the other party or moral duty. Bhishma, to safeguard the happiness of his father, caves in to all the demands of the Dasharaja. For Drona, the cost of denying the happiness of his favourite and devoted student outweighs the cost of inflicting a significant cruelty on Ekalavya. Note that once Ekalavya offers his tribute to Dronacharya, he is treated as an insider and taught by Drona to still become a skilled archer despite his new handicap. Recall further that Ekalavya's cheery sacrifice is a product of his respect for the teacher that he has adopted and respects to the utmost. Yudhishthira—the son of Dharma—recognizes the justice-based prior claim of the Yaksha on the waters of the lake and agrees to meet all his demands rather than attempt to negotiate a creative solution. Arjuna, albeit initially half-hearted in his battle against Bhishma, complies fully and completely with Krishna's wishes (not only the avatar of Vishnu, but also his trusted ally and close friend) when he realizes that his own negligence is driving Krishna to break his vow. Even Ashwatthama resists the attempt to negotiate his way out of surrendering his powerful jewel; his compliance on this is driven, in good measure, by the fact that his moral superiors—the two sages Vyasa and Narada, and the lord of the universe himself—are making the demand of him.

Third, although we come across instances when concessions are made to an outside party, here the concessionary dynamic is one that occurs under duress and under extreme conditions. Hence, for example, we see Indra finally bow to the sage Chyavana's wishes, but only after Chyavana sets upon him a demon of dreadful power and Indra's life is in great peril. Faced with this extreme condition, Indra is left in no position to bargain and gives in to Chyavana's demands.

Occasionally, we see genuinely integrative bargaining. Shukracharya, we saw, when faced with the death either of himself or of Kacha—the two individuals who were dearest to his daughter—manages to find an interesting solution at the integrative end of the spectrum. But the cost of teaching Kacha the Sanjeevani proved to be high: not only was the secret knowledge revealed to Shukra's opponents, but even his daughter's happiness was denied when Kacha left having accomplished his mission of espionage. This story begins to indicate that integrative strategies actually end up imposing costs: the proverbial pie may expand, but the other side often takes advantage of this expansion and ends up not just with larger relative gains but even leaves the first party worse off than before. We illustrate this by discussing the case of Karna and his magical armour and earrings below.

2.5.2. Karna's bargaining with Indra

Karna was the only Kaurava who was skilled enough to defeat Arjuna, and a history of minor and major slights from the Pandavas made him a determined and fierce opponent. Karna, akin to his Pandava brothers, was of divine lineage: Surya, the sun god, was his father.[21] His royalty and celestial beauty were evident from his birth: he was born wearing an armour and earrings of gold that protected him from death and made it impossible for anyone to kill him. Knowing that he would be a formidable foe for his son, Arjuna, to defeat in the forthcoming battle, Indra hatched a plan to deprive Karna of his protective amulets. Surya was aware of this plan and came to warn his beloved son in a dream. Surya told Karna that Indra would come to him in the guise of a Brahmin. Taking advantage of Karna's renowned generosity, and knowing that Karna never declined the requests of virtuous supplicants and petitioners, Indra would ask him for his armour and earrings. Surya urged Karna that he should propitiate the disguised Indra with the offer of other gifts, but under no circumstance should he surrender his celestial gifts.

Karna was grateful to have the blessings and advice of his father and favourite deity. But his response to Surya's warning was initially of resistance on the grounds of a deeply held honour code. He insisted that if Indra himself, disguised as a Brahmin, entreated him for his earrings and armour for the advantage of the Pandavas, he would willingly give them up to retain his glory in all three worlds.

मद्विधस्यायशस्यं हि न युक्तं प्राणरक्षणम्
युक्तं हि यशसा युक्तं मरणं लोकसंमतम्
III.284.28

Honourable men like me must protect our renown and reputation, not our lives.
To choose death in protecting one's renown wins respect in all worlds.

Surya, however, was deeply concerned about the well-being of his son, and offered a vital counterargument. Renown is of use only to the living; what use are fame and reputation to the dead man whose body has been turned to ashes? And besides this pragmatic counterargument to Karna's idealistic one, Surya

---

[21] Yudhishthira was the son of Dharma, Bhima of Pavana, Arjuna of Indra, and Nakula and Sahadeva were fathered by the two Ashwins.

reminded him of his long-standing enmity with Arjuna; as long as Karna wore his earrings, Arjuna would never be able to defeat him in battle.

After considerable debate, Surya was finally able to persuade Karna that if he insisted on propitiating Indra—a god who was clearly seeking his destruction—he must at least demand Indra's spear of tremendous power that would strengthen Karna's hand in the impending war. Surya had managed to convince his noble and stubborn son to use an integrative strategy from which both parties would walk away with some gains, in contrast to the all-out concessions to which Karna was initially committing.

Karna followed his father's advice and engaged in genuinely integrative bargaining. He first attempted to redefine the issue space by offering alternative riches to Indra. When these were turned down, he offered compliance with Indra's demands but in return for some gains:

यदि दास्यामि ते देव कुण्डले कवचं तथा
वध्यतामुपयास्यामि त्वं च शक्रावहास्यताम्
III.294.16
तस्मादिवनिमयं कृत्वा कुण्डले वर्म चोत्तमम्
हरस्व शक्र कामं मे न दद्यामहमन्यथा
III.294.17

Lord Indra, if I give both my armour and earrings to you, I will become vulnerable to my enemies and you will be a laughing stock in the world. I will exchange my supreme armour and earrings with you in return for something; without such an exchange, I cannot give these to you.

A bargain was thus struck: Indra secured Karna's precious armour and earrings, and in return granted him his spear and also a boon that his body (to which the armour and earrings were inseparably attached from birth) would retain its radiance when the amulets had been removed. One might think that this integrative bargaining had transformed a game of conflict into one of cooperation. In reality, Indra had driven a hard bargain, and Karna would be severely disadvantaged as a result of this integrative negotiating strategy. First, Indra's weapon could only be used under a very specific and limited set of conditions—which were specified in the deal that was struck. These included a single use, and that too only against one enemy of comparable prowess. Further, were Karna to use the spear carelessly, or when his own life was not in extreme danger, or if other weapons were available, then the weapon would turn on him and ensure the wielder's destruction. Second, the Pandavas were aware of these conditions, and would be extremely effective in forcing Karna to use the weapon on a more immediate danger—the demon Ghatotkacha who fought on the Pandava side—and thereby ensure that its intended target, Arjuna, would remain unscathed. Karna's integrative bargaining with Indra thus sowed the seeds of the noble and courageous hero's certain destruction.

2.5.3. Insights for negotiation

We can see that integrative bargaining is less commonly used in the Maha-bharata than distributive bargaining. In fact truly integrative bargaining—a genuine attempt to redefine and expand the issue space—is rare. If we equate integrative moves with primarily concessionary moves (where concede versus resist are seen as binary choices rather than presenting the extreme ends of a spectrum), our case set expands. Concessions are more likely if one of the following two conditions is met: a) there is either a moral or familial bond that underpins the negotiation relationship, which may lead the negotiator to give in relatively quickly and completely, and b) the negotiation reaches a level of extreme pressure, when capitulation becomes the only option available after a period of persistent resistance. Perhaps unsurprisingly, when negotiating in terms of an all-or-nothing mentality and then surrendering all, the costs are usually high. Bhishma's vow of celibacy takes his entire clan into a very costly war of succession; Ekalavya's readiness to meet his guru's demands deprives him of his status as supreme archer; Ashwatthama's willingness to surrender his jewel does not win him the compassion of Krishna or the mitigation of the curse, and only exposes him further to the terrible ordeals that the curse entails.

Occasionally, it is true that we see reward for graciously conciliatory behaviour, for instance in the case of Yudhishthira's compliance with the demands of the Yaksha. But Yudhishthira is the one and almost consistent exception in the story—he is, after all, the son of Dharma. And as we shall see in the next chapter, even Yudhishthira does not escape some of the costs that entirely concessionary diplomacy entails. His insistence on obeying his elders—even when he is well aware of their intentions to deprive the Pandavas of their kingdom and honour—generates extremely heavy costs on the five brothers and Draupadi. Nor is Yudhishthira ever allowed to forget the costs that his 'impotent' and 'cowardly' behaviour has cost them, particularly by Draupadi (but also his brothers) in piteous recriminations and bitter jibes.

When integrative strategies, in the sense of a real give and take are used, they often end up generating costly results. We have already come across the Kacha–Devyani–Shukracharya story. Karna's attempt to bargain with Indra using integrative moves brings him one clear and major step closer to his own downfall and death.

If the classical insights still hold today, we would expect Indian negotiators to be wary of concessionary moves and integrative bargaining. In the following section, we explore how far the insights into bargaining from the Mahabharata are applicable to India's negotiations as a rising power.

2.6. NEGOTIATION STRATEGY OF A RISING INDIA

In this section, we investigate the negotiation strategies that a rising India has used across two regimes: trade and nuclear non-proliferation. The two regimes allow us the study of India's behaviour across areas of soft and hard power, and also allow us to observe some variation amidst the dominant trends. In both cases, we highlight India's negotiation behaviour over time. This allows us to investigate the extent to which India's behaviour has changed as its power has risen or a negotiation *mentalité* persists. Before conducting this analysis, however, we recap the major lessons on negotiation strategy from the stories of the Mahabharata. Five stand out, and are analysed with reference to the two issue areas.

1. The distributive strategy is the dominant one, and shared by heroes and villains alike. This could partly be because of the slightly better performance of the distributive strategy. In contrast, instances of integrative bargaining are few, and they generate even fewer successful outcomes. The relative success rates of the different bargaining strategies are illustrated in the table at the end of this chapter.
2. Negotiation behaviour suggests that strategy is often viewed as a binary choice—resist or cave in—with instances of finding the negotiating space for compromise between these extremes (i.e. genuinely integrative behaviour) rare. The middle ground remains largely elusive.
3. The concept of honour and face recurs, providing a powerful deterrent against making concessions. A related characteristic that derives from this is the willingness of heroes to go it alone, that is, to face isolation and endure defeat if necessary, rather than lose face/sacrifice one's honour.
4. Strategy varies depending on whom one is negotiating with, with more scope for concessions towards insiders/allies. But even allies and friends can be at the receiving end of the distributive bargaining strategy, especially under extreme circumstances.
5. Instances of genuinely integrative bargaining strategy provide exceptions to the tendency to choose the distributive strategy amidst choices that are perceived as largely binary. These few instances further reveal that integrative strategies are used a) often under duress, or b) under pressure from a sense of moral or familial duty, and c) almost always impose costs on the character making concessions.

2.6.1. International trade

India's negotiation strategy in the multilateral trade regime has been almost consistently distributive. India was an active participant in the negotiations of the aborted International Trade Organization and a founding member of the General Agreement on Tariffs and Trade (GATT). Characteristic features of India's negotiation strategy in the first few decades of the GATT were a reluctance to engage in reciprocal concessions and support for developing country exceptionalism. In 1960, the Indian delegate S. T. Swaminathan argued: 'We feel that the contracting parties have, in the past, not been able to sufficiently come to grips with the problems of expanding the trade of less developed countries...It would, in our view, be a thousand pities if the concentration of pressures from imports on certain limited sectors of production in particular countries leads to a general reversal of the efforts to expand international trade and, in particular, exports from the less-developed countries.'[22] The costs of this reluctance to make concessions, however, were not high at the time, as several institutional features of the GATT, including negotiation on the basis of the Principal Supplier Principle, meant that developing countries could free-ride on concessions exchanged by major players.

Fast forward to the Uruguay Round of trade negotiations, which lasted from 1986 to 1994 (the pre-negotiation phase extended back to 1982). In this round the stakes were higher than ever before, especially as some countries sought an expansion of the GATT's agenda to the new issues of trade in services, Trade Related Intellectual Property Rights (TRIPs) and Trade Related Investment Measures (TRIMs). India took the lead in organizing a coalition of ten countries that resisted the introduction of the new issues in the GATT. While India's coalition politics are addressed in detail in Chapter 4, suffice it to note at this point that India's strategy as the leader of the coalition was distributive, which also influenced the coalition's bargaining strategy. Particularly striking in the pre-Uruguay Round negotiations was the somewhat self-righteous manner in which the G10 presented its position on a take-it-or-leave it basis. Both the distributive mode of bargaining and the reluctance to find solutions in the common middle ground came to the fore. The result of this bargaining was that India and its allies had only minimal impact on the agenda of the Uruguay Round that was agreed upon at Punta del Este. The G10 continued as a coalition in the early years of the Uruguay Round, albeit with a dwindling membership as allies were bought off with various carrots and sticks. India stood isolated in the endgame, still defending the collective position of the coalition to the hilt.[23]

It was not just in coalitions that India maintained a distributive bargaining strategy with outside parties; individually too it continued to actively, vociferously, and sometimes single-handedly fight for the cause of development and the interests of the South, maintaining a heroically critical attitude to the

[22] GATT, L/1229, 20 June 1960.
[23] For a detailed account of the coalitions of the Uruguay Round, see Narlikar 2003. India's coalition strategy is discussed further in Chapter 4 of this book.

expansion of the GATT agenda. For instance, in 1987, Ambassador S. P. Shukla stated in a largely critical survey statement of developments in the GATT that 'This survey would not be complete without a reference to the most serious development in the trade policy area in recent years, namely, the tendency on the part of some developed countries to seek linkages between trade in goods and other matters such as developing countries' policies in regard to foreign direct investment, protection of intellectual property, services and fair labour standards. Trade, which is a means of self-reliant development for developing countries, is in danger of becoming an instrument in the hands of certain developed countries for imposing unacceptable linkages on developing countries dependent on trade.'[24] The statement, in a fashion reminiscent of India's position in the 1950s, raised demands for Special and Differential Treatment, and went further in arguing against the attempt to include the 'new issues' of TRIPs, services, and others into the GATT agenda. It offered no compromise positions, no meeting ground for those who advocated an inclusion of the new issues and its own position. Ultimately, India was left isolated in the endgame, and, faced with multiple pressures from outside and within (including a very serious economic crisis in 1990 that finally prompted its programme of economic reforms in 1991), had little choice but to give in to the demands put upon it.[25] In the run-up to the launch of the Doha Development Agenda in 2001, India's strategy of holding the fort for developing countries persisted. It led the Like Minded Group of developing countries in resisting the launch of another new round until the implementation concerns of developing countries were met. Once again, it was left isolated in the endgame, and then found itself having to give in to the demands of the North.[26] The pattern that we identified in the Mahabharata stories—of a default strategy of distributive bargaining, and a turn to concessions in the form of complete capitulation when one's position is greatly worsened—is thus reflected in India's GATT behaviour as well as early years of the WTO.

India's defensive negotiating stance may perhaps have made some sense in the first four decades of its independence: Nehru's rhetoric of self-sufficiency amidst a licence-permit raj may have readily prompted caution on any concessions towards trade liberalization. But what of India's behaviour in the aftermath of its well-established programme of economic liberalization,

---

[24] GATT 1987.

[25] In fact, all the new issues—services, TRIPS, and TRIMS—ended up becoming an integral part of the trade regime with the completion of the Uruguay Round. Ironically, India benefited from at least some of these developments in spite of its distributive strategy: for example, even though it was the last bastion in the defence against the inclusion of services, it has now become one of the chief beneficiaries of services liberalization.

[26] For an account of the Like Minded Group and India's role in it, see Narlikar and Odell 2006.

and its increasing integration into a reforming WTO that has worked hard to ensure that the rising powers have a place and voice at all small-group consensus-building meetings? Surely, one would expect to see a decline in India's naysaying behaviour, a greater willingness to make trade-offs that help preserve the system (in which it has ever-increasing stakes), and engage in the give and take that are the hallmark of trade bargaining? In fact, we see strong continuities in India's negotiation strategies despite the changes in its own economic policies and also in the institution in which the negotiations take place.

India, while never afraid of standing up for certain principles, now has economic heft to back its positions as well. The closest that trade negotiators came to reaching an agreement towards concluding the current round of trade negotiations—the Doha Development Agenda—was in July 2008. They were not helped in this task by India: Minister Kamal Nath arrived at the conference and declared, 'The position of developed counties is utterly self-righteous . . . This self-righteousness will not do. If it means no deal, so be it . . . I am obviously not here to hand around freebies without getting something in return.'[27] India persisted with this position through much of the negotiation, which was conducted among an inner core of seven countries (several of which, however, reported back to their coalition allies who were not invited to attend the meetings). When Director-General Pascal Lamy put together a compromise package, Nath's reaction was unequivocal: 'I reject everything.' Other countries were willing to accept an offer that would place a cap on US farm subsidies. India's close ally, Brazil, pushed for a compromise, with its foreign minister Celso Amorim stating, 'As a package, I can swallow it.' One veteran journalist reports Nath's reaction to the Brazilian position as one of shock, 'who couldn't believe that his erstwhile G20 comrade in arms was failing to back him up. At last the inherent contradictions in the Brazilian–Indian alliance were coming to the fore . . . it became clear that Nath was the only G7 participant who was firmly saying no . . .'[28] The July Package negotiation of 2008 ended in failure, thereby closing a vital window on concluding the deal.

The above example gives illustrations of India's continued use of a distributive bargaining strategy, where choices are seen as polarized, and further one where the middle ground is often avoided in favour of an extreme position. We also see an important illustration of the concept of honour/face. For example, although the Indian delegation attracted considerable criticism from the international media, Kamal Nath received a hero's welcome at home.[29] In fact, we could not have a better illustration of the importance of

---

[27] TNC Meeting, Statement of Shri Kamal Nath, 23 July 2008.
[28] Blustein 2009, pp. 265–7. Journalistic and diplomatic accounts further report that Brazil attempted to build bridges between the extreme positions and canvassed for support for the Lamy Package, e.g. Ismail 2009.
[29] Lakshmi 2008.

honour and face at all costs than an admission made by an Indian negotiator in a private interview with one of us in 2003: 'It is easier for our minister to come back home empty-handed as a wounded hero, rather than to come back with something after having had to make a compromise.'[30]

2.6.2. Nuclear non-proliferation

While India's negotiation strategy on trade issues offers a close fit with the insights from the Mahabharata, confirming four of the five themes that were highlighted at the start of this section, what instances do we see of integrative bargaining? India's negotiation behaviour in the nuclear non-proliferation regime provides some interesting points of comparison. As an undeclared nuclear power, India's negotiation behaviour prior to the nuclear tests of 1998 was predominantly distributive. But in the aftermath of these tests, India's behaviour could be seen to have taken a strongly integrative turn, and it is perhaps no coincidence that this change coincided with the process of India's rise. In terms of signalling the turn towards integrative bargaining, India bound its own hands, for instance via its declaration of a No First Use policy and a self-imposed moratorium on testing, and it demonstrated responsible behaviour by guarding against proliferation to other nuclear aspirants in the developing world. The most concrete manifestation of this integrative bargaining was perhaps the transformation of India's prickly relations with the US into an entente (if not a fully fledged alliance)[31]—an entente whose lynchpin lay in the US–India nuclear deal. It is not surprising that there are a good many analysts who argue that India's negotiations on nuclear issues provide a powerful illustration of India's growing accommodativeness as it emerges as a global player: as India's power rises, we effectively see signs of greater willingness to engage in integrative bargaining.[32]

We offer a different interpretation by providing a brief overview of India's bargaining in the non-proliferation regime in the past, and further analysing India's re-entry into the nuclear regime. We argue that far from being an illustration of integrative bargaining, India's return from the cold is a product of hard-nosed distributive bargaining that persisted until all its major demands were met. Limited concessionary diplomacy did have a role to play as well, but only after the rules of the non-proliferation regime had been effectively rewritten to accommodate India's position and nuclear status.

Until very recently, India's bargaining behaviour regarding nuclear non-proliferation closely resembled its distributive bargaining behaviour in the GATT (as outlined in Section 2.6.1). Except for signing on to the Partial Test

---

[30] Interview, Indian trade negotiator, May 2003.   [31] Hagerty 2006.
[32] See, for example, Mohan 2006.

Ban Treaty in 1963, India's role in the regime was predominantly of opposition. Akin to its role in the GATT, India played an active role in drafting the Nuclear Non Proliferation Treaty (NPT) as a member of the Eighteen Nations Committee on Disarmament. Its participation was not in vain. The NPT came to include two key principles in good measure, thanks to India's diplomatic efforts: that non-nuclear states would have access to nuclear energy technology for peaceful purposes, and that non-proliferation was not an end in itself but a step towards universal nuclear disarmament.[33] Nonetheless, it refused to sign the NPT in 1968 on the grounds that by recognizing only five Nuclear Weapon States (NWS) and by grouping all other countries into the category of Non-Nuclear Weapon States (NNWS), the treaty discriminated between the nuclear haves and have-nots. In 1974, India went a step further in its rejection of the non-proliferation regime by conducting its first 'peaceful nuclear explosion' (PNE) at Pokhran. This was a clear signal on India's part of its intentions to play hardball. The repercussions were serious: resounding international condemnation was accompanied by a stop to nuclear technology transfers and also foreign aid. The Nuclear Suppliers Group (NSG) institutionalized these penalties and pre-emptively extended them to any other nuclear aspirants that chose to follow India's example: formed in the aftermath of and as a direct reaction to India's PNE, it tightened the regime on the export of even peaceful nuclear technology that could be misused for weaponization. Nonetheless, India stood firm in its nuclear stance, neither admitting to being a NWS nor denying it. When 177 countries signed the extension of the NPT in 1995, India resisted pressures to join the regime. Despite its near-isolation at the Conference on Disarmament in 1996, it refused to sign the Comprehensive Test Ban Treaty (CTBT).

With a history of distributive bargaining behind it in the nuclear regime, in 1998, India made another explicitly distributive move: it conducted a series of tests in Pokhran II in 1998 and declared itself a NWS.[34] Retribution followed in the form of international opprobrium and trade sanctions, and heavy pressure particularly from the P-5. In an attempt to manage this situation, a dialogue began between the US Deputy Secretary of State, Strobe Talbott, and the India Minister for External Affairs, Jaswant Singh. Interestingly, however, even in the face of this international isolation, India's negotiating position with the US was distributive. Jaswant Singh stated, for instance: 'I was not there to negotiate, either to give or to ask for anything. I was there only to engage in dialogue . . .'[35] Talbott recognized this gambit: 'the Indian government was,

---

[33] Ganguly 1999.

[34] Pakistan followed with a series of tests as well. Both the Indians and the Pakistanis claimed—and continue to claim—that their emergence as NWSs does not violate the NPT, as neither country actually signed the treaty.

[35] Singh 2007, p. 253.

from the outset, disinclined to compromise . . . By weathering the storm of US disapproval—by outlasting and outtalking the Americans in the marathon of diplomacy spurred by the test, in short by *not* compromising—the Indians would prove their resolve and their resilience, thereby giving a boost to their national self-esteem and self-confidence.' Talbott even admits in his account, 'as one of the architects of the Indian strategy, Jaswant Singh came closer to achieving his objective than I did to achieving mine'.[36] In other words, akin to the characteristics of India's negotiation behaviour highlighted earlier, we see that Indian negotiators persisted with distributive bargaining in the face of adversity, isolation, and reprisals. And even after dialogue was underway, the middle ground proved elusive, with the Indian side remaining in distributive bargaining mode.

Even though India's bargaining behaviour on non-proliferation remained largely unchanged before and after Pokhran II, the attacks of 9/11 injected a new urgency into the Indo–US dialogue.[37] The joint declaration by Prime Minister Manmohan Singh and President George W. Bush was a powerful signal of growing cooperation. A key barrier to the US–India relationship, however, was India's isolation on nuclear matters. A crucial step towards overcoming this barrier was the Henry J. Hyde US–India Peaceful Atomic Energy Cooperation Act of 2006, which allowed the amendment of Section 123 of the US Atomic Energy Act, and thereby enabled potential nuclear cooperation with India. In July 2008, albeit after much horse-trading, the Indian Parliament approved the US–India nuclear deal. In August, the IAEA cleared the India-specific safeguards agreement. And it is no small irony that the NSG, which was formed as a reaction to Pokhran I, was now persuaded to adopt an India-specific waiver that allowed the transfer of non-weapons nuclear technology to India. India had been brought back from the cold as at least a recognized de facto NWS if not a de jure one.

At first glance, these developments may perhaps be seen as involving some concessionary moves on India's part, which might even amount to integrative bargaining. Indeed, such perceptions on the part of Indian politicians nearly brought down the Manmohan Singh government in 2008 when it attempted to secure parliamentary approval for the strategic partnership. The suspicions of a near majority of politicians derived partly from the ideological concerns with autonomy that underpin Indian distributive bargaining in most issue areas. The nuclear deal with the US was seen as imposing autonomy costs on India. For the political right, these stemmed from the required separation between India's civilian and military programmes, which could potentially constrain India's ability to improve and expand its nuclear deterrent. For the

---

[36] Talbott 2004, p. 5.
[37] Joint Statement between President George W. Bush and Prime Minister Manmohan Singh, 2005.

political left, these costs derived from India's having to cosy up to the US and thereby jeopardize its historical stance of non-alignment. Especially when posited against the limited gains that the deal would offer—for example, only 3 per cent of India's energy consumption would be met through technology thus secured—the autonomy costs for both sides seemed especially high. But such an interpretation overestimates the concessions that India had to make to secure the deal, and underestimates the gains.

First, it remains to be seen what exact shape the required inspections would take. India will, most likely, exercise considerable leeway in which facilities it designates as civilian and opens up for inspection, and also in its interpretation of the safeguards agreement. Second, and even more importantly, the deal effectively allows India to escape the constraints imposed by the existing non-proliferation regime. India's BATNA (best alternative to negotiated agreement) on this issue area was poor: to remain outside the fold of recognized and legitimate nuclear powers and keep company with a group of slightly dubious outliers including rogue and pariah states. The gains are thus not just the relatively small increases in energy production that the deal would directly facilitate, but the systemic changes that the deal has induced, including the NSG waiver. The non-proliferation regime has in fact been turned on its head to include India in the fold, with the NPT taking the biggest hit. To make some small bilateral concessions and successfully avoid legally binding obligations (for instance, the deal does not bind India into signing the CTBT, despite pressures towards this by the US) *after* a regime has been completely rewritten to accommodate India is hardly an example of integrative bargaining.[38]

If anything, India's negotiation behaviour on non-proliferation illustrates its firm commitment to distributive bargaining as its power rises. Some concessions, some integrative moves, might occur, but only after all of India's demands have been met. Recall here Dronacharya's integrative moves towards Ekalavya after he had secured complete capitulation, and entirely on Dronacharya's terms, and further the generalization that was offered earlier that genuinely integrative bargaining would be rare to see if the examples of the Mahabharata are anything to go by. India's international diplomacy as a rising power seems to largely confirm this, and offer us an added spin: any integrative moves are likely to be framed entirely in voluntary terms rather

---

[38] As Leonard Weiss (2010), p. 267 notes, 'India can test any time it wishes, does not need CIRUS [research reactor] any longer for plutonium production, can block any FMCT [Fissile Material Cut-off Treaty] proposal it does not like in the CD [Conference on Disarmament], and its entire breeder reactor programme is exempted from safeguards under the agreement . . . one can only conclude that the Indian weapon programme has not been compromised in the least by the agreement.' Weiss further cites a particularly insightful editorial written at the time of the deal: 'Why is this deal important? Because for the first time, someone has decided to let India have its cake and eat it too. You stay out of the NPT, keep your weapons, refuse full scope safeguards, and yet get to conduct nuclear commerce in a system that is dead against such a formulation. That's the bottom line of this deal.'

than committed to in the form of reciprocal and legally binding commitments. In international trade, we have evidence of this in the 'water in the tariffs', where India's applied tariffs are far lower than its bound tariffs (though India is very far from being the only country guilty of this discrepancy). In non-proliferation, we see this in its voluntary moratorium on testing but its refusal to commit to the CTBT. In climate change, we see it in the much-vaunted concessions on voluntary emissions restraints that India has led and committed to, but as indicated by the name, these are voluntary and not legally binding in any way. Towards agreements that generate costs and have the ability to bind, rising India's negotiation strategy remains as distributive as ever.

2.7. CONCLUSION

In this chapter, we highlighted ten stories from the Mahabharata to investigate if a pattern might be found regarding how its characters negotiated. We found a strong proclivity on the part of its characters—heroes and villains alike—to use distributive strategies. Other characteristics included the tendency to view bargaining in strongly polarized either–or terms of 'resist' or 'give in' rather than find the middle ground to expand the pie that typifies integrative bargaining. The notion of honour and face recurs in the stories. Memories die hard, and forgiveness is not easy to find. Conciliatory behaviour is observed, but only in one's dealings with friends, or when left with no other choice. Truly integrative bargaining appears only rarely, and it usually leaves the person employing such strategies worse off.

Several of these lessons translate into India's foreign policy behaviour. We see that the dominant bargaining strategy is distributive, irrespective of India's rapidly transforming trajectory to power. Integrative bargaining is indeed rare and occurs either when distributive bargaining has failed and the country has few other choices left (i.e. from a position of extreme weakness) or when the other side has caved in to all of India's demands and some small face-saving concessions may therefore be allowed (i.e. from a position of considerable strength). Examples of the former can be found in India's negotiations in the GATT, while India's behaviour in the rewritten non-proliferation regime offers an illustration of the latter. An added feature in modern Indian diplomacy appears to be that concessions—when they happen to be made from a position of equality or power (rather than a capitulation that follows in the aftermath of the failure of iterative distributive moves)—are made on voluntary terms rather than through legal bindings. Exactly how this negotiating behaviour is presented and justified is explored in the next chapter.

Table 2.1 Success of Distributive versus Integrative Strategies in the Mahabharata

	Episode	Distributive strategy	Integrative strategy
1.	Bhishma–Dasharaja	Success for Dasharaja	Partial success (achieves Bhishma's objective of father's marriage, but produces heavy costs in the long run including Bhishma's own life of loneliness and the war of succession)
2.	Arjuna–Ekalavya–Dronacharya	Success for Arjuna and Dronacharya	Failure (Ekalavya pays heavy price)
3.	Pandavas–Yaksha	Failure for the four younger brothers	Success for Yudhishthira
4.	Ashwasena–Karna	Failure (for both Karna and Ashwasena)	Not attempted
5.	Krishna–Arjuna	Success (Arjuna's commitment to the battle against Bhishma is renewed)	Not attempted
6.	Kripacharya–Duryodhana	Failure (Duryodhana is killed)	Not attempted
7.	Ashwatthama's Jewel	Success (Ashwatthama is defeated and disempowered; the future of the Pandava clan is preserved)	Not attempted
8.	Indra–Chyavana	Success (Indra is deterred through show of force)	Failure (Indra is unresponsive to reasoned argument)
9.	Shukra–Kacha–Devyani	Partial success (Devyani manages to limit Kacha's use of the Sanjeevani)	Failure (Shukracharya is unable to protect the secret of the Sanjeevani from the Asuras, nor Devyani from heartbreak)
10.	Karna–Indra	Not attempted	Failure (Karna is killed in the war because he no longer has his protective earrings and armour).
		Success: 5 episodes Failure: 4 episodes Partial success: 1 episode	Success: 1 Partial success: 1 Failure: 3

REFERENCES

Barry, Bruce, and Raymond Friedman. 1998. Bargainer Characteristics in Distributive and Integrative Negotiation. *Journal of Personality and Social Psychology*, 74:2, 345–259.

Blustein, Paul. 2009. *Misadventures of the Most Favored Nations*. New York: Perseus.

Cohen, Raymond. 2004. *Negotiating across Cultures: International Communication in an Interdependent World*. Washington DC: United States Institute of Peace Press (1st edition 1991).

Cohen, Stephen. 2001. *India: Emerging Power*. Washington DC: Brookings.

GATT. 1987. Statement by HE Mr S. P. Shukla, Ambassador, Permanent Representative. SR. 43/ST/16. 22 December. Accessed at <http://gatt.stanford.edu> on 7 January 2012.

GATT. 1960. Statement by Mr. S.T. Swaminathan at the Meeting of the Contracting Parties, 31 May. L/1229, 20 June 1960.

Hagerty, Devin. 2006. Are we Present at the Creation? Alliance Theory and the Indo-US Strategic Convergence. In Sumit Ganguly, Brian Shoup, and Andrew Scobell eds., *US-Indian Strategic Cooperation into the 21st Century: More than Words*. London: Routledge.

Hopmann, P. Terrence. 1995. Two Paradigms of Negotiation: Bargaining and Problem Solving. *The Annals of the American Academy of Political and Social Science*, 542, 24–47.

Ikenberry, John. 2008. The Rise of China and the Future of the West. *Foreign Affairs*, 27:1, January/February, 25–57.

Ismail, Faizel. 2009. Reflections on the WTO July 2008 collapse. In Amrita Narlikar and Brendan Vickers eds., *Leadership and Change in the Multilateral Trading System*. Leiden: Martinus Nijhoff.

Janosik, Robert. 1987. Re-thinking the Culture Negotiation Link. *Negotiation Journal*, 3:4, 385–95.

Johnston, Alastair Iain. 2003. Is China a Status Quo Power? *International Security*, 27:4, Spring, 5–56.

Joint Statement between President George W. Bush and Prime Minister Manmohan Singh, 2005 <http://georgewbush-whitehouse.archives.gov/news/releases/2005/07/20050718-6.html>, accessed on 3 June 2012.

Kang, David. 2007. *China Rising: Peace, Power, and Order in East Asia*. New York: Columbia University Press.

Lakshmi, Rama. 2008. Hard Line at WTO earns India Praise. *The Washington Post*. 1 August.

Lax, David and James Sebenius. 1992. The Manager as Negotiator: The Negotiater's Dilemma—Creating and Claiming Value. In Stephen Goldberg, Frank Sander, and Nancy Rogers eds., *Dispute Resolution*. Boston: Little Brown and Co.

Lewicki, Roy J., Bruce Barry, and David M Saunders. 2009. *Negotiation*. New York: McGraw-Hill (6th edition).

Mohan, Raja. 2003. *Crossing the Rubicon: The Shaping of India's Foreign Policy*. Delhi: Viking.

Mohan, Raja. 2006. *Impossible Allies: Nuclear India, United States and the Global Order*. Delhi: India Research Press.

Moshaver, Ziba. 1991. *Nuclear Weapons Proliferation in the Indian Subcontinent*. Basingstoke: Palgrave Macmillan.

Narlikar, Amrita. 2003. *International Trade and Developing Countries: Bargaining Coalitions in the GATT and WTO*. London: Routledge.

Narlikar, Amrita. 2006. Peculiar Chauvinism or Strategic Calculation: Explaining the Negotiating Strategy of a Rising India. *International Affairs*, 82:1, January, 59–76.

Narlikar, Amrita and John Odell. 2006. The Strict Distributive Strategy for a Bargaining Coalition: The Like-Minded Group in the World Trade Organization. In John

Odell ed., *Negotiating Trade: Developing Countries in the WTO and NAFTA*. Cambridge: Cambridge University Press.

Nehru, Jawaharlal. 1963. Changing India. *Foreign Affairs*, 41:3, April, 453–65.

Odell, John. 2000. *Negotiating the World Economy*. Ithaca: Cornell University Press.

Odell, John. 2006. *Negotiating Trade: Developing Countries in the WTO and NAFTA*. Cambridge: Cambridge University Press.

Schelling, Thomas. 1966. *Arms and Influence*. New Haven, CT: Yale University Press.

Shay, Theodore L. 1968. Non-Alignment Si, Neutralism No. *The Review of Politics*, 32:3, April, 228–45.

Singh, Jaswant. 2007. *In Service of Emergent India: A Call to Honour*. Bloomington: Indiana University Press.

Swamy, Arun R. 2001. Déjà Vu all over again? Why Dialogue won't solve the Kashmir Dispute. *Asia Pacific Issues: Analysis from the East-West Center*, 56, November.

Talbott, Strobe. 2004. *Engaging India: Diplomacy, Democracy and the Bomb*. Washington DC: Brookings Institution Press.

Weiss, Leonard. 2010. India and the NPT. *Strategic Analysis*, 34:2, March, 255–71.

WTO 2008. TNC Meeting, Statement of Shri Kamal Nath, 23 July.

Zins, Max-Jean, and Gilles Boquérat eds. 2004. *India in the Mirror of Foreign Diplomatic Archives*. Delhi: Manohar, with Centre de Sciences Humaines.

3

Framing from a Moral High Horse

Crucial to successful bargaining and negotiation is how one *frames* one's demands. Certain formulations of the problem at hand can persuade the other side to alter its negotiation strategy and sometimes even change its preferences to thereby alter bargaining outcomes. In this chapter, we investigate the dominant pattern of framing demands in various bargaining situations in the Mahabharata, and further examine how far the negotiation behaviour of a rising India reflects continuities with the classical trends.

We start in Section 3.1 with a brief overview of the concept of framing, and the role that it plays in international negotiation. Using secondary sources, we also highlight the dominant framing trends associated with independent and modern India's negotiations with the outside world. Sections 3.2 to 3.5 discuss specific episodes of bargaining from the Mahabharata, which fit within the four categories that were outlined in Chapter 1 (i.e. pre-war negotiation, wartime negotiation, post-war negotiation and related stories and exceptions). Working in parallel with Chapters 2 to 6, each section also provides an analysis of the lessons offered by the stories. Section 3.6 of this chapter draws on the insights of the stories and investigates the extent to which they are reflected in India's bargaining as a rising power. Section 3.7 concludes.

3.1. WHAT IS FRAMING, AND WHY IT MATTERS FOR INTERNATIONAL NEGOTIATION

In their pioneering work on the subject of framing, Tversky and Kahneman summarize their findings as follows: 'The psychological principles that govern the perception of decision problems and the evaluation of probabilities and outcomes produce predictable shifts of preference when the same problem is framed in different ways. Reversals of preference are demonstrated in choices regarding monetary outcomes, both hypothetical and real, and in questions pertaining to the loss of human lives. The effects of frames on preferences are compared to the effects of perspectives on perceptual appearance. The dependence of preferences on the formulation of decision problems is a significant concern for the theory of rational choice.'[1]

While Tversky and Kahneman's work was most directly related to theories of decisions, it naturally generated important implications for negotiation analysts too. If the formulation of decision problems could potentially alter preferences, effective framing could be a vital mechanism in the negotiation process to sway outcomes in one's favour. Or, as Bazerman and Neale put it, 'The way the options available in a negotiation are framed, or presented, can strongly affect a manager's willingness to reach an agreement.'[2] The results of studies that focus on the effects of framing on negotiation are exciting and surprising. For example, in a study on framing and gender, Small et al. have argued that how opportunities are framed has a vital effect on gender differences in initiating negotiation: gender differences in initiating negotiations are high (with women showing reluctance to initiate a negotiation) when situations are framed as opportunities *for negotiation*, but are much lower when situations are framed as opportunities *to ask*.[3] There are several other studies with similarly valuable generalizations. Bazerman and Neale, for instance, argue that one can induce one's opponent to make more concessions by couching the proposal in terms of his potential gain, and thereby inducing him to adopt a more positive frame of reference, or by emphasizing the certainty of gain that one's offer entails, and framing these gains against the risks inherent in the negotiation situation.[4] Odell and Sell point to the attempt by Northern non-governmental organizations (NGOs) to reframe the debate on Trade-Related Intellectual Property Rights (TRIPs) in the WTO by changing the reference point of TRIPs as preventing piracy (which had been used as a justification to negotiate the TRIPs regime under the umbrella of the GATT) to a different reference point: even though medicines were available, the TRIPs patent regime was allowing rich pharmaceutical companies to deny poor people in the developing world access to life-saving drugs. The attempt was successful, and resulted in the TRIPs and Public Health Declaration of 2001, which clearly set out the conditions under which the strict patents regime could be relaxed in favour of the world's poor. The authors thus conclude: 'In a world of bounded rationality, much of the negotiation process is a contest of partisans trying to establish the dominant frame of reference. The more a weak-state coalition can do to prevail in this subjective contest, the larger its gains are likely to be.'[5]

---

[1] Tversky and Kahneman 1981, p. 453.   [2] Bazerman and Neale 1992, p. 31.
[3] Small et al. 2007.   [4] Bazerman and Neale 1992, p. 40.
[5] Odell and Sell 2006.

Given the broadness of the concept, framing can be and has been conceptualized across several different lines, for instance representation of one's demands in a negotiation as losses versus gains, or interests versus ideas. For our purpose, interesting dimensions along which we can study India's framing behaviour are twofold: a) prolixity versus brevity and b) moralization versus pragmatism.

The prolix and moralistic frames adopted by Indian negotiators have invited comment from practitioners and scholars alike. Often highlighted as characteristics of India's traditional negotiation style, these two aspects of framing are important also in the debate on whether a rising India's negotiation behaviour represents a break with its past (as summarized in Chapter 1). If the socialization/interest-convergence variants of the argument are right, we would expect to see some change in India's negotiation behaviour in both style and substance. If, however, prolixity persists and, even more importantly, India continues to frame its demands in moralistic frames, we would have cause to argue for greater continuity in a rising India's behaviour with its past than change.

While we conduct this analysis, it is important to bear in mind that our central purpose is primarily analytic rather than normative or prescriptive. We do not assume, for instance, that moralistic framing necessarily generates better or worse results than pragmatic framing. Negotiation demands are usually framed in a context, and contexts too can change and thereby affect the success of the framing strategy. For example, moralistic framing that might not have proven so effective in the past may find a more sympathetic ear in a different international context, wherein concerns with legitimacy and accountability are higher for several reasons (including the demonstrated veto power and potential agenda-setting power of large developing countries). Prolix arguments, framed in moralistic terms, may sometimes work to the negotiator's strategic advantage, depending on the audience and context; our investigation focuses on whether these framing characteristics typify India's negotiation culture in the past and present.

The prolixity variable in Indian politics in general has been nicely captured by Amartya Sen, who writes:

> Prolixity is not alien to us in India. We are able to talk at some length. Krishna Menon's record of the longest speech ever delivered at the United Nations (nine hours non-stop), established half a century ago ... has not been equaled by anyone from anywhere. Other peaks of loquaciousness have been scaled by other Indians. We do like to speak.
>
> This is not a new habit. The ancient Sanskrit epics the Ramayana and the Mahabharata, which are frequently compared with the *Iliad* and the *Odyssey*, are colossally longer than the works that the modest Homer could manage ... they proceed from stories to stories woven around their principal tales, and are engagingly full of dialogues, dilemmas, and alternative perspectives. And we encounter

masses of arguments and counterarguments spread over incessant debates and disputations.[6]

Sen's observations apply to different aspects of Indian politics, including its foreign policy behaviour. But perhaps an even more significant characteristic of India's framing style than prolixity is our second variable: moralism.

Raymond Cohen persuasively argues that Third World states have often compensated for the limitations of their economic and military power by positioning themselves on a moral high ground, particularly in their negotiations with Washington: 'From the high ground of moral superiority and self-righteous indignation, they can direct their rhetorical fire at Washington's exposed moral positions.' In his comparative study, Cohen points out that for some Third World states this moralism is a flip side of the role of the dependant, even supplicant. The Indian case, he rightly argues, is different: although reluctant to accept a subordinate or supplicant position in a negotiation, post-independence India has seldom been reluctant to adopt the path of moral indignation. The Indian negotiator, even at the outset of the negotiation, is cited as tending to 'parade "a litany of all your past failures, abuses of them, sins," while India's record is presented as one of "great principle and universal approbation."'[7] Stephen Cohen's analysis reinforces these findings, and he argues: 'Indian officials believe they are representing not just a state but a civilization. Few state-civilizations are India's equals . . . Indians believe that India-as-civilization has something to offer the rest of the world. Contemporary Indian leaders also see India as playing a global, albeit benign, role. These beliefs explain Nehru's tendency to moralize, and the Indian propensity to lecture other powers, great and small.'[8] Importantly, one negotiator's moral high horse could well be another negotiator's fight for justice and fairness. And the underpinnings of such a fight can be seen in India's negotiations across issue areas. Details of particular cases are discussed later in this chapter, but a brief overview of the dominant trend is provided here.

Recall India's position of considerable relative weakness in the early years of the GATT. That it sought exemptions and exceptions from its GATT obligations at the time is perhaps not surprising in itself. But in framing its proposals in terms of more generalizable principles of fairness and equality, with considerable eloquence, India's negotiation behaviour was striking. An illustration can be found in the memorable statement of India's chief negotiator at the GATT, Sir Raghavan Pillai, made in 1954:

> Equality of treatment is equitable only among equals. A weakling cannot carry the same load as a giant . . .[9]

---

[6] Sen 2005, p. 3.   [7] R. Cohen 1998, p. 95.   [8] S. Cohen 2001, p. 52.
[9] GATT 1954. Just how visionary the statement was is not the main subject of our study, though it is worth noting that provisions relating to Special and Differential Treatment (which

Trade was not the only area where we find India's moralism high. Jawaharlal Nehru's address to the UN General Assembly on 3 November 1948 is but one illustration of this commitment to moral principle as he outlined India's position on world affairs:

> We do not think that the problems of the world or of India can be solved by thinking in terms of aggression or war or violence. We are frail mortals, we cannot always live up to the teaching of the great man who led our nation to freedom. But that lesson has sunk deep into our souls and so long as we remember it, I am sure we shall be on the right path. And, if I may venture to suggest this to the General Assembly, I think that if the essentials of that lesson are kept in mind, perhaps our approach to the problems today will be different. Perhaps the conflicts that always hang over us will appear a little less deep than they are and in fact gradually fade away.[10]

Nor was this cheap talk or the naïve idealism of a newly independent India; the commitment to moral principle persisted in areas of high politics and matters of national security.

We have several examples of India's moralistic framing of its negotiation demands over nuclear technology and nuclear weapons. When faced with renewed pressure to sign up to the nuclear Non-Proliferation Treaty (NPT), India framed its own position against the failure of the superpowers to adhere to their own duty of disarmament. Raymond Cohen paraphrases this framing as follows: 'How unjust, it thundered, taking the moral high ground once again, for states authorized under the treaty to possess nuclear weapons . . . to perpetuate their own monopoly while evading their ethical and legal obligations to the human race to disarm.'[11] In fact, rather interestingly, India continued to adopt a moral high ground even after it conducted the nuclear tests of 1998. Jaswant Singh, while also alerting the world to India's nasty nuclear neighbourhood, offered the following moral defence of India's position in an article in *Foreign Affairs* that was entitled 'Against Nuclear Apartheid', thereby skilfully turning the condemnation that India had faced at the time on its head:

> The basis of Indian nuclear policy . . . remains that a world free of nuclear weapons would enhance not only India security but the security of all nations. In the absence of universal disarmament, India could scarcely accept a regime that arbitrarily divided nuclear haves from have-nots. India has always insisted that all nations' security interests are equal and legitimate. From the start, therefore, its principles instilled a distaste for the self-identified and closed club of the five permanent members of the U.N. Security Council.[12]

---

were incorporated in the GATT in 1979 via the Enabling Clause), or indeed the ideas of 'policy space' that developing countries advance today, echo many of Pillai's sentiments.

[10] Nehru 1948.   [11] R. Cohen 1998, p. 97.   [12] Singh 1998a.

We find few exceptions to this dominant trend in independent India's negotiations in different multilateral regimes. But there is one interesting line of variation: while the previous examples are those where moralistic framing was used to support India's perceived strategic interests, we also have a few instances when moralism pervaded India's negotiation positions even when this ran counter to India's interests. An important example of this can be found in the window of opportunity that opened up for India immediately after China's nuclear tests in 1964. J. N. Dixit records that the Americans had advance information of China's developing nuclear programme, and had indicated to Dr Homi Bhabha that 'they would be generally supportive of India becoming a nuclear weapons power'. Nehru, however, refused to make use of this opportunity, reiterating his moral stance against all types of weapons of mass destruction. Dixit interprets this as one of India's diplomatic failures: 'We lost a valuable opportunity of transmuting our capacities into operational reality . . . Had we exercised the nuclear weaponisation option in the early 1960s, we would have been able to sign the nuclear non-proliferation treaty as a nuclear weapons power, instead of getting enmeshed in all the controversies and the isolation which we have gone through from 1966–68.'[13] Effectively, moralism sometimes served as more than a framing device, and came to constitute the substance of the negotiation position. And it was used in instances not only when it reinforced India's interests but also when it may have proven detrimental to them.

India's framing strategies to some extent are reflective of a phenomenon identified by Pratap Bhanu Mehta, who argues that India's approach to its foreign policy is 'through the language of entitlement more than a language of bargaining'.[14] He suggests that negotiation entails two objectives. The first is 'to get others' thoughts around to what you think you are entitled to'. The second is to strike a deal, success in which depends on 'how many cards you hold'. He correctly argues that India's approach to most negotiations emphasizes the former objective. This sense of entitlement leaves very little space to negotiate indeed.[15] Note that this observation resonates strongly with the

---

[13] Dixit 2003, p. 358–9. Dixit was a veteran of the Indian Foreign Service; having joined it in 1958, he rose to its highest echelons to become the Foreign Secretary in the early 1990s.

[14] Mehta 2009 in fact argues that India lacks a culture of bargaining, but this claim displays a rather limited understanding of the concept. We would argue, as would many other negotiation analysts, that the language of entitlement that India uses in its negotiations forms a distinctive characteristic of its bargaining style.

[15] Mehta 2009, p. 228, notes another interesting characteristic besides that of intransigence caused by the sense of entitlement; the resistance to engage in give and take 'makes India peculiarly inert in trying to hold onto or amass as many bargaining chips as possible'. The two characteristics together produce a paradox: 'India can sometimes be too ready to concede others' entitlement when it thinks they are legitimate, but too intransigent when it comes to cutting deals that seem to reduce its own entitlement to a bargaining game.' Our findings in Chapter 2 regarding negotiation strategy reinforce this analysis: recall, for instance, the readiness of

findings of Chapter 2, which illustrated a broad tendency of negotiators in the Mahabharata, and also modern India, to negotiate on a take-it-or-leave-it basis. As the rest of this chapter illustrates, using examples from the Mahabharata and also of India's modern-day negotiations as a rising power, India's prolix and moralistic framing of its demands is targeted at the art of persuasion (however aggressive and non-conciliatory at times) and legitimization, rather than the more direct, almost crude, give and take that typify many bargaining situations.

3.2. FRAMING STRATEGIES OF THE MAIN PROTAGONISTS, PRE-WAR

The pre-war part of the epic offers us several instances of how the chief protagonists frame their negotiating demands. Three stories follow below.

3.2.1. Yudhishthira's negotiation with the Yaksha

Recall from Chapter 2 that the five Pandava brothers encountered a magical being, a Yaksha, of the lake. Four of the five brothers disregarded the warnings they were given, and Arjuna explicitly challenged the disembodied voice. Having drunk from its waters, all four fell lifeless to the ground. Yudhishthira—the eldest Pandava and the son of Dharma—alone complied with the terms of the Yaksha. Although tormented initially by thirst and subsequently by grief and loss, he agreed to answer the riddles of the Yaksha with humility and patience, and did not touch the water until he had permission to do so. The Yaksha's questions were philosophical puzzles that only the wisest could answer. Yudhishthira passed the test. Impressed, the Yaksha granted him a boon, besides allowing him access to the waters of the lake: one (and only one) brother, of Yudhishthira's choosing, would be brought back to life.

Yudhishthira had a difficult moral decision before him. He chose his stepbrother, Nakula. The Yaksha was surprised by this choice. He pointed out that not only were Bhima and Arjuna Yudhishthira's real brothers, but also that they offered greater strategic value to him. Bhima bore the strength of a hundred thousand elephants and was a great favourite of Yudhishthira's; Arjuna was matchless and much admired for his dexterity with the bow. Why then had he chosen to revive Nakula?

Bhishma to concede to his father's demands, but his subsequent refusals to break his vow in the face of multiple imperatives demanding that he did so.

Yudhishthira appealed to the principle of Dharma as he offered his explanation. He presented the argument as follows:

धर्म एव हतो हन्ति धर्मो रक्षति रक्षितः
तस्माद् धर्मम् न त्यजामि मा नो धर्मो हतोसवधीत्

III.313.128 (Gita Press Edition)

When Dharma is destroyed, the destroyed Dharma also destroys its destroyer. When Dharma is protected, it also protects its protector. This is why I never forsake Dharma for fear that the destroyed Dharma might also destroy me.

And having presented the moral argument, Yudhishthira further explained that his devotion to his own mother, Kunti, equalled his devotion to his stepmother, Madri (even though she was no longer alive). He did not wish either mother to be rendered childless, and therefore believed it only fair that as his own life was being preserved, the life of one of Madri's sons should also be restored:

यथा कुन्ती तथा माद्री विशेषो नास्ति मे तयोः
मातृभ्याम् सममिच्छामि नकुलो यक्ष जीवतु

III.297.73

As Kunti is to me, so also was Madri; there is no distinction for me between the two. I wish to treat them both equally, and, therefore, please revive Nakula.

The choice of morality over personal preferences and strategic advantage dictated that Yudhishthira choose his stepbrother over Arjuna and Nakula. Yudhishthira, as the noblest and most virtuous of the Pandavas, willingly embraced this choice.

For his kindness, which he distributed in equal and fair measure to all, the Yaksha praised Yudhishthira. As a reward, he revived not just Nakula but all the other Pandava brothers. The Yaksha further revealed his true identity: he was Dharma himself, the father of Yudhishthira, who had come to learn more about his son's character. And he granted Yudhishthira several additional boons as a reward for his virtue.

The story is interesting in the insights that it offers us on the importance attached to morality by a key protagonist, and how the opponent reacts to this morality-laden negotiation. In his exchange with the Yaksha, Yudhishthira frames his demands in terms of fairness and virtue rather than interest. In fact, even the choice that he makes—rather than the mere framing of this choice— is determined by his choosing Dharma over and above strategic advantage. And rather than end up with the sucker's payoff, he is abundantly rewarded for this moralistic framing and moral choice. As per this story, the moral course of action is not only the path of idealistic heroes, but morality and moralization also yield high returns.

3.2.2. Draupadi urges Yudhishthira to stand up to the Kauravas

The excesses of the Kauravas against the Pandavas were many and grievous. When Yudhishthira was declared the heir to the throne, the Kauravas attempted to assassinate the Pandavas and their mother, Kunti, by building a house of wax and setting fire to it. The Pandavas escaped this assassination plot. Recognizing that Duryodhana would never accept Yudhishthira as king, Dhritarashtra now attempted to find a compromise solution by dividing the kingdom between the two factions. Duryodhana was crowned king of Hastinapur; the Pandavas built their own capital, Indraprastha, from scratch, and transformed a desolate land into a fertile and rich kingdom. Their ambitions unappeased and their jealousies reignited, however, the Kaurava brothers now attempted to seize the Pandava kingdom through a rigged dice game. Loaded dice ensured their victory, and the Pandava princes and their wife Draupadi were subject to heinous insults and cruelties, and were reduced to the status of slaves of the Kauravas. The Kauravas' excesses and transgressions violated all the precepts of Dharma, and many inauspicious signs burst forth. Wolves and jackals howled, donkeys brayed, and vultures circled the skies. The elders in the Kaurava court observed these signs and were filled with fear, sorrow, and regret. Vidura (the king's chief consul and half-brother) and Gandhari (the queen) then entreated Dhritarashtra to correct some of these wrongs. Upon their advice, and in his attempt to save his son from sin, Dhritarashtra restored to the Pandavas their kingdom and their freedom. But even before the Pandavas had a chance to return to their kingdom, upon Duryodhana's insistence, they were recalled for another game of dice. The game was again rigged with their uncle Shakuni's loaded dice. The Pandavas lost again, and were exiled for 13 years. Having survived the attempt on their lives by their envious cousins and endured grievous and public humiliation at their hands in the courts, the diktat of exile was the last straw for the usually patient and stoic Pandavas. In the forest, the brothers and Draupadi urged Yudhishthira to finally take action against the Kauravas.

Draupadi, whose suffering had been the greatest at the hands of the Kauravas, was particularly eloquent in presenting the case for action. Drawing on the stories presented in religious and secular texts, she counselled Yudhishthira that strategies of constant forgiveness are counterproductive, as are strategies of constant reprisal, and advised him on the importance of employing suitable strategies of forgiveness and power according to the particular situation.

काले मृदुर्यो भवति काले भवति दारुण:
स वै सुखमवाप्नोति लोकेसमुष्मिन्निहैव च
III.29.23

He who is able to adopt strategies of gentleness and harshness depending on the requirement of the particular situation, he alone is able to achieve happiness in this world and the next.

And given Yudhishthira's strong predilection to forgive, she then offered him a specification of the conditions under which forgiveness made sense.

Importantly, her argument was framed primarily in ethical terms. Draupadi's maxims on forgiveness, despite the bitter and cruel lessons that life had taught her, showed considerable magnanimity. Many, as per the maxims that she presented, are worthy of forgiveness. For example, if someone had caused one grave injury, a prior kindness by the same person should not be forgotten; for this prior kindness, the transgressor was still deserving of forgiveness. Wrongs caused by ignorance or poor understanding were also to be forgiven. The first offence always deserved pardon. An offence committed unwillingly also deserved forgiveness. In contrast, however, if someone deliberately committed a wrong and then pleaded ignorance, he deserved to be punished. Second offences, however trivial, deserved retribution. In other words, one could not adopt forgiveness as one's sole strategy in dealing with opponents; the timing and situation dictated strategy choice.

The Kauravas had caused the Pandavas constant pain and great suffering. This was not the time to shower them with forgiveness. Those of a forgiving disposition were being victimized, while the powerful indulged in persecuting others. Under these circumstances and in these difficult times, a display of power was the correct course of action for Yudhishthira.

न हि कश्चित्क्षमाकालो विद्यतेसद्य कुरून्प्रति
तेजसश्चागते काले तेज उत्स्रष्टुमर्हसि
III.29.34

There is now no excuse or opportunity to show forgiveness towards the Kauravas. Now is the time to use force, and the only strategy that you should employ towards them is one of force.

This discussion of forgiveness is important for at least two reasons. First, it is significant because it is Draupadi who pronounces these maxims. Were Yudhishthira to wax eloquent on the virtue of forgiveness (as he was indeed wont to do), this would have been unsurprising. But even Draupadi, one of the most formidable and fierce characters in the epic, and the victim of grave injustice, extols some of the virtues of forgiveness, and is generous with regard to the conditions under which it can be exercised. Second, the discussion is pertinent to this chapter because even though the Pandavas are enduring great adversities in the forest during their exile, Draupadi does not restrict herself to making the strategic case by reminding Yudhishthira of the responsibility of the Kauravas for causing the undeserved downfall of the noble Pandavas. Rather, she frames her demand for action by the Pandava brothers by appealing to their ethics. Admittedly, this is the language that Yudhishthira—the son of Dharma and renowned for his virtue—best understands. But it is also language that one of the angriest protagonists has internalized.

3.2.3. Sanjaya and Vidura advise Dhritarashtra against war

Despite the foul play of the Kauravas, the Pandavas returned from their 13 years in exile and demanded their just share of the kingdom. In fact, in the spirit of conciliation, Yudhishthira did not demand the whole kingdom, or even half the kingdom; he promised that the Pandavas would be satisfied with just five villages. The story of the Kauravas' rejection of this magnanimous offer is covered in detail in Section 5 of this chapter. Relevant to our immediate concern, however, is the advice offered by two protagonists—Sanjaya (a trusted courtier) and Vidura to the Kaurava king, Dhritarashtra—when the Pandavas send word of their offer via Sanjaya. The importance of their advice derives from their position as trusted counsellors to Dhritarashtra, who nonetheless managed to preserve their reputations of impartial judgement even through the divisive and polarizing war.

War seemed imminent. In a last-ditch effort to avoid war with his kinsmen, Yudhishthira asked Sanjaya to return to Hastinapur with major concessions from the Pandava side in return for peace. Sanjaya communicated the offer of the Pandavas to the blind king. But this communication was not a straight-forward statement of the final negotiating position of the Pandavas; Sanjaya placed the offer in an eloquent moral frame. First, he presented Dhritarashtra with a litany of his many transgressions and sins (which included his constant inability to stand up to the excesses of his son, Duryodhana), and contrasted them with the virtues of Yudhishthira.

त्वमेवैको जातपुत्रेषु राजन्वशं गन्ता सर्वलोके नरेन्द्र
कामात्मनां इलाघसे द्यूतकाले नान्यच्छमात्पश्य विपाकमस्य
V.32.28

O King, in the entire world, you alone continued to shower praise on your wilful and wayward son; you were under his control at the dice game, and here too, you were unable to abate your admiration for him; the terrible situation that we face today is a consequence of your actions.

Second, he placed the blame of the impending war firmly on Dhritarashtra's shoulders, owing to his excessive paternal doting on his wayward son. Third, while his argument was primarily a moralistic one, Sanjaya also appealed to strategic pragmatism. The Pandavas had just cause behind them and also matchless ability as warriors. They had shown great restraint until now, but if they were further provoked, they could and would ensure the certain and complete annihilation of the Kurus.

Sanjaya's severe moral rebuke and strategic warning greatly perturbed Dhritarashtra. As soon as Sanjaya retired for rest, he sent for Vidura, who was known for his measured and unbiased counsel, and sought his advice.

Vidura's advice was candid and unrestrained (it runs for nine chapters in the text!). And even more than Sanjaya's counsel, his advice was couched in even greater moralistic detail. He began by praising the righteous and kind Yudhishthira, who had suffered many wrongs at the hands of the Kauravas. He asked Dhritarashtra how he possibly imagined peace and prosperity for himself, given that he had entrusted the management of the kingdom and its policies to the likes of Duryodhana, Karna, and Dushasana. Vidura then offered the king a detailed account of the principles of virtue, and the qualities of an intelligent and righteous man. And at the end of each chapter, he reminded Dhritarashtra of the virtues of the Pandavas, and urged him to return their just share of the kingdom.

सर्वैर्गुणैरुपेताश्च पाण्डवा भरतर्षभ
पितृवत्त्वयि वर्तन्ते तेषु वर्तस्व पुत्रवत्
V.35.67

King of the Bharatas, the Pandavas are bestowed with many virtues and they show you the same respect as they would their own father. You should also regard them likewise and treat them appropriately as your own sons.

Vidura's teachings to Dhritarashtra provide us with a striking illustration of the attempt to frame a negotiation in prolix and moralistic terms. Vidura did not, for instance, emphasize the military might of the Pandavas and the near certainty of defeat for the Kauravas (which Sanjaya had at least highlighted, although only as an additional argument to the moral one against war). Nor did he mince his words in pouring censure on Dhritarashtra for his weak and irresponsible behaviour. The righteous action that he urged Dhritarashtra to take by restoring their share of the kingdom to the Pandavas would save the entire clan from a destructive war, but would above all offer redemption to the king for his many sins of omission and commission over the years.

3.2.4. Insights for negotiation

Two themes emerge from these episodes. First, the righteous in the Mahabharata, in general, seem to attach considerable importance to providing a moral justification of their actions; an interest-based frame (even when appealing to the opponent's interest) is secondary at best. In fact, in Yudhishthira's case when he negotiates with the Yaksha, we see that the appeal to morality is more than a justification; it determines and frames the very content of his negotiating position. It was on moral grounds that Yudhishthira agreed to comply with the Yaksha's demands and answer his questions in the first place (as discussed in Chapter 2). He also took the path of fairness, particularly in refraining from causing injury to another, when he was given the choice of saving one brother's life. Similarly, the greatly wronged and vengeance-seeking Draupadi attempts to persuade Yudhishthira to battle with the Kauravas by providing him with an eloquent discourse on the virtues of forgiveness. When Sanjaya and Vidura urge Dhritarashtra to accept the Pandava offer of peace, they base their arguments only partially on pragmatic grounds (i.e. the power of the Pandavas) and primarily on moral grounds. The expectation, in this process of argumentation, seems to be that the moral argument is more likely to produce the desired outcome.[16]

Second, the moral argument admittedly does not consistently win. Of the three episodes here, we find that only Yudhishthira is rewarded by the Yaksha for his ethical behaviour. Draupadi's considered moral arguments do not persuade Yudhishthira—at least at the time—to adopt the course of war that she believes to be the just course of action. And neither the Pandavas' willingness to surrender their claim to the throne for just five villages in the interest of peace nor Sanjaya's nor Vidura's moral counsel are able to persuade the blind king (physically blind, but also blinded by his love for his wilful son) to embrace the offer of peace. In other words, moralism pays, but only in certain unusual conditions. But interestingly, heroes and villains alike predominantly reject pragmatism over moralism. Why this might be the case is discussed in greater detail in Section 3.6 of this chapter.

3.3. NEGOTIATIONS IN WARTIME

3.3.1. The Bhagwad Gita: Krishna counsels Arjuna

All efforts at mediation and conciliation had failed, and finally the two magnificent armies of the Pandavas and Kauravas stood facing each other on the battlefield of Kurukshetra. Amidst the sound of drums, conches, and war cries, both sides stood poised for battle. But Arjuna gazed upon his elders, teachers, and kinsmen in the Kaurava army, and his heart was overcome with doubt, remorse, and confusion. What gain could possibly be had from destroying one's own kinsmen? Not for the sovereignty of all three worlds would Arjuna incur such great sin, let alone the sovereignty of a kingdom. Speaking thus, Arjuna set his bow and arrows aside, refusing to fight. And in his dejection he turned to Lord Krishna. What followed

---

[16] In contrast, we have evidence of negotiation in other cultures where the pragmatic argument trumps the moral one. For example, see the contrast that Kumar and Worm 2004 draw between China and India.

remains one of the greatest sermons in philosophy, the Bhagwad Gita. The clamouring armies on either side could neither interrupt Krishna's exposition nor distract Arjuna from it. The discourse runs for 18 chapters, and covers a great breadth of difficult philosophical questions in considerable detail. While we cannot even begin to cover the range or depth of its teachings here, it provides us with a particularly useful example of framing behaviour in the Mahabharata.

Note that the discourse took place at a time of considerable urgency, that is, when the two armies eyeballed each other, ready to do battle. Both Arjuna's doubt at the eleventh hour, and Krishna's method of persuasion, might come as a surprise to negotiating cultures that work with tight deadlines (the Indian negotiator's attitude to deadlines, and time more generally, is discussed in detail in Chapter 5). In this case, however, moral concerns trumped all other considerations. Arjuna's doubt derived from a fundamental moral question: could any circumstance justify a war against one's own kin?

Krishna's reply was not one delivered in haste. It delved deep into the nature of the body and soul, Dharma, Moksha (liberation from the cycle of life and death), and details of the different types of Yoga whereby Moksha could be attained. In particular, Krishna explained to Arjuna that it was foolish to mourn the impending deaths in battle, as such mourning misunderstood the relationship between the material body and the eternal soul. Though the body perishes, the soul is eternal and timeless, and can never be destroyed. Arjuna's grief was misguided: though Arjuna would wreak great destruction upon the Kaurava army, the souls of his kinsmen were indestructible, and it was thus wrong to mourn their loss.

वासांसि जीर्णानि यथा विहाय नवानि गृह्णाति नरोसपराणि
तथाशरीराणि विहाय जीर्णान्यन्यानि संयाति नवानि देही
VI.24.22

Just as one discards old robes and dons new ones, so also the soul discards the old body and acquires a new one.

Krishna also provided the moral justification for Arjuna's role in the war, and why he must choose the pathway of detached action rather than renunciation:

कर्मण्येवाधिकारस्ते मा फलेषु कदाचन
मा कर्मफलहेतुर्भूर्मा ते संगोसस्त्वकर्मणि
VI.24.47

Focus always on your actions, but never on the fruits of your actions. The reward should not be the purpose of your actions, nor should you allow yourself to be tempted by inaction.

Krishna also showed Arjuna the pathway of enlightenment by narrating the qualities of the 'Stitah Pragyah'—the individual with stability of mind—and also thus the individual who was dear to Krishna.

तुल्यनिन्दास्तुतिर्मौनी सन्तुष्टो येन केनचित्
अनिकेतः स्थिरमतिर्भक्तिमान्मे प्रियो नर
VI.34.19

He who reacts in the same way to praise and blame alike, is equally content with the inflows and outflows of worldly goods, treats the whole world as his home (rather than is attached to a particular home), has a stable mind, and shows me devotion, such an individual is dear to me.

Finally, towards the end of this sermon laden with the precepts of Dharma and Moksha, Krishna revealed his divine and infinite form to Arjuna, which encompassed the universe in its entirety. Through the teachings of Krishna and the divine vision that he had been given, Arjuna's doubts finally disappeared. With renewed resolve, he seized his arms and readied himself for battle.

3.3.2. Karna's defeat and death

Karna and Arjuna met almost as demigods on the battlefield. There was a certain inevitability to this battle. The two sons of Kunti were equally gifted in the skills of archery, unmatched by any other warriors, and fierce rivals since the days of their youth. They were both equally courageous. Karna, rejected and abandoned by his mother at birth, had been approached by Kunti prior to the war in an attempt at reconciliation. Constant in his loyalty to Duryodhana, however, Karna refused to defect to the Pandavas. But upon discovering that Kunti was in fact his mother, he made her a promise: amongst the Pandava brothers on the opposing side, Karna would kill only Arjuna or die in the attempt, and thereby ensure that she would continue to have five sons even after the war (i.e. the same number that she had claimed for many years by failing to acknowledge the existence of her sixth—and firstborn—son, Karna). It was also known that Karna would pick Arjuna as his opponent, and the fight would be unto the death of one brother or the other. This day arrived on the 17th day of the war, in the shape of a duel between Karna and Arjuna. The brothers fought bravely and ferociously, each as powerful as the other, with no end in sight. Then the wheel of Karna's carriage began to sink into the earth, and Karna was thrown into a state of agitation and confusion.[17]

---

[17] The sinking of Karna's wheel was significant, and this was not an overreaction by Karna. He had been cursed by the sage Parashurama, from whom Karna had acquired the knowledge of the use of the supreme weapon, the Brahmaastra, under false pretences (Parashurama had a

Karna's immediate reaction, amidst his confusion and as Arjuna's powerfully accurate arrows continued to rain on him (causing him insufferable, near-fatal injuries), was to rant bitterly about the failure of Dharma to protect its worshippers. He had good reason to feel thus deserted. After all, he had tried hard to pursue the path of Dharma; recall, for instance, Karna's extreme generosity, which was discussed in Chapter 2. But then, Karna, despite being distraught with pain, also resorted to a more rational framing of a request to Arjuna, which was based on the laws and ethics of war. He asked Arjuna to pause in his onslaught for a moment, and reminded him of the laws of war. Only a coward would attack an opponent whose carriage wheel was stuck. The righteous warrior would refrain from attacking an opponent under several conditions, for instance if the opponent had run out of arrows or had lost his armour. Would the noble and heroic Arjuna not give Karna a moment to free his wheel from the earth? For Arjuna to shoot at Karna from his carriage, when Karna himself was displaced and unprepared on the ground, was unbecoming and unworthy.

अबाणे भ्रष्टकवचे भ्रष्टभगनायुधे तथा
न शूराः प्रहरन्त्याजौ न राज्ञे पार्थिवास्तथा
VIII.66.63

The brave do not attack one who is dismounted from his carriage, has no arrows left in his quiver, whose shield is broken, and whose weapons have been destroyed.

Karna had made a strongly framed plea on the grounds of morality. But Krishna gave Karna an equally strong response, reiterating and reframing the situation through a different appeal to morality.

अथाब्रवीद्वासुदेवो रथस्थो राधेय दिष्ट्या स्मरसीह धर्मम्
प्रायेण नीचा व्यसनेषु मग्ना निन्दन्ति दैवं कुकृतं न तत्तत्
VIII.67.1

Is it not fortunate, son of Radha, that you remember the laws of Dharma now? Unworthy men are wont to blame Dharma when they face difficult situations, seldom accepting responsibility for their own actions that have in fact led them to their doom.

And Krishna then gave Karna a fierce reminder of his many sins and transgressions against the Pandavas and the blameless Draupadi. Infuriated by the reminders of Karna's excesses against his family, Arjuna renewed his attack

long-standing hatred of Kshatriyas and would only instruct Brahmins in the arts of war; Karna had thus concealed his Kshatriya roots, and pretended to be a Brahmin in order to be accepted as a pupil of this great teacher). The curse was a dreadful one: when Karna's life was in peril, and his need to use this knowledge was the greatest, he would be afflicted by a forgetfulness that would make it impossible for him to use the Brahmaastra. The curse of another Brahmin on Karna had also stated that when his life faced the greatest jeopardy, the earth would swallow the wheel of his chariot.

with even greater vigour. Karna had no argument left against Krishna's indictment of his actions (and, indeed, all the actions that Krishna had listed were reprehensible and condemnable), nor did he attempt any further argument. He fought bravely against the divine weapons that Arjuna continued to use with much skill, all the while attempting to raise his sinking wheel. Finally, however, Arjuna loaded his bow, Gandiva, with the Anjalika weapon (which was said to hold the same prowess of destruction as the Chakra of Lord Vishnu or the Pinaka of Lord Shiva), and fired it laden with prayers and much determination. Karna's head was severed, and it fell to the ground, resplendent as the magnificent and blazing sun. And thus was the mighty and noble Karna defeated and killed.

3.3.3. Kripacharya's failed attempts to restrain Ashwatthama

Recall the story of Ashwatthama, which we discussed in Chapter 2, Section 2.4.1, when possessed with grief, fury, and the desire for vengeance, he chose to attack the sleeping Pandava camp in violation of the most fundamental laws of war. Of particular relevance to this chapter was the debate that took place between Kripacharya and Ashwatthama between the genesis of his idea of vengeance and his implementation of it. The debate was effectively a negotiation over the legitimacy—perhaps even the morality—of Ashwatthama's proposed course of action.

Ashwatthama began first by justifying the action to himself. He framed it, repugnant though it was to the Kshatriya code, in terms of the treacherous and dishonest strategies that even the Pandavas had used in the war. He reminded himself of his promise to Duryodhana, his trusted friend and leader who had been rendered so pitiful in his dying hours, to destroy the Pandavas who had killed him using unlawful tactics of combat. And he then made a strategic argument that led back to the fundamental moral point: the Pandavas were invincible; if he did not resort to some treachery, Ashwatthama would not be able to fulfil the promise he had made to his dying friend. Having thus justified his action to himself, he awoke Kritavarma and Kripacharya, and unveiled his plan. On being met with shocked silence on the part of the two elders, Ashwatthama made a passionate speech reminding them of the unlawful and remorseless way in which the Pandavas had killed the valiant Duryodhana, and how they had also wreaked havoc and destruction on the many greats of the Kaurava army, leaving just three survivors. Many of these actions had violated the laws of war and morality. And thus, Ashwatthama argued:

निन्दितानि च सर्वाणि कुत्सितानि पदे पदे
सोपधानि कृतान्येव पाण्डवैरकृतात्मभिः
X.1.49

At every step, the impure Pandavas have taken actions that are worthy of blame and contempt. They bear responsibility for many deceitful deeds.

Kripacharya—trusted teacher of the Kauravas and also Ashwatthama's maternal uncle—urged Ashwatthama to exercise restraint. He offered him three arguments. First, he offered a discourse on the relationship between destiny and effort, to finally arrive at the argument that emphasized the importance of *good action*. Second, he reminded Ashwatthama of Duryodhana's many faults and wicked transgressions. Third, he reminded Ashwatthama of the importance of relying on the advice of good friends (something that Duryodhana had consistently failed to do, having surrounded himself by wicked counsel), and his own intention to return to the Kaurava king and queen, Dhritarashtra and Gandhari, and act only upon their advice.

Ashwatthama remained unpersuaded. His response was now framed in terms of relativism in understanding: that individuals differed in their understanding depending on their own circumstances and also on altered external conditions. He argued the following:

तस्मैव तु मनुष्यस्य सा सा बुद्धिस्तदा तदा
कालयोगविपर्यासं प्राप्यान्योन्यं विपद्यते
X.3.7

Every individual is different, and differs accordingly in his or her thinking. But when circumstances change, the same individual stands the original reasoning on its head.

Individuals often pursue a course of action with the best intentions, but can end up committing acts of great violence. Effectively, Ashwatthama was considering this admittedly terrible and unlawful action because of altered circumstances. Further, though he was a Brahmin by birth, he had been brought up in the practices of the Kshatriya; he could not now abandon his Kshatriya duty to fight and avenge the deaths of his friends and allies by turning to the spiritualism of the Brahmin. He was resolved to destroying the sleeping Pandavas, and only this vengeance would allow him peace of mind.

As a final attempt, Kripacharya appealed to strategy and morality. First, he assured Ashwatthama that were he to postpone his cause to the following day, both Kripacharya and Kritavarma would fight by his side and ensure the devastation of the Pandavas. Ashwatthama's devotion to his cause, accompanied by their combined skills as warriors accomplished in the use of divine weaponry, would ensure their victory. And second, Ashwatthama had a clean record, having resisted recourse to any deceit or treachery in the war. The act of killing a sleeping foe was a condemnable one; were Ashwatthama to purse it, it would blot his clean record as blood that stains a white sheet.

Ashwatthama remained unmoved: he would neither change his intended course of action nor delay it. He provided Kripacharya with a list of the

Pandava transgressions, and asked why he should not censure them for their evil acts. Ashwatthama would prefer to accept the penalties for his own act of revenge, including the possibility of being reincarnated as a worm. Paramount in his preferences was that he fulfil his duty and avenge the deaths of his father and his friends, who had been mercilessly persecuted by the nefarious and deceitful methods employed by the Pandavas. And having thus attempted to justify his action, Ashwatthama mounted his carriage to advance stealthily towards the Pandava camp in the middle of the night.

The story is important for several reasons. First, it gives us an indication of the importance that the characters of the Mahabharata attach to justification of their actions, not just to external audiences but also to themselves. Second, while both Kripacharya and Ashwatthama make some strategic arguments, the central and ultimate argument always revolves around the question of what constitutes one's rightful duty, and, by extension, morality.

3.3.4. Insights for negotiation

The previous stories illustrate that even under extreme conditions, which include war, framing continues to be prolix and takes the shape of heavy moralizing. Three themes stand out.

First, recall the dire conditions that face some of our protagonists, with Karna being the prime example. In accordance with the curses and prophecies afflicting him, it is obvious to Karna that his time has come. Nonetheless, he thinks it is worth his while to reason with his arch-rival and enemy. Importantly, Karna's arguments never descend into a straightforward entreaty that his life be spared. Rather, they are framed wholly in terms of the legality and morality of certain actions in war. Similarly, in Arjuna's discourse with Krishna, recall that Arjuna's doubts emerge at the eleventh hour, when the two armies stand facing each other in the battleground. Moral questioning and doubt, however, trump the urgency of the battleground. Krishna responds to them with patient and detailed moralization. He does not resort to alternative and pithier lines of reasoning, which could legitimately include Krishna's supreme position as the divine lord whose advice and precepts Arjuna is duty-bound to obey (it is only at the end of his discourse, in fact, that Krishna reveals his divine form to Arjuna). Nor does he resort to a military or nationalistic style of argument, that is, it is Arjuna's duty to fight for king and country. He does not even use the highly emotive—and legitimate— arguments of the wrongdoings of the Kauravas in this case. Arjuna's qualms about the morality of war will only be quelled through a moral discourse on the same terms, and we thus get the eloquence of the Bhagwad Gita.

Second, we find that moralization is not a one-way street. Moralistic—and often prolix—framing is not only the domain of wise elders advising the young, but works the other way round too. Nor is it used only as a stick to brandish at enemies; friends also are donors and recipients of moralistic advice. An example of the former is Ashwatthama's legitimization of his proposed course of action to Kripacharya and Kritavarma, who are his teachers and elders. An example of the latter is the discourse of Krishna to his closest and dearest friend, Arjuna, or indeed Draupadi's discourse with her husband, Yudhishthira. This observation is significant. In most cultures, a position of moralization is usually associated with a patronizing attitude, perhaps even an assumed superiority, on the part of the negotiator choosing the moral high ground. Additionally, an element of confrontation is associated with such positioning: after all, one would only use such arguments if one wanted to establish oneself as the moral superior, which is hardly a position that one normally adopts when negotiating with friends. The Mahabharata shows us that neither assumption is necessarily valid in the Indian case.

Third, akin to the pre-war stories, we do not find that moral framing necessarily leads to success. Only in the story of Krishna's advice to Arjuna on the morality of his intended actions do we find Arjuna persuaded, and thereby agreeing to a change in his behaviour. In Karna's case, moralistic framing is met with counterframing on similar grounds by Krishna. He is unable to win his argument, and is killed. Ashwatthama is unable to convert Kripacharya or Kritavarma to his proposed plan; they accompany him stealthily into the night, but they do not battle by his side against the Pandavas. In fact, Ashwatthama's elaborate pre-emptive moral justifications of his actions satisfy no one except himself, and Krishna's curse ensures that he will be haunted by his unlawful and immoral actions for the next 3,000 years (as discussed in Chapter 2).

3.4. POST-WAR AND RELATED STORIES

3.4.1. Bhishma's discourse from his deathbed

The Pandavas were victorious, but their bloodstained victory filled Yudhishthira with despair. Dejected, he wished only to take refuge in the forest as a hermit and seek redemption. All the Pandava kinsmen then pressed upon Yudhishthira his duties as a king; they reminded him that the exorbitant loss of life would be rendered futile if he now chose the path of abdication and hermitage. Yudhishthira was finally brought round to assuming the responsibilities of kingship, and was duly crowned. Not long afterwards, Krishna, in sombre mood, advised Yudhishthira to seek counsel from the grandsire Bhishma before his death. Recall, from Chapter 2, that Bhishma had been granted a boon that he would be able to choose the time of his death. He had been fatally wounded on the tenth day of the war, and had lain since then on a bed of arrows to depart from life at a time of his choosing. Krishna anticipated that Bhishma would renounce his life immediately after the winter solstice (known to be an auspicious time for ascent to heaven), and recommended that Yudhishthira draw on the teachings of the grandsire on the conduct of kingship.

Krishna and Yudhishthira hastened back to the battlefield where Bhishma lay. What followed was a long and detailed discourse on the duty and discipline of kingship. In fact, however, it went significantly beyond the precepts of statecraft and kingship. Bhishma, even while lying on his deathbed, gave Yudhishthira an exhaustive philosophical exposition on Dharma, morality, duty, the caste system, crime, punishment, sacrifice, redemption, and the attainment of heaven. In doing so, he drew on numerous and detailed examples from the ancient texts. He offered practical advice too—for instance, on day-to-day administration, the constitution of the army, law enforcement—but the discourse laid great emphasis on the morality that underpins good kingship, and the pathways that the king must follow to attain heaven. Bhishma's advice, moreover, was not just a collection of random thoughts, but a carefully selected treasurehouse of wisdom taken systematically from many scholarly and religious texts as well as from Bhishma's own experiences:

नैतच्छुध्दागमादेव तव धर्मानुशासनम्
प्रज्ञासमवतारोसयं कविभिः संभृतं मधु
XII.140.3

Child, this discourse on Dharma is not one that I have gathered for you simply by listening to the Shastras. Just as the honey bee gathers the nectar from different kinds of flowers in distant places, so also is this discourse a collection of the wisest thoughts gathered by the most astute scholars from different sources.

Bhishma revealed to Yudhishthira the secrets of Dharma. Peace, stability, and the happiness of subjects were important goals, and war could be a vital instrument towards the achievement of these goals under certain conditions. But ultimately, all the duties that the king performed, including different types of charity, law enforcement, and war, were directed towards the accumulation of good Karma and the attainment of the goal of salvation.

एतावन्मात्रमेतध्दि भूतानाम् प्राज्ञलक्षणम्
कालयुक्तोसप्युभयविच्छेषमर्थम् समाचरेत्
XIII.150.4

The mark of intelligence of any being is that he has faith in the fruits of Karma, and puts this faith into practice.

He who understands his duty, and also those actions that are to be avoided, must even in difficult times and even when one's life is afflicted with ill luck and misfortune act according to Dharma.

Bhishma's discourse, focusing on Samkhya and Yoga as pathways to salvation, is a deeply philosophical one. Rather than restrict himself to easy and practical answers relating to public administration and law enforcement, Bhishma, even while lying on his deathbed of arrows, manages to find the energy and motivation to tackle some of the most fundamental and universal questions of existence. And, interestingly, this elaborate lecture on morality turns out to be just the 'buck-u-uppo' tonic that the dejected Yudhishthira needs to embrace his duties of kingship.

3.4.2. Arjuna and Babruvahana

After the Pandavas accepted their destiny as rulers of Hastinapur, tradition required them to perform the Ashwamedha Yagya. This was the horse sacrifice ceremony, which involved releasing a royal horse to wander through the lands adjacent to the kingdom, followed by an army. These lands would become the dominion of the king performing the ceremony, unless the ruler of the state (whose sovereignty was being thus threatened) challenged the king to a battle. Arjuna led the Ashwamedha Yagya on behalf of Yudhishthira, and conquered many kingdoms; until he arrived in the northeast state of India, Manipur.

The state was ruled by Babruvahana, the son of Arjuna and Chitrangada. Delighted at the prospect of meeting his father and his troops, Babruvahana stood at the gateway to offer a respectful welcome to Arjuna. Brahmins stood by his side, and he brought with him offerings of many treasures. Arjuna, however, was enraged by Babruvahana's attempted hospitality, and berated him severely and repeatedly. Such conduct was unbecoming of a warrior, Arjuna said; the duty of the Kshatriya was to fight and protect his kingdom from the protector of the sacrificial horse.

धिक्त्वामस्तु सुदुर्बुध्दिदम् क्षत्रधर्मविशारदम्
यो मां युध्दाय संप्राप्तं साम्नैवाथो त्वमग्रही:
XIV.78.5

Shame on your addled and misguided brain! You have clearly abandoned your Kshatriya Dharma by greeting me thus—an invader into your kingdom—with such respect and attempts at appeasement.

Babruvahana was hurt and dejected on being thus reprimanded. At this point, the serpent princess Ulupi (Babruvahana's stepmother) arose from the depths of the earth. She urged him to do battle with his father because this was indeed his father's wish. Babruvahana obeyed, and in his enthusiasm to please and impress his father, fired his arrow and struck him lifeless to the ground. Ultimately, Arjuna's life was restored with the power of a magical jewel that Ulupi was able to conjure up.

तस्मिन्न्यस्ते मणौ वीर जिष्णुरुज्जीवितुः प्रभुः
सुप्तोत्थित इवोत्तस्थौ मृष्टलोहितलोचनः
XIV.81.12

When the Sanjeevani jewel was placed on Arjuna's chest, the powerful and brave Arjuna was brought back to life, almost as if he were awoken from a deep sleep, rubbing the redness from his eyes.

Ulupi revealed that the reason why Arjuna was subject to death was because he had committed a grievous and sinful crime by destroying Bhishma through unfair means. As a consequence, the Vasus had cursed Arjuna to descend to hell for his treachery. Ulupi's father, however, had been able to secure a mitigation of the curse: were Arjuna to fall in battle at the hands of his son, he would be saved from hell.

This story is interesting from our perspective, first and foremost because of Arjuna's negotiation position towards his son. Long years of separation do not prompt a demonstration of fatherly love from Arjuna; Kshatriya morality trumps paternal affection. Further, Arjuna refuses to accept an easy takeover of the kingdom through his son's acquiescence; the recently reunited father and son must take the costly route of battle rather than a costless route of peace because this is what the warrior code dictates. Arjuna frames his response to Babruvahana's welcome accordingly. Finally, as the plot is unveiled, it becomes obvious that Arjuna's killing has also served a moral purpose; Arjuna's death is a form of retribution for a major transgression that he committed in battle. In other words, not only is the attempted negotiation between Arjuna and Babruvahana framed in moralistic terms, but the sequence of events serves a moral purpose.

3.4.3. Yayati and the reattainment of heaven

Yayati, the ancestor of our main protagonists, was residing in the heavens, but was banished by Indra for his hubris (on being asked, by Indra, who equalled Yayati in his asceticism, he had replied that he was unequalled). As he fell to the earth, he requested Indra to let him fall only amongst virtuous men. Indra granted him this wish. In his fall, Yayati encountered four sages—Ashtaka, Pratardana, Vasumana, and Shivi—all of whom were impressed by his resplendent and celestial beauty, and questioned him on many issues relating to Dharma. Yayati offered detailed answers on a range of issues. But from our perspective, of great significance were the offers that all four sages made to him, all of which he refused. These offers, albeit framed somewhat differently, all pertained to the reacquisition of heaven for Yayati.

The first offer was from Ashtaka. Persuaded by Yayati's glorious appearance and enlightened answers, he offered him his own portions of heaven (which he had acquired through religious merit), and thereby curtail Yayati's fall and return him to heaven. This was a unilateral offer made freely by Ashtaka, rather than a bargain of any kind. Nonetheless, Yayati refused on moral grounds. He argued that it was only a Brahmin who could accept a gift. As a Kshatriya, Yayati had bestowed many such gifts on Brahmins. He would be straying from the pathway of virtue, which he had so aspired to, were he to accept charity now.

नास्मद्विधोसब्राह्मणो ब्रह्मविज्ञ्च प्रतिग्रहे वर्तते राजमुख्य
यथा प्रदेयं सततं व्दिजेभ्यस्तथाददमं पूर्वमहं नरेन्द
I.87.11

Following the code of charity and giving, I have always given generously to the Brahmins. A true Brahmin alone is entitled to accept charity, never a Kshatriya like me.

Pratardana then made him a similar, unilateral offer. Again, Yayati refused on broadly the same grounds.

Vasumana now tried to reframe the offer, and suggested not a gift (which could be interpreted as charity) but a token exchange or trade: Vasumana would willingly give up his share of heaven acquired through his own merit to Yayati in return for a piece of straw. Yayati again turned down this offer, by arguing that he had never engaged in unfair trade.

न मिथ्याहं विक्रयं वै स्मरामि वृथा गृहीतं शिशुकाच्छंकमानः
कुर्यां न चैवाकृतपूर्वमन्यैर्विवित्समानः किमु तत्र साधु
I.88.4

I do not remember any occasion when I might have engaged in unfair dealings, nor do I recall my gratuitously having acquired any object through deceit. Always wary of the circle of time and Karma, I wish to do only good deeds; I cannot take actions which other great men have also been reluctant to commit.

Finally, Shivi turned to Yayati, and suggested that he accept Shivi's share of heaven as something borrowed, especially as Shivi was certain that he would never reclaim this loan because he had no wish to reside in heaven. Yayati refused again, this time arguing that he had never taken, nor would take, something that belonged to another. He would not enjoy the fruits of heaven if they rested on the virtues of another.

Effectively, Yayati had turned down generous unilateral offers from the sages—offers that had been differently framed as charity/gift, trade, and security—and remained firmly committed to his moral principles. This moral commitment generated positive results: Yayati and the four sages saw five chariots of blazing gold, which would carry each one of them to heaven. The four sages had acquired heaven by their willingness to sacrifice it, and Yayati had regained heaven by his refusal to accept the easy route, that is, the shares of his fellow men.

3.4.4. Insights for negotiation

The three episodes in this section reveal four bargaining-relevant insights. First, and in keeping with some of the episodes discussed in the previous sections, we find that even urgent and extreme conditions—in Bhishma's case, even as he lies on his deathbed—produce prolix and moralistic discourses. This suggests that the engagement with moral issues—and legitimization and moralization—is more than indulgence or mere lip service; the commitment to moral questions is real, and persists even when facing situations of war and death.

Second, that the commitment to moral frames is great and genuine is revealed particularly with the story of Yayati. Yayati is offered a seemingly costless bargain, where the other sages present very attractive proposals of unilateral concessions. The prize of accepting these offers is a big one—the reattainment of heaven. Nonetheless, Yayati refuses these offers, even though the high cost of this refusal is his fall from heaven. Arjuna similarly puts his own life in jeopardy, which from an external perspective can only be seen as taking on an unnecessary risk, when he provokes his long-separated son to battle. Moralistic framing in the Mahabharata may sometimes have a strategic end depending on the addressee of the offer, but it is certainly not 'cheap talk'.

Third, all three stories in this section reveal the importance that the characters attach to the concepts of Dharma—particularly doing one's duty—when framing their negotiating positions. Bhishma's long discourse to Yudhishthira revolves fundamentally around the question of the duties of kingship, which he conceptualizes in great philosophical detail. Arjuna berates his son Babruvahana for his welcome because he equates it with cowardice: he only wishes his son to do his duty and protect his kingdom from an invader (even when the invader is his own father). Yayati bases his refusal to accept the gains of heaven that the other sages offer him in charity, trade, and as a loan, all on the grounds that the duty of the Kshatriya disallows him from accepting charity, engaging in unfair trade, or accepting what belongs to another. In all the stories, there is an emphasis on adherence to one's duty, even if one incurs costs in doing so.

Finally, where does duty derive from, before it gets translated into the moralistic frame? In all three cases, it seems to have its roots in one's position in the social hierarchy. Hence, for example, Bhishma clearly elucidates to Yudhishthira how the just king must treat the four Varnas or castes, and also how the king's own position as Kshatriya will require him sometimes to take up the path of violence and war. Arjuna's fury with Babruvahana emanates from his conceptualization of the warrior code, which his son seems to be denying in favour of his filial duty. In fact, by doing his duty and through the act of parricide, Babruvahana not only proves himself to his father but also wins Arjuna redemption for his sins. Yayati rejects heaven, which wise sages have offered him willingly, because he believes that he will be violating his duty deriving from his position as a Kshatriya. This is a potentially important insight: the characters of the Mahabharata frame their offers and demands in terms of moral duty, and the notion of this moral duty seems to derive centrally from one's position in the system of social stratification.

3.5. EXCEPTIONS TO THE RULE

3.5.1. Exceptions in the previous episodes: evidence of pragmatic framing in Sections 3.2–3.4

Prolix and moralistic framing dominates all the episodes discussed earlier in this chapter. However, we do have a few instances, within two episodes, where strategic and pragmatic arguments are presented in addition to the moral ones.

Sanjaya, when attempting to persuade Dhritarashtra to avoid the pathway of war, uses primarily the moral argument by pointing to the blameless conduct of the Pandavas (and contrasting it with the sins and transgressions of the Kauravas), but he also raises a pragmatic point. He reminds Dhritarashtra that not only do the Pandavas have right on their side, but their courage as warriors and the support that they enjoy from Lord Krishna together make them invincible. It would of course be immoral to pursue a war against them, but it would also be foolish.

Kripacharya also resorts to a more pragmatic framing of argument when he finds Ashwatthama unresponsive to the moral case against attacking the Pandava camp in the stealth of the night. Kripacharya first reminds Ashwatthama of Duryodhana's many reprehensible actions. These are the root cause of his sorry fate, rather than the treachery of the Pandavas, and Ashwatthama's case for vengeance is a weak one. The right thing to do is to go back to the Kaurava elders and seek their instruction. But Ashwatthama remains undeterred. Then Kripacharya urges Ashwatthama to wait until the morning, offering him the promise of two major advantages were he to do so. First, a night of rest would see him energized, and ready to exploit his overwhelming prowess to the fullest. Victory would be a near certainty, were the mighty Ashwatthama to fight with his energies renewed. Second, both Kripacharya and Kritavarma would be able and willing to fight by his side the next day. They would vanquish the Pandavas in battle, or die in the attempt. But this battle could only be fought in daylight (neither Kripacharya nor Kritavarma, as Ashwatthama knew only too well, would or could break the laws of war and attack the sleeping enemy). It is thus in Ashwatthama's moral interest (and salvation) to wait until daylight, and also in his strategic interest (and victory in battle), argues Kripacharya.

In both instances, we find that the pragmatic argument accompanies the moral one, rather than standing alone in its right. In both cases, the negotiators making use of the pragmatic argument know that they are making an especially difficult case and dealing with difficult opponents. Neither Dhritarashtra nor Ashwatthama are presented in a particularly heroic or noble light in the earlier parts of the epic (in contrast to some of the other Kaurava 'villains', such as Karna or even Duryodhana). They are thus unlikely to be swayed by moral argument alone, and may be more easily persuaded through an appeal to baser instincts of self-preservation and self-interest.

In neither instance does this framing strategy produce the intended results. Dhritarashtra had always maintained a deep ambivalence to the war; Sanjaya's harsh words struck deep but he was still unable to persuade Duryodhana to exercise restraint. Thus Sanjaya's strategy of combining moral and strategic framing failed to curtail war. In Ashwatthama's case, the use of the strategic argument proved to be even more limited. Ashwatthama countered Kripacharya's strategic argument with moral counterargument, pointing particularly to the cruel and deceitful way in which his father had been killed by the Pandavas. Ashwatthama then proceeded to attack the Pandavas, exactly as he had first proposed to Kripacharya and Kritavarma, with little evidence of the long moral and pragmatic discourse having had much impact on his actions.

3.5.2. Duryodhana insists on war

Before the outbreak of war, many counselled Duryodhana to exercise restraint. Even his ever-indulgent and devoted father, the blind king Dhritarashtra, urged him to renounce the pathway on which he was headed. Dhritarashtra offered him both moral and strategic argument to avoid the course of war. Morally, he pointed out, war was never the preferred course of action; besides, surely Duryodhana could be satiated with half the earth and would thus allow the other half to the noble and virtuous Pandavas. Strategically, he reminded Duryodhana that none of the illustrious warriors of the Kaurava army, on whom he would rely for victory, endorsed the war. Perhaps Duryodhana himself did not desire war? He was simply being misled and goaded into it by Karna and the malicious Dushasana.

Contrary to the practice of most characters of the Mahabharata to match moral argument with moral counterargument (and, indeed, sometimes even strategic argument with moral counterargument), Duryodhana offered no moralization. In fact, he made little effort to justify his position. He offered one counterclaim against the strategic argument that his father had made, and simply asserted that Duryodhana alone, aided only by Karna and Dushasana, would fight the war and emerge victorious; their troika did not need to depend on the ambivalent greats of the Kaurava side at all. Duryodhana would, in any case, prefer to sacrifice all that he had, including his life, rather than endure a life spent living alongside the Pandavas. Just how great his commitment was to waging this war was enunciated in the following shloka:

यावधि सूच्यास्तीक्ष्णाया विध्येदग्रेण मारिष
तावदप्यपरित्याज्यं भूमेर्नः पाण्डवान्प्रति
V.57.18

Not even the portion of land that can be pierced by the point of a needle will I surrender to the Pandavas.

Duryodhana repeated the same logic when Krishna attempted to mediate between the two sides. The pathway to war was now set.

3.5.3. Insights for negotiation

Exceptions to the dominant strategy of prolix and moralistic framing are few. In general, even when dealing with particularly difficult opponents, negotiators seek recourse in pragmatic framing only as an added frill to the moralistic frame. The logic could be that most opponents will primarily be concerned with Dharma, and the moral argument will therefore suffice. In dealing with most opponents—even if they are one's enemies—the appeal to base self-interest is not seen to be necessary.

Pragmatic framing of arguments need not necessarily produce pragmatic counterarguments. Only in Duryodhana's case do we get a reaction that is couched in pragmatic terms; and even here the resort to pragmatism is minimal: it is limited to Duryodhana's counter-assertion that he expects to be able to destroy the Pandavas assisted only by Karna and Dushasana. Having made this assertion, Duryodhana then simply and briefly reiterates his preference for death rather than coexistence with the Pandavas. In Ashwatthama's case, we see him respond to Kripacharya's strategic argument by reiterating the moral case against the Pandavas. Dhritarashtra accepts Sanjaya's advice (even though he is ultimately unable to deter Duryodhana from launching the war).

In the few instances that pragmatic framing is resorted to, the results are mixed. We discussed two cases in Section 3.5.1 and focused on the case of Dhritarashtra's attempted negotiation with Duryodhana in Section 3.5.2. We have partial success of pragmatic framing in the case of Sanjaya's discourse with Dhritarashtra: Sanjaya's mix of moral and pragmatic arguments further increases the blind king's reluctance to endorse the war. But he is still unable to stand up to his headstrong son and get him to change his mind; therefore war ensues, hence Sanjaya's strategy can be deemed to be only partially successful. Kripacharya's strategic framing to highlight the ineffectiveness of a night-time attack, comparing it with a much higher probability of victory in a daytime attack that adheres to the rules of war, fails to sway Ashwatthama's resolve. Dhritarashtra's attempt to awaken Duryodhana to both the moral and strategic folly that underpins his hawkishness fails to deter him from the course of war that he has already chosen.

The exceptions to moralistic framing are thus few, and even fewer of these exceptions result in successful outcomes.

3.6. FRAMING STRATEGIES OF A RISING INDIA

The episodes discussed in the previous pages offer us five important lessons, which bear relevance to the negotiations of a rising India. We recap these lessons here, and then, akin to Chapter 2, present an analysis of the extent to which these insights help us in understanding India's bargaining in the two regimes of international trade and nuclear non-proliferation. We investigate the pattern of India's framing behaviour as its power rises, and also analyse the different audiences towards which such framing is targeted.

1. Framing bargaining demands in moralistic terms stands out as the dominant framing strategy in the Mahabharata, where we find the negotiators also revealing a tendency towards a prolix form of framing. This prolixity takes not only the shape of very detailed and long arguments, but also substantiation of these arguments with an appeal to historical example and mythology.

2. Moralistic framing reveals a near universalism. Heroes and villains alike resort to moralism, and they do so when dealing with enemies and friends, and elders and juniors.

3. Only in a small set of exceptions do we see a resort to strategic arguments, which usually accompany the morally framed ones rather than standing alone in their own right. These seem to take place in a particularly difficult negotiation context, when the other party is regarded as not only taking a view that is the polar opposite to one's own, but is also stubborn, difficult, somewhat unscrupulous, and suspect. In other words, when dealing with 'normal' people— even one's own enemies—the assumption seems to be that the moral argument will suffice. The implications of this insight are interesting, particularly in relation to the claims of some authors that a rising India displays greater strategic pragmatism than the older India that proclaimed its adherence to Third Worldist values. If the practice of

the Mahabharata holds true to the present day, the use of strategic arguments may be less a function of India's growing power or socialization and more symptomatic of how Indian negotiators view their opponents. The more adversarial the relationship, and the greater the expectation that they will have to play hardball, the more we will find Indian negotiators using strategic arguments to accompany moral ones.

4. The moralistic and prolix framing strategy yields, at best, a mixed rate of success. Interestingly, however, this mixed rate of success does not dissuade the protagonists from resorting to the moral frame. It is almost as if the use of the moral frame is as much for the self (and perhaps other domestic audiences/people already on one's side) as it is for the opponent. Pragmatic framing is attempted only in three instances, with partial success in one case and failure in the other two (for a distribution of the successful, partially successful, and failed outcomes, see Table 3.1 at the end of this chapter).

3.6.1. India's framing strategies in international trade

The extent to which India resorts almost consistently to moralistic, and sometimes prolix, frames is evident in its trade negotiations. Even in the early years of its independence, India's appeal to moral principle (e.g. 'Equality of treatment is equitable only among equals') was high in the GATT. Its commitment to the moral high ground persisted in the later years of the GATT too. For example, the Indian Ambassador to the WTO, S. P. Shukla, offered several stringent critiques of the GATT, framing them not directly in terms of the *interests* of India or its allies, but in terms of the *principle* of development, which affected a large group of developing countries, and to which the GATT was paying inadequate attention: 'The participation of developing countries in GATT is necessarily centred on the contribution that such participation makes to their development process...Unfortunately, attention to the role and contribution of GATT towards the development of developing countries, as reflected in the ongoing work in the Uruguay Round process, is not commensurate with the unprecedented interest and participation of developing countries in this Round.'[18] The ambassador's speeches also placed considerable emphasis on the principle of Special and Differential Treatment. Shukla's critique provides us with a nice illustration of India's willingness to engage with several different and detailed lines of argumentation over principle, without necessarily engaging in the nitty-

---

[18] GATT 1988.

gritty of trade-offs that make up the give and take of bargaining. But India, in the days of the GATT, was not the rising power that it has become in the WTO. Could it be argued that framing demands in terms of moral principle represents a weapon of the weak? As India's power rises, we could perhaps expect it to embrace a more pragmatic framing of demands akin to the West. There is, however, little evidence of such a change in its framing tactics, as highlighted below.

At the WTO's Ministerial Conference at Doha in November 2001, India's Minister for Commerce and Industry, Murasoli Maran, was scathing in his critique of the draft ministerial declaration. Note that a significant portion of this critique was couched in general terms, appealing not to the straightforward national interest of his own country, but to the general principle of development and the concerns of developing countries:

> I am constrained to point out that the draft Ministerial Declaration is neither fair nor just to the view points of many developing countries including my own on certain key issues. It is negation of all that was said by a significant number of developing countries and least-developing countries . . . The only conclusion that could be drawn is that the developing countries have little say in the agenda setting of the WTO. It appears that the whole process was a mere formality and we are being coerced against our will. Is it not then meaningless for the draft declaration to claim that the needs and interests of the developing countries have been placed at the heart of the Work Programme? . . . WTO has to recognize the existing development deficit in various WTO agreements and take necessary remedial action. WTO has also to recognize that development strategy has to be related to country specific situations. The 'one size fits all approach' has clearly failed to deliver.[19]

The results of this framing strategy generated mixed results. India was left isolated at the end of the Ministerial Conference, having achieved few gains.[20] Guy de Jonguières went so far as to remark in the *Financial Times*, 'The only real loser was India. It achieved no obvious gains except for the dubious pleasure of delaying the close of the meeting.'[21] This did not, however, deter Indian negotiators from adopting similar strategies in future trade negotiations.

India's moralistic fervour continued in subsequent ministerial conferences. At the Cancun Ministerial Conference, Minister Arun Jaitley highlighted problems with processes of WTO decision-making, again taking up the collective cause of developing countries: 'Over the years we have seen gradual increase in lack of internal transparency as well as reduced participation of

---

[19] WTO 2001.   [20] Narlikar and Odell 2006.

[21] In fact, insofar as trade liberalization is a positive-sum game, India also stood to gain from the launch of the new round that it had so avidly resisted. But from a bargaining perspective, India did not emerge as a winner in the ministerial negotiations. Arvind Panagariya 2001 thus rightly points to the many gains that the conference produced for India, but also recognizes: 'the initial position of India was so extreme as to effectively rob it of any room to claim an unqualified victory at the end of the day. Given the fact that Maran had publicly opposed the launch of the round altogether, his critics can now point to the newly agreed round as evidence of his defeat.'

developing countries in the decision-making process in the WTO. We should not let the developing countries perceive the decision-making process of the multilateral trading system to be discriminatory, opaque and unresponsive to their needs.' And while his tone may have been somewhat less combative than his predecessor's, his commitment to articulating the cause of development and the concerns of developing countries remained high. He thus argued:

> We are engulfed in a sense of deep disappointment that the development dimension envisaged under the Doha Work Programme has been given short shrift. In our view the draft Cancu*i*n Ministerial Text is grossly inadequate on implementation issues and would severely affect the interests of developing countries in agriculture, industrial tariffs and Singapore issues. We cannot escape the conclusion that it does not accommodate the legitimate aspirations of developing countries and instead, seeks to project and advance the views of certain developed countries.[22]

Kamal Nath continued to keep up the tradition of moralistic eloquence in subsequent negotiations. In July 2008, his opening speech resorted to some important moral arguments. But perhaps indicative of the considerable and increasing polarization in the Doha negotiations, he did not rely solely on an appeal to the social conscience of the North. Rather, he discussed several technical details, and also signalled India's bottom lines by pointing to the pragmatic imperatives facing the country. For example, he argued the following on agriculture, combining both moral and pragmatic reasoning:

> As far as developing country agriculture is concerned, the challenges are well known. Most of Indian agriculture is subsistence level agriculture. For us, agriculture involves the livelihoods of the poorest farmers who number in the hundreds of millions. We cannot have a development Round without an outcome which provides full comfort to livelihood and food security concerns in developing countries. There has been some progress in discussions on SPs and SSM but important gaps still remain. The poor of the world will not forgive us if we compromise on these concerns. These concerns are too vital to be the subject of trade-offs.[23]

In other forums too, India has reinforced its vision through a moralizing frame. For example, at a meeting of the UN General Assembly in 2008, the Indian delegate invoked principles of fairness for managing globalization:

> Unfavourable international regimes, in which developing countries have a marginal say, have also prevented developing countries from taking full advantage of globalization in other areas. Agricultural production in developing countries has been severely undermined by massive subsidies in developed countries. Developing countries continue to face non-trade barriers in accessing markets of

---

[22] WTO 2003.   [23] WTO 2008.

developed countries, while a steady reduction in their industrial tariffs has greatly enhanced the risks of de-industrialization of developing countries. Further, in the area of technology access, critical technologies in the area of public health and climate change remain inaccessible and unaffordable for developing countries due to the existing Intellectual Property Rights regime . . . If globalization is to succeed, it must be fair, and benefit the whole of humanity. Developmental considerations must be at its core . . . The practical way to achieve this is through a comprehensive restructuring of the international decision making and norm-setting structures in a time bound manner, with greater voice and participation of developing countries. This process must be overseen by the United Nations, which has a unique legitimacy and universality.

Interestingly, the moralism that underlies the framing of India's negotiating position is not reserved for the domain of North–South relations or in adversarial relations. Illustrative of the universalism inherent in its moralistic framing is Pranab Mukherjee's address to the India–Africa conclave:

India has always had a vision and a message for the world. From the very beginning of our civilization, we have believed that humanity is a single family. We are committed to establishing ties of friendship and co-operation with all countries. Our ties with Africa are special and we will continue to work with Africa and the international community to create a better world—a world free of terror, poverty, disease, ignorance and inequality.[24]

Effectively, Indian negotiators have relied considerably on attempting to frame their negotiating positions via an appeal to norms that shows continuity over time and consistency across different types of negotiating partners (strong and weak, adversaries and friends).[25] In some of the particularly tough negotiations in recent years, such as the Doha negotiations, we do see a greater measure of pragmatic framing, but never as a substitute for moralistic framing. In other instances, when negotiations are conducted with allies and friends, the dominant framing device continues to be the moralistic one.

3.6.2. Framing the nuclear non-proliferation negotiations

In the negotiations over the nuclear non-proliferation regime, independent India's stance was traditionally moralistic. Nehru was renowned for his impassioned views and utterances on disarmament, which he took seriously in word and deed (and hence even went so far as to decline the possible opportunity for India to become a nuclear weapons state following China's Lop Nor test). Raymond Cohen gives the example of 'India's dash for the moral high ground' in the early 1980s and its skill in 'cannily turning the

---

[24] Mukherjee 2008, p. 1954.   [25] Natchippan 2008, p. 2657.

ethical-legal argument upside down': when the US insisted that India accept new restrictions on its nuclear fuel imports, India accused the US of being in violation of its own legal obligations. And similarly, when the NPT came up for renewal in 1995, India's refusal to sign it was again couched in moral terms, referring to the treaty as one that discriminated between 'nuclear haves and have-nots...India will not sign the NPT in its current form but will continue to work for achieving genuine non-proliferation through the elimination of all nuclear weapons.'[26]

Even at the time of India's nuclear tests of 1998, India's rationalization was only partially strategic (framed in terms of the nuclear environment of its neighbourhood). The moral high ground was never abandoned in offering explanations and justifications, and included references to India's historical and often pioneering role in launching disarmament initiatives and its record as a responsible player in the regime (despite having refused to sign major treaties such as the NPT and the CTBT—the Comprehensive Test Ban Treaty). Illustrative of this was the following statement by Jaswant Singh:

> Since independence, India has been a staunch advocate of global nuclear disarmament. We have participated actively in all such efforts, convinced that a world without nuclear weapons will enhance both national and global security. India was the first to call for a ban on nuclear testing in 1954, for a non-discriminatory treaty on non-proliferation in 1965, for a treaty on non-use of nuclear weapons in 1978, for a nuclear freeze in 1982, and for a phased programme for complete elimination in 1988. Unfortunately, many of these initiatives were not accepted by the nuclear weapon states who still consider these weapons essential for their own security, and what emerged has been a discriminatory and flawed non-proliferation regime which affects our security adversely. For many years, we have conveyed our apprehensions to other countries but this did not lead to any improvement in our security environment. As a result, we were left with no choice but to develop the capability that had been demonstrated 24 years ago.[27]

At least some of the attention to the moral rhetoric continues to find resonance in the language of practitioners even in rising India: Shashi Tharoor, for example, argued in 2008 that 'India's refusal to sign the NPT was based on principle, for the NPT is the last vestige of apartheid in the international system, granting as it does to five permanent members of the United Nations Security Council the right to be nuclear weapons states while denying the same right to others.'[28] But could it not be argued that a fundamental switch—from moralism to pragmatism—is taking place in India's framing strategy, as evidenced most strongly by the Indo–US nuclear deal? At the very least, could this case be seen as an important exception to the dominant framing

---

[26] Cohen 1998, pp. 96–7.   [27] Singh 1998b.   [28] Tharoor 2008.

strategy? Such an interpretation, if correct, would reinforce the argument that was examined and challenged in Chapter 2, that is, that India's negotiated exception to the NPT is indicative of the use of integrative bargaining. In fact, the argument might be pushed even further to argue that the willingness to reframe issues pragmatically rather than moralistically has allowed India greater and more effective use of integrative strategies. A closer inspection of just how India attempted to rationalize its nuclear deal with the US reveals that the situation is less clear-cut than such an account would suggest.

An insightful illustration of how Indian negotiators themselves viewed their own bargaining position and sold it to their populace can be found in a detailed speech given by Shyam Saran, the PM's Special Envoy, in February 2008. The speech offers some important pragmatic arguments for improving relations with the US (discussed in the context of coalitions in Chapter 4), and also emphasizes that 'India was justified in exercising its nuclear weapons option at a time when nuclear disarmament seemed all but abandoned by the existing nuclear weapon states. Its security was also being threatened by clandestine proliferation in its own neighbourhood, without any remedial action being taken at the international level.' But Saran never loses sight of the moral dimension. Hence, for instance, he argues, 'we must not forget that despite being a nuclear weapon state, India remains convinced that its security would be enhanced, not diminished, if a world free of nuclear weapons were to be achieved... Therefore, even as we work to strengthen our credible minimum deterrent, we ought to take a fresh initiative to realize Rajiv Gandhi's vision of a non-violent world, free from the scourge of nuclear weapons.'[29]

The Lok Sabha debate, when the government was put on trial for what some saw as its overly friendly relations with the US in the shape of the civilian nuclear energy agreement, offers us further interesting examples.[30] As the government sought to get a confidence motion passed, its allies and members made a strong argument on pragmatic and strategic grounds. They highlighted India's energy needs, which the US–India deal would help fulfil, and further emphasized that the agreement neither jeopardized India's sovereignty nor curtailed its nuclear options. But they also expended some effort in making the moral case. For instance, the Minister for Shipping, Road Transportation and Highways (and leader of the DMK, which constituted the coalition government) offered one interesting legitimization of the deal by attributing deep historical roots to the prime minister's engagement with the US (since 2005):

This dialogue is not a new one. The genesis of this dialogue lies in the Nehruvian era. When Pandit Jawaharlal Nehru was the Prime Minister of India, he initiated

---

[29] Saran 2008, pp. 384–5.   [30] Lok Sabha Debate 2008.

this dialogue. That dialogue has been renewed now. That is all. The genesis lies there. It is not a new one.[31]

Representatives of the Congress also combined moral and strategic arguments. Rahul Gandhi illustrated this clearly when he made an explicit link between poverty reduction and energy supply with the help of an emotive story. This story referred to a woman living in Vidarbha, whose husband had committed suicide because of poverty and who had no resources to feed or educate her nine children. The story was told at considerable length, not only for emphasis but also to highlight the ethical and moral implications of an inadequate and unreliable energy supply (which the Indo–US cooperation on civilian energy supply would help correct).[32]

There is undoubtedly some evolution in the way that India frames its nuclear debate. The pragmatic slant to the argument is high—indeed perhaps higher than ever before, albeit still combined with moralist framing—when justifying the Indo–US nuclear agreement to domestic audiences. Going by the insights offered by the Mahabharata negotiations, the mixing of moral and pragmatic in this instance may be less a function of India's emergence as an increasingly 'socialized' power that has learnt the language of the West, and more a function of the fact that the government was dealing with a particularly difficult sell domestically. When faced with opponents who are especially stubborn and who adopt positions that are the polar opposite of one's own, the moral argument is unlikely to hold much sway by itself. Hence, when trying to persuade the opposition, and the sceptical public at large, of the merits of a nuclear deal, some recourse to a strategic cost–benefit analysis becomes necessary.

When we see Indian negotiators declaiming on non-proliferation to international audiences, the balance in the argument seems to swing back towards the moral (although still retaining a good component of the strategic, given the persistent difficulties of incorporating India within the NPT de jure). Indian negotiators thus frame the exceptions that India has secured for itself from the regime, not in straightforward power terms alone, but to reinforce the story of it being a responsible international player. The letter of the Indian Permanent Representative to the UN, Ambassador Hardeep Puri, is illustrative of this discourse, which combines an element of the strategic with a strong component of the moralistic:

> India has an unwavering commitment to global efforts for preventing the proliferation of weapons of mass destruction and their means of delivery. These efforts are in India's interest as the infirmities of the non-proliferation regime have had an adverse impact on our security... India's position on the Nuclear Non-Proliferation Treaty (NPT) is well-known. We cannot accept any obligations

[31] Baalu 2008, p. 475.   [32] Gandhi 2008.

arising from treaties that India has not signed or ratified. This position is consistent with the fundamental principles of international law and the Law of Treaties. India cannot accept calls for universalization of the NPT. As India's Prime Minister stated in Parliament on 29 July, 2009, there is no question of India joining the NPT as a non-nuclear weapon state. Nuclear weapons are an integral part of India's national security and will remain so, pending non-discriminatory and global nuclear disarmament . . . India is a nuclear weapon state and a responsible member of the world community, and would approach these negotiations as such . . . India has an impeccable non-proliferation record and is committed to working with the international community to advance our common non-proliferation and disarmament objectives so that we are able to fulfill the vision of a world free of nuclear weapons.[33]

The logic of, and importance attached to, moralistic framing also leads India to remain committed to movements such as the Non-Aligned Movement (NAM), in parallel with its nuclear agreement with the US and some of the other members of the Nuclear Suppliers Group. The prime minister, in 2009, for instance, pledged at the NAM summit that 'India will play its part in helping NAM to regain its *moral high ground* to address issues which are of direct concern and relevance to developing countries such as sustainable development, climate change, food security, energy security, terrorism and reform of the architecture of international governance.'[34]

3.7. CONCLUSION

As this chapter has illustrated, moralistic framing dominates the stories in the Mahabharata. Detailed, prolix, and often deeply philosophical arguments are offered when the characters negotiate, often with little scope for making trade-offs or cutting deals. This moralistic strategy yields a mixed rate of success, but is pursued nonetheless. Strategic framing is used infrequently. In the few instances that pragmatic frames are resorted to, they almost always accompany moralistic frames rather than stand alone; negotiators only turn to them when dealing with a particularly difficult opponent who is seen to adhere to a different system of ethics and morality.[35]

---

[33] Puri 2009.   [34] Singh 2009.

[35] Note that this can, but does not necessarily, imply that strategic framing is used when bargaining with an enemy. Recall that Kripacharya and Ashwatthama were both allies and friends when the former used strategic arguments to dissuade the latter from attacking the Pandavas in the stealth of night; similarly, Dhritarashtra used the strategic line of argumentation in an attempt to bring his dearest but errant son into line after all moral arguments had failed to persuade him that the course of war (which he was so intent on pursuing) was a futile and fatal one.

Independent India used moralistic framing with eloquence and abundance; Nehru epitomized this strategy, but, as this chapter has shown, he was far from alone in adopting such a course of action. In the case of India as a rising power, we see a continued use of a moralistic framing strategy. In some, and possibly even an increasing number of, instances in recent times, we find the occurrence of pragmatic arguments, but only in addition to (and not as a substitute for) the moralistic lines of reasoning and justification. We observe this trend in international trade: as the polarization in the Doha Developed Agenda negotiations has increased and India's own power in the trading system has risen, it has begun to combine some strategic argumentation with the more traditional moralistic framing of its demands. In the nuclear non-proliferation regime, we see Indian practitioners emphasizing the strategic gains from India's cooperation with the West, particularly in their attempt to sell the recent developments to a skeptical public and an incensed opposition.

What are the implications of these trends? First, it is unlikely that moralistic framing will disappear any time soon. We see prolix and moralistic framing pervading different issue areas. We also see the persistence of this type of framing in India's negotiations with more powerful players and weaker players alike.

Second, the use of strategic arguments, while on the rise, seems to occur more in cases where the opposition is staunch and levels of confrontation are high. This is not only in line with the lessons that the Mahabharata offers, but it suggests that a rising India may not be viewing the world with the rose-tinted glasses of a fully socialized or like-minded power. Indeed, if the analogy from the Mahabharata holds, then it is even possible that the increasing use of strategic argumentation suggests perceptions of higher levels of potential confrontation from the Indian side.

Third, it is worth bearing in mind that moralistic framing is likely to push any actor towards a more distributive strategy. Climbing down from a moral high horse is seldom easier than having to reverse a decision that was justified initially on strategic grounds. There may then be a potentially interesting and paradoxical trajectory of negotiating behaviour: the use of strategic framing may reflect perceptions of a higher level of confrontation than the moral one in the first instance, but were strategic framing to eventually dominate moralistic framing, we could see greater scope for more conciliatory behaviour in the long run. Further empirical study on this subject, perhaps as India's own position as a rising power evolves as does its negotiation behaviour, would provide an exciting research area for the future.

Table 3.1 Success of Moralistic versus Pragmatic Framing Strategies in the Mahabharata

	Episode	Moralistic framing	Pragmatic framing
1.	Yudhishthira and the Yaksha	Success (Yudhishthira is rewarded)	Not attempted
2.	Draupadi and Yudhishthira	Failure (Yudhishthira refuses to change his behaviour)	Not attempted
3.	Sanjaya and Dhritarashtra	Partial success (Dhritarashtra becomes even more uncomfortable with the prospect of war, but is unable to dissuade Duryodhana)	Failure (when Dhritarashtra makes the pragmatic argument to Duryodhana, the latter responds with a counterargument, and continues on the course of war)
4.	Krishna's discourse to Arjuna	Success (Arjuna agrees to fight the war)	Not attempted
5.	Karna's defeat	Failure (Krishna offers moral counterargument and Karna is killed)	Not attempted
6.	Kripacharya and Ashwatthama	Failure (Ashwatthama remains undeterred)	Failure (Ashwatthama remains undeterred)
7.	Bhishma's discourse to Yudhishthira	Success (Yudhishthira wholeheartedly embraces kingship)	Not attempted
8.	Arjuna and Babruvahana	Partial success (Babruvahana is dejected by his father's moral criticism, but only agrees to battle with him when urged by his stepmother Ulupi for the purpose of pleasing his father).	Not attempted
9.	Yayati and the sages	Success (Yayati is rewarded with the attainment of heaven, as are the four sages, for resisting temptation)	Not attempted
10.	The exception of Duryodhana (no moralistic framing)	Not attempted	Partial success (Duryodhana gets his way and the brave Kaurava warriors fight by his side; he has not attempted to persuade them of the justice of his cause, however, and most fight out of duty to Hastinapur rather than for Duryodhana's cause; arguably, this influences the final outcome of the Kaurava defeat)
		Success: 4	Success: 0
		Failure: 3	Failure: 2
		Partial success: 2	Partial success: 1
		Not attempted: 1	Not attempted: 7

REFERENCES

Baalu, T. R. 2008. Extract from the Speech of Minister of Shipping, Road Transport and Highways, and Leader of Dravida Munnetra Kazhagam (DMK), on the Motion of Confidence in the Council of Ministers. New Delhi. 21 July. In Avtar Singh Bhasin ed., *India's Foreign Relations Documents—2008*. New Delhi: Public Diplomacy Division, Ministry of External Affairs.

Bazerman, Max E. and Margaret A. Neale. 1992. *Negotiating Rationally*. New York: Free Press.

Bhasin, Avtar Singh Bhasin ed. 2009. *India's Foreign Relations Documents—2009*. New Delhi: Public Diplomacy Division, Ministry of External Affairs.

Cohen, Raymond. 1998. *Negotiating across Cultures: International Communication in an Interdependent World*. Washington DC: United States Institute of Peace Press (second revised edition).

Cohen, Stephen P. 2001. *India: Emerging Power*. Washington DC: Brookings Institution.

Dixit, J. N. 2003. *India's Foreign Policy, 1947-2003*. New Delhi: Picus Books.

Gandhi, Rahul. 2008. Excerpts relevant to Nuclear Energy Cooperation Agreement from the Speech of Congress Leader Rahul Gandhi while participating in the debate in the Lok Sabha on the Motion of Confidence in the Council of Ministers. New Delhi. 22 July. In Avtar Singh Bhasin ed., *India's Foreign Relations Documents—2008*. New Delhi: Public Diplomacy Division, Ministry of External Affairs.

GATT. 1954. Speech by Sir N. Raghavan Pillai (India). Delivered in Plenary Session on 9 November 1954. Press Release GATT/185.

GATT. 1988. Statement by HE Mr S. P. Shukla, Ambassador, Permanent Representative. SR.4/ST/17. 23 November. Accessed at <http://gatt.stanford.org> on 18 December 2012.

Kumar, Rajesh and Verner Worm. 2004. Institutional Dynamics and the Negotiation Process: Comparing India and China. *International Journal of Conflict Management*, 15:3, 304–34.

Lok Sabha Debate. 2008. On the Motion of Confidence in the Council of Ministers, 21–22 July. Extracts relevant to Civil Nuclear Energy Cooperation. In Avtar Singh Bhasin ed., *India's Foreign Relations Documents—2008*. New Delhi: Public Diplomacy Division, Ministry of External Affairs.

Mehta, Pratap Bhanu. 2009. Still under Nehru's Shadow? The Absence of Foreign Policy Frameworks in India. *India Review*, 8:3, July, 209–33.

Mukherjee, Pranab. 2008. Valedictory Address at the 4th Africa-India Partnership Conclave. New Delhi. 21 March. In Avatar Singh Bhasin ed., *India's Foreign Relations Documents—2008*. New Delhi: Public Diplomacy Division, Ministry of External Affairs.

Narlikar, Amrita and John Odell. 2006. The Strict Distributive Strategy for a Bargaining Coalition: the Like-Minded Group in the World Trade Organization. In John Odell ed., *Negotiating Trade: Developing Countries in the WTO and NAFTA*. Cambridge: Cambridge University Press.

Natchippan, Sudarsana. 2008. Statement by Member of Parliament and Member of the Indian Delegation, Dr E. P. Sudarsana Natchippan, on Agenda 51—Globalization and Interdependence at the Second Committee of the UNGA. New York. 29

October. In Avtar Singh Bhasin ed., *India's Foreign Relations Documents—2008*. New Delhi: Public Diplomacy Division, Ministry of External Affairs.

Nehru, Jawaharlal. 1948. Address to the UN General Assembly. Paris. 3 November. Accessed at <http://www.un.int/india/ind13.pdf> on 18 December 2012.

Odell, John S. and Susan K. Sell. 2006. Reframing the Issue: The WTO Coalition on Intellectual Property and Public Health. In John Odell ed., *Negotiating Trade: Developing Countries in the WTO and NAFTA*. Cambridge: Cambridge University Press.

Panagariya, Arvind. 2001. India Arrives at the WTO. *Economic Times*. 21 November.

Puri, Hardeep Singh. 2009. Letter from Permanent Representative of India to the UN addressed to the President of the Security Council outlining India's Approach and Perspectives regarding the Security Council's Summit Meeting on Nuclear Non-Proliferation and Nuclear Disarmament. Accessed at <http://www.nti.org/media/pdfs/4_ea.pdf?_=1316627912> on 25 December 2012.

Saran, Shyam. 2008. Address of Special Envoy of Prime Minister Shyam Saran on 'India and the Nuclear Domain' at the India International Centre. New Delhi. 18 February. In Avtar Singh Bhasin ed., *India's Foreign Relations Documents—2008*. New Delhi: Public Diplomacy Division, Ministry of External Affairs.

Sen, Amartya. 2005. *The Argumentative Indian: Writings on Indian Culture, History and Identity*. London: Penguin.

Singh, Jaswant. 1998a. Against Nuclear Apartheid. *Foreign Affairs*, September–October.

Singh, Jaswant. 1998b. Press Statement by Shri Jaswant Singh, Deputy Chairman, Planning Commission. 18 May. Accessed at <http://www.sassu.org.uk/html/profiles/NuclearWeaponsrelatedDocuments/98%20tests/98testIndex.htm#indsta> on 21 December 2012.

Singh, Manmohan. 2009. June. In Avtar Singh Bhasin ed., *India's Foreign Relations Documents—2009*. New Delhi: Public Diplomacy Division, Ministry of External Affairs.

Small, Deborah A., Michele Gelfand, Linda Babcock, and Hilary Gettman. 2007. Who Goes to the Bargaining Table? The Influence of Gender and Framing on the Initiation of a Negotiation. *Journal of Personality and Social Psychology*, 93:4, October, 600–13.

Tharoor, Shashi. 2008. The Indian Exception. Project Syndicate, 6 October. Accessed on 21 December 2012.

Tversky, Amos and Daniel Kahneman. 1981. The Framing of Decisions and the Psychology of Choice. *Science*, 211:4481, January, 453–8.

WTO. 2001. Statement by the Honorable Murasoli Maran. WT/MIN(01)/ST/10. 10 November. Accessed at <http://www.wto.org> on 18 December 2012.

WTO. 2003. Statement by the Honorable Arun Jaitley. WT/MIN(03)/ST/7. 10 September. Accessed at <http://www.wto.org> on 18 December 2012.

WTO. 2008. TNC Meeting, Statement of Shri Kamal Nath, 23 July.

4

Coalitions: Choosing Allies, Sustaining Friendships

Isolationism is not a dominant trend in India's international politics. In modern times, a newly independent India embraced multilateralism with enthusiasm, and employed coalition diplomacy across regimes. In this chapter, we examine the coalition behaviour of the characters of the Mahabharata, and investigate the insights that this offers into India's evolving coalition diplomacy from the first decades of independence to its position as a rising power. As this chapter illustrates, there is little obvious about how one chooses one's friends, either as an individual or as a state. How a rising power chooses its friends and allies can offer important information regarding the vision of global order that the state is still in the process of developing, or may even be signalling, as outsiders speculate about its emerging role.

In the first section, we present an overview of the logic behind coalition formation and the various shapes that coalitions can take. It also provides a brief account of the coalitions that India has participated in historically, and the trends in its coalition diplomacy as a rising power. Sections 4.2 to 4.5 provide an analysis of the coalition patterns that we find in the Mahabharata, and also discuss their implications for understanding India's negotiating culture. Section 4.6 offers a detailed analysis of India's coalition behaviour in the two regimes of international trade and nuclear non-proliferation. Section 4.7 concludes the discussion.

4.1. THE IMPORTANCE OF COALITIONS, AND HOW TO CHOOSE ONE'S FRIENDS AND ALLIES

A coalition can be defined as a group of states that combine their resources and efforts to pursue a common end. While coalitions are used by states at all levels of the international hierarchy, they serve as a particularly useful weapon of the weak and can be likened in some ways to the collective bargaining efforts of trade unions.[1] At least four benefits stand out. First, coalitions offer a vital pooling of scarce resources. Smaller European countries, for example, benefited from the clout that the Common Market offered them in GATT negotiations, and the OPEC countries were able to hold the world to ransom through their cartel in 1973. Parallels in the security area are to be found in alliances and the benefits offered by collective security. The benefits of international collective action are, moreover, not just structural. The second significant benefit, of particular importance to countries from the developing world, is the pooling of information, research, and organizational resources to help improve their participation in various governance processes. Third, depending on the level of their institutionalization, coalitions can offer the asset of increased certainty, which is of considerable value for small, weak, or unstable states that cannot rely on domestic mechanisms to provide internal balancing. Finally, the power of large numbers cannot be overestimated. This was true in the era of anti-colonialism that India entered as an independent state, and it remains just as important in today's era of globalization. When the legitimacy of international rules matters, as does the legitimacy of the process that goes into the making of those rules, states that are able to find the backing of others are more likely to be able to exercise influence than if they were to go it alone.[2] It is not surprising, then, that a newly independent India, facing many difficult challenges at home and with few instruments of internal balancing available to it at the time, sought to assert its international position and build its prestige by participating in, and even leading, several coalition initiatives. But the choice of one's allies and friends is seldom an easy task. Choices had to be made along at least three axes.

The first fundamental choice that India faced, and one that most states seeking coalition formation must consider, is whether to bandwagon with or balance against the powerful. For some, the choice may appear to be at best an academic one: for example, what hope does a small island economy like Vanuatu have in balancing against the US, the EU, or the BRICs? Stephen Walt has thus argued that weak states are more likely to bandwagon than balance: 'Because weak states can do little to affect the outcome (and may suffer grievously in the process), they must choose the winning side.'[3] The case of India is particularly important here. India, in the first few decades of independence, was not a strong state (let alone a Great Power), and thus provides an 'easy' case study for bandwagoning behaviour. If, even under

---

[1] Narlikar 2003.

[2] Of course, some institutions are more amenable to the exercise of the power of large numbers, depending on the rules that they use for decision-making: the UN General Assembly, for instance, offers more opportunities for countries to exploit majoritarianism more effectively (owing to its one-member-one-vote system) than the UN Security Council (and its two-tier system of decision-making).

[3] Walt 1987, p. 20.

those difficult circumstances, we find that it was reluctant to bandwagon, we can assume that it will be even less likely to bandwagon as a rising power.

It is worth bearing in mind that Walt's logic is primarily a Realist one; a Constructivist line of argument would suggest that perceptions of like-mindedness might increase the proclivity of strong states to bandwagon with the expanding power, whereas perceptions of deep-rooted differences may lead even weak states to adopt risky strategies of balancing (rather than contribute, via bandwagoning, to the even riskier outcome of having an enemy state, with which differences are irreconcilable, emerge as the dominant one). We have some evidence of this: even small states have managed on occasion to exercise their independent voice as a collective when they work in coalitions, at least avoiding the course of bandwagoning, if not engaging in full-blown balancing.[4] This logic leads us to advance a different expectation for India from the one provided by Realist logic. We could argue, for instance, that as a relative outsider to the international system, India under Nehru would have seen its interests as strongly in opposition to those of the estab-lished powers. Hence, even though in a position of weakness, it would have done its utmost to avoid bandwagoning and may have preferred balan-cing. In contrast, as a rising power, India's calculations might change: efforts to accommodate it may produce socialization, leading it to bandwagon with the established powers even as its power rises.

Note that the Realist and Constructivist accounts offer contradictory in-sights for India's coalition behaviour. Going by the Realist account, we would expect to see a transformation of India's behaviour towards external threats from bandwagoning to balancing as its power rises. The Constructivist ac-count, however, suggests the opposite trajectory: if perceptions are altered and outsiders are socialized, states that previously saw themselves as outsiders will change their behaviour from balancing to bandwagoning as their increasing power is accompanied by increasing socialization. As this chapter illustrates, neither theory is fully validated in the Indian case; some congruence between the modern-day examples and the stories from the Mahabharata suggests that the deviation from the theoretical expectation may perhaps be partly explained by culture-specific approaches and attitudes to negotiation.

The second choice that states are faced with involves formalization of cooperative endeavours: even if a state is fully committed to coalition diplo-macy, to what extent should this take the shape of formal alliances? Or are the state's interests better served by forming coalitions that are largely informal? These choices were particularly stark for independent India in the years of the Cold War, when it was (along with other former colonies) courted by the US and the Soviet Union to join the Western and Eastern blocs (and their alliance

---

[4] Narlikar 2011, on small states. For a useful analysis of the important nuances in balancing and bandwagoning, see Hurrell 2006.

systems) respectively. But they remain relevant even today; for instance, in the context of US–India relations some see improved cooperation as a stepping stone to a formal alliance, while others see persistent and powerful resistance towards this from the Indian side.

Third, states also have a choice available to them regarding whether their coalitions will be narrow and specific to particular issue areas, or if they will form coalitions that transcend issue areas and take the shape of blocs.[5] The former are united by shared interests over a specific issue; the latter can be much more heterogeneous, with diverse countries coming together through a logrolling of their different interests into a grand and complex collective programme of action that transcends issue areas. Often, bloc-type coalitions involve the sharing of ideas and even identity that go beyond interests. Issue-based coalitions allow their members greater flexibility, whereas bloc-type coalitions allow for reduced transaction costs and greater reliability of allies, albeit at the cost of negotiating flexibility. Weak states, in general, are likely to prefer the certainty of coalition allies, while their limited diplomatic resources may make it difficult for them to exercise the flexibility offered by issue-based coalitions. We would thus expect to see the transformation of India from a post-colonial state to a rising power to be accompanied by a transition from bloc-type coalitions to issue-based coalitions. Groupings such as the G77 in the UNCTAD, the G10 in the GATT, and the Non-Aligned Movement (NAM) are examples of bloc-type coalitions in which India has traditionally played an active role. In contrast, the US–India agreement may be seen as the start of an issue-based coalition on nuclear energy and non-proliferation, especially if it does not transform into a fully fledged alliance involving other aspects of security. But as we illustrate below, bloc-type coalitions are far from dead in India's diplomacy, even though they are no longer framed as such. Their persistence goes against the grain, and reinforces our purpose to investigate how far this behaviour is rooted in India's negotiating culture.

4.1.1. Bandwagons or balances?

Historically, India's coalition behaviour showed relatively clear trends along the three axes. The general pattern that we observe is an opposition to bandwagoning (often accompanied by vehement assertions of preserving one's independence and autonomy), a suspicion of formal alliances, and a proclivity to work in bloc-type coalitions. Within this pattern, however, we see nuances and three important exceptions: India's brief period of closeness with

---

[5] In trade, from where this categorization originates (Narlikar 2003), bloc-type coalitions normally brought together developing countries, whereas issue-based coalitions transcended North–South boundaries.

the West resulting directly from the Indochina war of 1962; its several periods of closeness with the Soviet Union, which were epitomized in the Treaty of Friendship and Cooperation of 1971; and, more recently, a rising India's closer relations with the US. A brief overview of the general trends follows, with a further discussion of the two exceptions.

In his detailed and careful study that relies extensively on primary sources, Dennis Kux has provided some telling examples of India's impending resistance to bandwagoning even before it had acquired formal independence. For example, Nehru had the following advice to offer Asaf Ali (who was to become India's first ambassador to the US): 'The United States are a great power and we want to be friendly with them for many reasons. Nevertheless, I should make it clear that we do not propose to be subservient to anybody . . . We have plenty of good cards in our hands and there is no need whatever for us to appear as supplicants before any country.'[6]

Under Nehru's premiership of an independent India, this position persisted, taking the shape of India's leadership in the NAM. There was nothing inevitable about India's role in the NAM; recall the many other states, operating from positions of weakness, that had readily aligned themselves with one or other bloc in the Cold War era. Raymond Cohen offers a useful comparison: 'If a Japan chastened by defeat and ruin had made a virtue of necessity and fully aligned itself with the West in the postwar world, India— like Egypt of the 1950s and 1960s—resolutely set its face against such a course. The policy of nonalignment, defined as India's right to determine its foreign policy orientation freely and without duress, became sacrosanct . . . Not only was alignment in the Cold War rejected, but fierce opposition was consistently expressed to anything that smacked of limiting Indian sovereignty.'[7]

Non-alignment was not an easy path to follow, guaranteeing as it did the chagrin of the superpowers and their allies. For example, India's 'neutralism' in the Korean War attracted trenchant criticism from the US, with the *New York Times* delivering the following indictment in 1950: 'Pandit Nehru purports to speak for Asia, but it is the voice of abnegation, his criticism turns out to have been obstructive, his policy appeasement.'[8] Nehru himself was well aware of the risks involved in the pursuit of non-alignment, but pursued it nonetheless. Even in the aftermath of the devastation that India occurred from the war with China, Nehru's commitment to the policy persisted:

What is called 'non-alignment' has . . . not fared badly . . . 'non-alignment' has become a summary of this policy of friendship towards all nations, uncompromised by adherence to any military pacts. This was not due to any indifference to issues that arose, but rather to a desire to judge them for ourselves, in full freedom

---

[6] Cited in Kux 1992, p. 51.   [7] R. Cohen 2004, p. 57.
[8] Cited in Kux 1992, p. 74.

and without any preconceived partisan bias. It implied, basically, a conviction that good and evil are mixed up in this world . . . Essentially, 'non-alignment' is freedom of action which is a part of independence. This attitude no doubt displeased some people to begin with, but it has been of service to the cause of world peace at some critical moments in recent history. A large number of countries, including most of the newly independent states of Asia and Africa, have adopted a similar outlook on international affairs . . . 'Non-alignment' is now an integral part of the international pattern and is widely conceded to be a comprehensible and legitimate policy, particularly for the emergent Afro-Asian states.[9]

While grateful for the timely assistance of the US and Britain at the time of the Indochina war, Nehru emphasized that India's pathway still lay in the direction of self-reliance rather than towards external balances or bandwagons:

> It is obvious . . . that the defence of India in any long-term view calls for a sustained effort by India herself—an effort, moreover, which cannot be conceived entirely or directly in narrow military terms. In the past, our preoccupation with the human problems of poverty and illiteracy was such that we were content to assign a relatively low priority to defence requirements in the conventional sense. We will now clearly have to give considerably more attention to strengthening our armed forces and to the production within the country, to the extent possible, of all weapons and equipment needed by them.[10]

The motivation for self-reliance was driven not only by a suspicion of the reliability of external balancing, but also India's leadership of and responsibility for the NAM: 'India is such an outstanding member of the non-aligned community that her defection, whether voluntary or enforced, cannot fail to bring grave or far-reaching consequences in its train.'[11]

The policy of non-alignment continued in future decades. By the 1970s, the NAM was transforming 'from a grouping of newly independent Afro-Asian countries seeking to stand apart from the two quarrelling power blocs into a platform for the world's poorer nations, the so-called Third World, to press their economic claims against the developed world'.[12] India's role continued to be a very proactive one in this arena too, both in the G77 and the UNCTAD and the push for the New International Economic Order, and in the GATT in advancing the cause of developing countries via the Informal Group of Developing Countries.

It is noteworthy that even over two decades since the end of the Cold War not only does the NAM survive, but so does India's involvement in it. In fact, the concept is being reinvented as India rises, as is illustrated in an important

---

[9] Nehru 1963, pp. 456–7.   [10] Nehru 1963, p. 459.   [11] Nehru 1963, p. 461.
[12] Kux 1992, p. 288.

(and controversial) report that was published by the Centre for Policy Research in New Delhi, and also the reactions to it.[13] The report recognizes the significantly altered context that provides the backdrop to India's rise, but goes on to argue that the core objective of India's strategic approach should be to 'enhance India's strategic space and capacity for independent agency . . . which in turn can be described as "Nonalignment 2.0"—a reworking for present times of the fundamental principle that has defined international engagements since Independence'.[14] It states that in its modern-day incarnation, nonalignment 'will no longer be limited to avoiding becoming a frontline state in a conflict between two powers. It will instead require a very skilful management of complicated coalitions and opportunities . . .'[15] The fact that the report uses non-alignment as its central frame in identifying India's foreign policy strategies is revealing of the legitimacy that the concept still enjoys, while its content reveals some important continuities in India's persistent aversion to bandwagoning.

Parallels to the strategy of non-alignment, or at least avoidance of bandwagoning, have flourished in a rising India's negotiations in other issue areas too. In climate change negotiations, India has participated actively in the BASIC (Brazil, South Africa, India, and China) group presenting an agenda that is often in opposition to that of the developed countries. The BRICS (Brazil, Russia, India, China, and South Africa) grouping has begun to evolve from an annual summit to more frequent meetings and a more detailed agenda on specific issues (including the idea of the BRICS development bank that was announced at the New Delhi summit in March 2012). And we have several examples of India's leadership of coalitions involving developing countries in multilateral trade, which have presented a direct challenge to the agendas of the EU and the US, and contributed to the deadlock in the Doha negotiations (discussed in detail in Section 4.6).

The possible exceptions to this dominant trend of resistance to bandwagoning are India's brief turn to the West in 1962 and the deepening of India's pro-Soviet proclivities in 1971. For a rising India, we have one possible exception: India's emerging cooperation with the US as a rising power.

Before the two more explicit turns—the first towards the West and the other towards the East—it is worth bearing in mind that post-colonial India's intrinsic ideational affinity had been with the Soviets. Stephen Cohen writes: 'At the time of independence, it saw the United States as an overdeveloped, materialistic power driven by a Manichaean view of the world. The Americans had stepped into the shoes of the British, and even non-communist Indians suspect the United States wanted to undercut India's natural and rightful regional dominance. It saw the Soviet Union as an errant but fundamentally

---

[13] Khilnani et al. 2012. For reactions to the report, see Singh 2012; Tellis 2012.
[14] Khilnani et al. 2012, p. 8.   [15] Khilnani et al. 2012, p. 9.

friendly state. Nehru had written in 1927 that it was inconceivable that Russia could ever become a threat to India . . . It was admired for its economic accomplishments and defiance of the West, although Nehru and the Indian non-communist left understood its essentially totalitarian structure.'[16] India's non-alignment thus traditionally had a pro-Soviet bent (reflected in its voting patterns in the UN General Assembly), even though it did not form a part of the Soviet bloc system or show any explicit signs of bandwagoning with the Soviets or balancing against the US.

The only times when we see any suggestion of bandwagoning from India are under conditions of extreme crisis. The Indochina war in 1962 was one such traumatic experience, while the prelude to the Indo–Pakistan war of 1971 provided the other. In the case of its devastating encounter with China, India found itself unable to rely on the assistance of the Soviets,[17] and had little choice but to turn to, and accept, Western aid. This was a turning point in India's behaviour in some forums: its voting pattern in the UN General Assembly, for instance, showed a very dramatic switch away from the Soviet Union and towards the US through the 1960s. But closer inspection reveals that India was far from willing to throw in its lot with the US, or the West more generally. For example, even as soon after the war as January 1963, Nehru was firmly opposed to India's accepting any Western defence guarantees: while some help from the US and others may have been acceptable, anything beyond this 'will be purchased at the expense of giving up our basic policy of non-alignment. That is not merely some kind of moral issue but something which makes our people feel that they have to be self-reliant and it also helps greatly in the balance of the world and our search for peace.' Dennis Kux is right to note that Nehru, even in the aftermath of a humiliating defeat, 'managed to maintain the basic thrust of Indian foreign policy . . . He was willing to accept military aid from the West—with his teeth clenched, rather like a child swallowing castor oil—but he resisted a closer policy embrace.'[18] India's evolving relations with the Soviet Union in the late 1960s, which took the shape of the Indo–Soviet Treaty of Peace, Friendship and Cooperation that was signed in 1971, show just how short-lived the honeymoon with the West was.

The treaty with the Soviet Union was just short of a formal alliance. For most external observers, it was a step too far by a country that had always expressed some admiration for the Eastern bloc, and presented a serious challenge to the credibility of India's commitment to non-alignment. But the

---

[16] S. Cohen 2001, p. 272.

[17] In fact, the Indians were disappointed not just by the Soviet Union's failure to offer them support; most of the NAM countries (other than Nasser of Egypt and Tito of Yugoslavia) were 'standoffish' in their reactions (Kux 1992, p. 205).

[18] Cited in Kux 1992, p. 212.

context prompting this swing was an extreme and urgent one. As an impending war with Pakistan loomed on the horizon, a major concern for India was 'to obtain political and military reinsurance against interference from China'. The treaty achieved this through articles that 'provided for consultations in the event of crisis and pledged that neither country would support a third party against the other'.[19] Further, even with such a treaty in place, several observers have noted India's continued attempts to maintain its independence. David Malone, for instance, writes that Delhi 'could never be included entirely in the Soviet "camp", however much Washington and some of its allies resented India's close relationship with Moscow'.[20] Even in the face of such extremities as war, India's attempts to preserve the independence of its policy persisted.

A third, and more recent, instance that we have of a possible break in India's dominant behaviour of avoiding bandwagons is its agreement with the US on civilian nuclear energy cooperation. We discuss this in further detail in Section 4.6. Suffice it to note at this point that the agreement is still far from serving as an alliance with the US; and even the minimal cooperation that this deal signals has proven controversial with domestic audiences in India, as was indicated in Chapter 2. A comment by the leader of the opposition, L. K. Advani, in the parliamentary debate on this topic is revealing: 'sometimes, I feel that the Deal is not a deal between two sovereign countries . . . it does not give me happiness to find that a Deal is being gone into in a way which makes India a junior partner in the agreement. I do not want the world to be a unipolar world as it has become now. No. It must be a multipolar world and in that multipolar world, I want to see India as the principal pole; and in order to be a principal pole, you cannot agree that these countries are nuclear weapon States whereas India is permanently a non-nuclear weapon State; and this is in the agreement.'[21] The comments illustrate (a) the importance of building coalitions as at least an equal, and certainly not as a lesser party (or what Nehru had referred to as a 'supplicant') and (b) the importance attached to multipolarity rather than the hierarchy that accompanies bandwagoning. In this chapter, we investigate the extent to which these ideas resonate with principles governing negotiations in the Mahabharata.

Note that neither the Realist nor the Constructive accounts are borne out thus far. Contra the Realist prediction, India, even at its weakest and facing dire circumstances, showed at best only short-lived and occasional dalliances with bandwagoning. The dominant tendency was either towards hedging or balancing. Thus the strategy of non-alignment took on an explicit balancing element when presented as a third force, and at other times a form of hedging. And contra the Constructivist account, we do not see a clear tendency towards bandwagoning via the route of socialization.

---

[19] Kux 1992, pp. 295–6.   [20] Malone 2011, p. 235.   [21] Advani 2008, pp. 455–6.

4.1.2. Formal alliances or alternative groupings?

The second axis on which coalitions are defined is formalization of different types of coalitions. Inherent in India's historical association with non-alignment was also its refusal to be drawn into any formal alliances. Others have also noted this tendency. Pratap Bhanu Mehta, for instance, has observed that even though it has entered into strategic partnerships with a number of countries, 'India has been reluctant to enter into comprehensive alliances of the kind that NATO represents.'[22] He explains this in terms of Indian pragmatism and a concern regarding the preservation of its foreign policy autonomy. It is certainly true that India's overwhelming concern about maintaining the independence of its foreign policy has traditionally rendered it reluctant to join alliances that other countries (including other developing countries with their own colonial baggage) have willingly embraced. Effectively, the means (foreign policy autonomy) are seen as just as important as the ends (e.g. wider goals, such as the preservation of national autonomy, sovereignty, and economic growth).

Interestingly, a historical suspicion of alliances has not deterred India from participating in, and even leading, looser groupings towards collective action and what Stephen Cohen has called the pursuit of global diplomacy.[23] Hence, for instance, its role in not just the NAM but also the G77 in the UN, and various coalitions in the GATT, including the Informal Group of Developing Countries and the G10 in the Uruguay Round. Note that all these coalitions involve developing countries. The importance of coalitions continues to be evident even today as India's power is rising. For instance, the report entitled *NonAlignment 2.0* places considerable emphasis on coalitions. Other examples in which India participates are groupings such as the IBSA (India, Brazil, South Africa) and the BRICS. And in the WTO it has been proactive in several coalitions that involve developing countries, including the G20 and G33 on agriculture.

It is perhaps worth noting again that all the examples given in the previous sections are coalitions of developing countries. Examples of India's activism on coalitions with developed countries are few. This 'imbalance' may be a product of what Mehta refers to as 'an inordinate quest for international recognition of its status'. As Tanham notes perceptively, 'status and symbolism, rather than a hard nosed assessment of interests, have marked this quest . . . India is likely to remain an extraordinarily status conscious power.'[24] Stephen Cohen has

---

[22] Mehta 2009, p. 221.

[23] S. Cohen 2001, pp. 72–3, contrasts India's global diplomacy (with a wide range of strategic and diplomatic priorities) with that of Pakistan, which has limited and clear priorities that include a focus on India, and 'intense engagement' with only three or four countries and the Islamic world.

[24] S. Cohen 2001, p. 217.

pointed to a similar trend in the day-to-day workings of India's diplomacy, and notes the importance that negotiators assign to 'establishing the moral and political equality of the two sides'.[25] What this translates into most obviously is that Indian negotiators would prefer to bargain with an opponent who accords them the status they believe is due to them, rather than opponents who might offer them a better deal but would somehow expect India to adopt the role of a supplicant. For a long time, this resulted in difficulties in negotiations with the West; in contrast, India's negotiations with a good proportion of the developing world were easier because they were seen to be either on equal terms or on terms favourable to India.

The three arguable exceptions discussed in the previous subsection are even less persuasive examples of formal alliances than they were of bandwagoning. In the two instances from the Cold War era, neither the turn to the West for aid in 1962 nor the Indo–Soviet Treaty of 1971 were fully fledged alliances. In other words, even in times of great difficulty (with war either already upon the country, as in 1962, or imminent, as in 1971), India avoided the pathway of formal alliances. And as we elaborate in Section 4.6, even after the Indo-US agreement paved the way to recognition and legitimacy for India as a de facto nuclear power (at a cost to the credibility of the regime), India's civilian nuclear energy deal remains just that. India and the US are no longer the 'estranged democracies' that had sparred in the Cold War years, but they are still far from being 'allies' in any formal sense.

4.1.3. Bloc-type or issue-based coalitions?

The third axis along which states must choose their alignments relates to bloc-type versus issue-based coalitions. India, led by Nehru, had always been emphatic in its refusal to join the Eastern or Western bloc, and had insisted upon the freedom to decide its position on particular situations after assessing them on their own terms, rather than an ideological pre-commitment. Somewhat paradoxically, though, India's leadership of the NAM produced a bloc of its own kind, that is, a group of states united by an ideology, transcending issue areas, and comprising developing countries. As was argued in Section 4.1.1, India's commitment to non-alignment was high, which it attempted to preserve even when faced with such extreme conditions as war. It is noteworthy that India was willing to bear considerable costs for its

---

[25] S. Cohen 2001, p. 85, further offers a useful point of comparison with China: 'Just as the Chinese try to establish a set of agreed-upon principles before negotiations can proceed, Indians tacitly (and sometimes explicitly) try to get their Western counterpart to agree to the principle of equality, usually via a series of arguments over seemingly irrelevant issues . . . The Soviet Union had considerable success in negotiating with New Delhi, partly because it was willing to treat India as a "major" power, whatever its private views.'

leadership of the NAM. Recall, for example, the discussion in Chapter 3, where Nehru turned down the opportunity to develop nuclear weapons, with the blessing of the US, in the 1960s, on the grounds that this violated the principle of disarmament that India had constantly espoused, individually and collectively.

The economic parallel to India's participation in the NAM was the G77 in the UNCTAD, and also other coalitions that involved developing countries, such as the Informal Group of Developing Countries in the GATT. In the UNCTAD and the GATT, India took the lead in pushing for the cause of development. In the former, this involved the call for the New International Economic Order. In the latter, it took the shape of a call for what would come to be known as Special and Differential Treatment (or Less Than Full Reciprocity in the WTO today) for developing countries, and attempting to limit mandate expansion of the institution until these concerns had received due attention.

In some instances, India's commitment to bloc-type coalitions united by a developmentalist ideology brought it into direct conflict with issue-based coalitions. Such a conflict took place in the GATT in the 1980s, when India led the G10 in resisting the inclusion of the 'new issues' of Trade Related Intellectual Property Rights (TRIPs) and Trade Related Investment Measures (TRIMs), and services. Overtures by issue-specific coalitions, which proposed a joint exploration of the implications of services liberalization by developed and developing countries, were firmly resisted. In effect, on several occasions, commitment to particular ideational loyalties trumped opportunism.

It could be argued that a newly independent India found value in the certainty offered by bloc-type coalitions; but as a rising India's power increases, would it not abandon its defensive commitment to blocs and exploit the opportunities of dynamic and flexible coalitions that would change according to issue areas? One might expect this to be the case, especially as bloc-type coalitions are more effective at blocking than agenda-setting, and are hence often the default strategies of weaker and defensive states. As India's power rises, would it not be better served by issue-based coalitions that are more effective at agenda-setting?[26] Interestingly, however, India's reliance on bloc-type coalitions has largely continued, with non-proliferation providing the one exception to the rule. In this area, as discussed in Section 4.6, India seems to have indeed formed a coalition with the US, specifically on the issue of nuclear energy cooperation, which in turn has contributed to its securing the NSG waiver. The waiver is granted to India alone, rather than a group of its developing country allies. Compare this with Nehru's willingness to turn down the opportunity for nuclear weaponization in the 1960s and instead to stand by the NAM, and a departure in policy in this issue area is significant.

---

[26] Narlikar 2003; Narlikar and Tussie 2004; Narlikar 2009.

That said, in most other issue areas, ranging from global economic governance to climate change and global governance, India continues to form coalitions with other developing countries. They are seldom presented with the same ideological fervour that guided groupings such as the G77 or the NAM, and it is true that they sometimes take an issue-specific focus (e.g. the BASIC on climate change, the G20 and G33 on liberalization of agricultural trade, or the BRICS on matters of global governance). But they are often restricted to a subset of developing countries (often with diverse interests, that are held together by some shared identity), and are relatively successful at blocking but less effective at agenda-setting. Section 4.6 compares the example of India's bloc-type coalitions in trade, which represent the persistent norm in its coalition strategy in contrast to its go-it-alone strategy on the issue of nuclear non-proliferation. Before doing so, however, we investigate the coalition behaviour of protagonists in the Mahabharata, and explore the insights that they offer towards understanding the Indian negotiator's approach to coalitions.

4.2. NEGOTIATING PRE-WAR COALITIONS IN THE MAHABHARATA

In the Mahabharata, coalitions are viewed not only as a strategy towards strengthening one's position in a war, but as a vital part in the conduct of the politics of the everyday. The first story in this section is an illustration of how two key protagonists—Duryodhana and Karna—form a friendship in the early part of the epic, which becomes a vital source of strength for Duryodhana many years later in wartime. The second story illustrates the cooperation and aid that the Pandavas extend to their future enemy when Duryodhana is faced with a more immediate threat. The third is an example of how coalitions are built when war is imminent.

4.2.1. Karna and Duryodhana: A long-lasting coalition is forged

When Dronacharya deemed that the Kauravas and Pandavas had completed their martial education, he arranged an exhibition of their skills for the public. Much of the display took the form of a tournament between the Kauravas and the Pandavas, with the warriors demonstrating their skills with different weapons. While the two sides turned out to be well matched, Arjuna impressed the crowds with his many skilful feats. Just as the proceedings were about to draw to a close, with Arjuna emerging as the star of the show, a handsome stranger with a most formidable countenance, shining with the splendour of the sun, appeared. This stranger was Karna, and he issued a public challenge to Arjuna, claiming that he would outperform Arjuna in all his exploits. The spectators were awed by this, and Arjuna was disconcerted and angered. Duryodhana, however, was delighted (for the rivalries between the cousins went back to the days of their childhood), and offered Karna a warm and gracious welcome:

स्वागतम् ते महाबाहो दिष्ट्या प्राप्तोससिमानद
अहं च कुरुराज्यं च यथेष्टमुपभुज्यताम्
I.126.14

Oh brave warrior, welcome, it is our great honour that you have come amongst us. I am at your service, and the entire Kuru kingdom stands at your disposal.

Karna, in turn, said that he wished only for Duryodhana's friendship, and the opportunity to engage with Arjuna in single combat. Duryodhana gave Karna his blessing, and a powerful alliance began to take shape.

Arjuna, in contrast, met Karna with hostility, accusing him of being an uninvited and unwanted visitor, and promising to destroy him. Karna responded calmly: the tournament's arena was not reserved exclusively for Arjuna; and what need was there for words when they would soon be speaking with arrows anyway? At this point, none of the characters (not even Karna himself) knew that Karna was, in fact, the eldest Pandava, the illegitimate son of Kunti. Kunti, however, had recognized Karna immediately from the golden armour and amulets that he had been born with, and fainted on witnessing the hostilities and impending confrontation between her two sons.

Kripacharya, as master of the ceremonies, then invited Karna to reveal his royal lineage; this would determine whether Arjuna would agree to fight with him or not. Karna, who had no knowledge of his royal lineage, knowing his only parents to be the kindly charioteer and his wife who had adopted him, paled at the prospect of having to reveal his humble origins in this class-bound and hierarchical setting. Duryodhana noticed Karna's discomfort and leapt to his defence. He reminded the onlooking crowds that royalty could be claimed not only by those of blue blood, but also by those of heroic deeds and the leaders of armies, and then declared:

यद्ययं फाल्गुनो युध्दे नाराज्ञा योध्दुमिच्छति
तस्मादेषोसंगविषये मया राज्येसभिषिच्यते
I.126.35

If Arjuna will not engage in combat with one who is not a king, I, at this very moment, crown Karna the King of Anga.

Duryodhana ensured that Karna's coronation was completed within a few moments. This act of kindness and generosity won Duryodhana the undying loyalty and friendship of Karna, which he avowed in gratitude immediately after his coronation. As it turned out, Karna was an extremely powerful ally for Duryodhana.

The story is important because it reveals the value of investing in even seemingly weak allies. Karna may have been regal in his appearance, but for all accounts and purposes he was a nobody when he arrived at the tournament, and a target of contempt and derision for the Pandavas. Nonetheless, Duryodhana chose to help the underdog, and secured a strong and reliable friend through his act of kindness. Simultaneously, Arjuna's insults to Karna cut deep. Even if Karna had not been the abandoned son of Kunti, his hatred of the Pandavas was ingrained at the tournament, which in turn reinforced his loyalty to the opposing Kaurava clan.

The story also suggests a slight proclivity to balancing. Duryodhana knew nothing of Karna when he arrived, but his brave challenge to the people's favourite, Arjuna, naturally endeared him to the Kaurava side. In keeping with the axiom attributed to Kautilya, by assisting the rival of a rival Duryodhana was effectively assisting a friend. This was, in effect, balancing behaviour. But given the absence of any information about Karna at the time, this was not balancing at its best planned or strategic; for all he knew, Duryodhana could have been investing in a boastful but incompetent warrior or an unreliable turncoat. That he did so nonetheless suggests almost an intrinsic proclivity to balance *against* a major centre of power, rather than *with* alternative centres of power in premeditated design.

4.2.2. The Pandavas rescue Duryodhana

One day, when the Pandavas were still in exile, Duryodhana led a party of the Kauravas into the forest. The pretext that the Kauravas used was that they wished to conduct cattle inspections; the real purpose of the journey, however, was to witness and delight in the miseries of the exiled Pandavas. The Kauravas reached a scenic spot in the forest beside the sacred lake, where birdsong filled the air. Duryodhana commanded his men to set up camp by the lakeside. But before the arrival of the Kauravas, the Gandharvas—celestial beings—led by their own king, Chitrasena, had already set up camp there. The Kauravas' attempt to enter the wood adjoining the lake was thus stopped by the Gandharvas. When Duryodhana's men returned to their king, explaining that they had been thwarted from following his orders because the lakeside was already occupied by the Gandharvas, Duryodhana was furious. Despite all warnings that were issued to him, Duryodhana ordered his men to remove the celestial beings with the use of force. A full-scale battle began. The Gandharvas were not only divine musicians but also ferocious warriors, and although the Kauravas fought bravely their troops were devastated. Karna, who battled most valiantly, was finally struck down by what seemed to be a fatal blow, while Duryodhana, for all his courage, was taken captive, along with three of his brothers. Panic-stricken, the routed remains of the Kaurava army fled to the nearby Pandava camp and sought assistance.

Bhima, often easy to anger and perhaps the most fiery of the Pandava brothers, could not resist the opportunity to point to the poetic justice in this situation. He guessed (rightly) that the intention of the Kauravas had been to gloat over the miseries of their unfortunate cousins, and delighted in the misfortune that had befallen them as comeuppance for their malign intentions. He lauded the Gandharvas for the task that the Pandavas should have performed themselves—defeating the Kauravas. 'Those who are unable to help themselves often find that others more powerful come to their rescue. The Gandharvas have proved this.' But his sarcasm and glee were both cut short by Yudhishthira, who chided Bhima firmly. The eldest Pandava argued that all families had their disputes and disagreements, but one had to take action to protect the family honour:

यदा तु कश्चिज्ज्ञातीनां बाह्यः प्रार्थयते कुलम्
न मर्षयन्ति तत्सन्तो बाह्येनाभिप्रमर्षणम्
III.232.3

If an outsider attacks any one of the members of their family, then individuals of a noble heart cannot tolerate this insult (and must take action).

And rather than commend the Gandharvas for their actions, he expressed much displeasure: the Gandharvas were well aware that the Pandavas resided close by; by choosing to attack their kinsmen, the Kauravas, they had insulted the shared family honour of the Kauravas and the Pandavas. Besides, argued Yudhishthira, it was the Kshatriya duty to protect one who sought one's help or refuge. And finally, argued Yudhishthira, not completely forgetting the enmity between the cousins and the many wrongs that the Kauravas had inflicted on the Pandavas, by liberating one's foe one can secure more good Karma than the blessings that one accrues by performing many good deeds together. And having thus argued the case, he urged the Pandavas to hasten to the rescue of Duryodhana and their other captive cousins. He suggested that they first attempt to use persuasion for the rescue effort, and then light force. If neither strategy proved effective, they must use all the force necessary to secure the release of their brethren. On receiving Yudhishthira's instructions, Arjuna thus vowed:

यदि साम्ना न मोक्ष्यन्ति गन्धर्वा धृतराष्ट्रजान्
अद्य गन्धर्वराजस्य भूमिः पास्यति शोणितम्
III.233.20

If the Gandharvas do not release the sons of Dhritarashtra after our attempts to persuade them to do so, the earth will drink the blood of the Gandharva king today.

Duryodhana and his men were duly rescued by the Pandavas.

The story is illustrative of how one's allies are chosen in the Mahabharata. Remember that the Pandavas had endured much suffering at the hands of the Kauravas. But when it came to a challenge posed by an outsider, the only course of action that the virtuous Pandavas saw as being open to them was to come to the aid of their nefarious cousins. Recall that Yudhishthira gave his brothers several reasons as to why they should hasten to the rescue. He emphasized the good Karma that they would reap by rescuing their rivals and enemies, and also reminded them of the Kshatriya duty to aid those who sought assistance. But his primary justification was that of defending the family honour. As the Mahabharata later explains, the Gandharva king and the Pandavas had a history of amicable relations. But when forced to choose, the Pandavas chose the Kauravas. The Kauravas had inflicted innumerable and extreme miseries on the Pandavas, and the Pandavas could have gained a major strategic advantage in their long-standing rivalry had they left Duryodhana and his brothers to the mercy of the Chitrasena. But the Kauravas were their cousins, and the Pandavas chose to sacrifice strategic advantage in favour of the principle of family loyalty.

On being released, as a result of the generous bravery of the Pandavas, Duryodhana was overcome with shame. The fact that he had been rescued by those whom he had greatly wronged, and was now in the debt of those whom he believed to be his enemies, was a matter of great insult and dishonour. He declared a preference for death in battle rather than a life thus rescued and lived subsequently in debt. Duryodhana's story resembles the 'wounded hero' story that we discussed in Chapter 2, where a trade negotiator representing modern India admitted that it was easier for an Indian minister to come back to the country from Geneva with no deal, rather than to return with a deal that was secured on the strength of concessions. Duryodhana, similarly, would prefer death to the humiliation of a rescue that indebts him to his enemies. He thus began a fast unto death. And though Dushasana, Karna, and Shakuni took it in turns to persuade and admonish him in order that he might regain his ardour for life, Duryodhana refused to change his proposed course of action.

Only demonic intervention was able to breathe the will to live into Duryodhana's heart again. The demons, upon hearing of his resolve to end his life, conducted a sacrifice to summon him to the netherworld. There they promised him great power, glory, and victory in the impending war with the Pandavas. Besides, the demonic cause would be lost without Duryodhana's proactive role. On thus being addressed by the demons and being entrusted with their cause, Duryodhana re-embraced life with a deepened resolve and confidence to annihilate the Pandavas. Effectively, the Pandavas had not only sacrificed a potential strategic advantage, but had stoked the wrath of Duryodhana through their kindness, and had thereby worsened their own strategic position in a significant way.

4.2.3. Preparations for war: Arjuna and Duryodhana seek a coalition with Krishna

When war became unavoidable and inevitable, both the Kauravas and the Pandavas decided to seek the help of Krishna. Duryodhana, representing the Kaurava side, reached Krishna first. Krishna was asleep, and Duryodhana took his seat on a grand chair near Krishna's head, and waited. Arjuna followed, and stood by the foot of Krishna's bed, hands folded in respect. When Krishna awoke, his eyes fell first on Arjuna, and he asked the cousins the purpose of their visit. Duryodhana presented his cause first. Having stated that he had come to ask Krishna for his assistance in the impending war, Duryodhana pointed out that Krishna's relationship with both sides was the same, and, by implication, his duty to both sides was also the same. But Duryodhana had been the first to arrive, and the ancient codes of righteous conduct dictated that those who arrived first should also be the first to be assisted. Duryodhana thus urged Krishna, known for his virtue and righteousness, to follow the prescribed code of conduct.

Krishna, in response, assured Duryodhana that while he did not doubt that Duryodhana had been the first to arrive, Krishna's gaze had fallen on Arjuna (at the foot of his bed) before he spotted Duryodhana (by the head of the bed). Duryodhana had arrived first, while Arjuna had been seen first, so both were deserving of Krishna's help and would receive it. One side would benefit from Krishna's massive force, comprising a hundred million cowherds, as strong as Krishna himself and skilled in the art of battle. The other side would have Krishna himself, but a Krishna who had forsaken his weapons and who would not do battle:

ते वा युधि दुराधर्षा भवन्त्वेकस्य सैनिका:
अयुध्यमान: संग्रामे न्यस्तशस्त्रोऽहमेकत:
V.7.17

One side will stand the most ferocious warriors, ready to do battle. I will be on the other side. But I will be alone, and I will not fight, nor will I don any weapons.

And while Krishna accepted Duryodhana's point about first-come-first-serve, the ancient code of conduct also stated that the younger party should be allowed the first choice. Which side of the bargain would Arjuna prefer?

Arjuna, without the slightest hesitation, chose Krishna. Duryodhana was elated: he had gained a hundred million soldiers of remarkable prowess, and Krishna moreover had vowed that he would not fight. Duryodhana regarded the war as good as won for the Kauravas, and he returned with his expanded armies to much rejoicing at home.

The story shows us that Arjuna's loyalty to Krishna remained unwavering amidst much temptation. By choosing his closest friend—despite Krishna's commitment not to fight—under the dire circumstances of an impending war, where the Pandavas were from the start outnumbered by the Kauravas, Arjuna behaved as we would expect an adherent to a bloc-type coalition would behave. The coalition is preserved even in the face of altered circumstances and transcends issue areas—in this case, times of peace and times of war. In fact, when Krishna asks Arjuna (after Duryodhana's departure) why he chose an ally who would not fight at all, Arjuna responded:

भवान्समर्थस्तान्सर्वान्निहन्तु नात्र संशयः
निहन्तुमहमप्येकः समर्थः पुरुषोत्तम
भवांस्तु कीर्तिमाँल्लोके तद्यशस्त्वां गमिष्यति
यशसां चाहमप्यर्थी तस्मादसि मया वृतः
V.7.32, 33

I do not doubt that you could slay them all unaided, and so could I, my Lord. But you have renown in the world and glory will accrue to you. I too wish to accrue such renown and glory, and thus have I chosen you.

Arjuna then asks if Krishna will assist him in the war as his charioteer, and Krishna agrees. Note that Arjuna's commitment to renown is supreme, in contrast to Duryodhana's commitment to victory.

Duryodhana, in contrast, sought an alliance with Krishna that was more akin to an issue-based coalition. Krishna, throughout the early part of the epic, had shown considerable sympathy towards the Pandavas, and criticized the Kauravas for their unwarranted excesses; his half-sister, Subhadra, moreover, was married to Arjuna. This history, however, did not deter Duryodhana from seeking Krishna's aid. And rather than be driven by affection towards Krishna's godliness, Duryodhana's pragmatism led him to delight in the fact that Arjuna's choice had ensured a marked increase in the size and prowess of the Kaurava army. In fact, as we know, Arjuna's choice was the wiser one, and Duryodhana's apparent pragmatism and willingness to form an issue-based coalition did not secure him the victory that he had anticipated.

4.2.4. Insights for negotiation

Four interesting tendencies emerge from the stories in this section. First, we see evidence of balancing by both Karna and Duryodhana against the Pandavas in the first story. By challenging the people's favourite, Arjuna, Karna wins the respect of Duryodhana (the fact that Karna is in fact challenging a rival Pandava brother undoubtedly also works in his favour). Duryodhana shows a willingness to take a risk on this courageous newcomer (of dubious origins and no social status), defending him against the derisive comments of the Pandavas and even bestowing the kingship of Anga on him, to enable him to fight with Arjuna on equal terms. Duryodhana, by befriending the enemy of his enemy, wins the unwavering and undying loyalty of the unfortunate Karna.

Karna, as it turns out later, is the only warrior skilled in archery to match Arjuna, and thus plays a crucial role in the balance of the Kauravas against the Pandavas.

Second, the tendency to form bloc-type coalitions predominates. When Karna states that he only seeks the friendship of Duryodhana, he means this in a literal sense; as we shall find in the story discussed in the next section, Karna refuses all temptations and firmly stands by Duryodhana (in spite of his foreknowledge that in doing so he will end up on the losing side). Arjuna displays a similar steadfast loyalty to Krishna, picking Krishna himself over a mighty army of a hundred million soldiers. Arjuna could easily have made the opposite choice, driven by the issue at hand, that is, the relatively small size of the Pandava force in contrast to the teeming numbers of the Kauravas. But he did not do so, for the presence of Krishna in his life in all circumstances outweighed all possible gains that he could wish for in the war. Arjuna was ultimately rewarded for this: Krishna's presence with the Pandavas was fundamental and indispensable to their victory. Duryodhana, in contrast, driven by the urgency of the impending conflict, did not have any qualms in asking Krishna for his assistance, despite the well-known closeness between the Pandavas and Krishna. He was further satisfied and enthused when offered Krishna's force rather than Krishna himself, for his immediate purpose—as is the purpose of issue-based coalitions—was to win the war, rather than seek glory or the friendship of Krishna. Duryodhana fared poorly in making this choice. In fact, as he lay wounded and dying, Duryodhana declared Krishna solely responsible for the victory of the Pandavas (by advising them on their war strategy) and the defeat of the Kaurava heroes.

Third, the second story in this section (the Pandavas rescuing Duryodhana from the Gandharvas) demonstrates some very interesting distinctions that are drawn between categories of friends and allies. The Gandharva king was on friendly terms with the Pandavas, and potentially a valuable ally: the Gandharvas were celestial beings with considerable martial skills. But Yudhishthira chose to come to the assistance of his cousin Duryodhana, despite the history of extreme and bitter rivalry between the two factions. Family loyalty, and possibly other potential gains (e.g. the virtue that one accrues by helping those who seek aid, and, even more so, the virtue that one accrues by helping a foe), trumped the immense strategic advantage that the Pandavas could have gained by leaving Duryodhana to his fate. In fact, Yudhishthira not only sacrifices a potential strategic advantage, but willingly embraces a strategic risk by having his brothers draw swords with the usually friendly Gandharva king.

Finally, recall that Duryodhana's reaction to the generous rescue operation taken on by the Pandavas is not one of gratitude but of shame (initially) and increased hatred (after his encounter with the demons). Both Yudhishthira and Duryodhana are driven by honour codes rather than 'rational' strategic behaviour, but their honour codes are different. For Yudhishthira, the honour code of family loyalty surpasses all potential strategic advantage. For Duryodhana, the honour code first requires him to end his life because he has become indebted to his foes. Subsequent demonic intervention that emphasizes the importance of his leadership for the cause of the netherworld leads him to return with renewed hatred of the Pandavas and reinforced determination to defeat them. Both are honour codes of heroism and for this reason command respect, even though Yudhishthira's honour code is ethically superior to Duryodhana's.

The interaction between the two codes might well lead a newcomer to the Mahabharata to walk away with the lesson that no good deed goes unpunished, given that Yudhishthira's generosity towards Duryodhana effectively provoked the latter's anger and vengeance even further, and firmed up his resolve to fight with the Pandavas. In fact, this is not the case. The Pandavas are rewarded for their many good deeds in heaven, and they also emerge as the victors in the war, in spite of Duryodhana's strengthened resolve against them.

4.3. COALITIONS IN WARTIME

Coalition-building is not just a pre-war activity but one that persists even amidst the pressures of war, as the conflicting sides try hard to secure an advantage over the other.

4.3.1. Karna refuses to switch sides

Karna, the firstborn and rejected son of Kunti, found a loving home with a humble charioteer and his wife. Even though in appearance he shone with the same glory as his father, Surya (the sun god), and even though he had taught himself martial skills that surpassed those of all the other accomplished warriors of his age and were matched only by Arjuna, Karna was constantly subject to jibes and put-downs about his allegedly humble birth. Recall, for example in Section 4.2.1, the refusal of Arjuna to accept his challenge on the grounds that Karna was not a Kshatriya. The jibes did not stop there. Bhima had ridiculed him as a mere sutaputra when Karna's aged father had arrived in the contest arena. Draupadi had subsequently turned down Karna as a suitor because of his humble origins. Contrast this constant humiliation with the status, respect, and recognition that the courageous Karna found with the Kauravas, and it is unsurprising that his loyalty towards the Kauravas ran deep. He was an extremely powerful ally for the Kauravas, and inspired fear in the hearts of those who supported the Pandavas.

As war became increasingly imminent and unavoidable, Kunti decided to go on a mission to persuade Karna to defect from the Kauravas and to embrace his real family by revealing to him the secret of his birth. When Karna introduced himself to her as the son of Adhiratha, the charioteer, and his wife Radha, Kunti told him that he was in fact her own firstborn son. She recounted the story of the boon that she had received, which allowed her to bear children fathered by the gods. Driven by youthful and misguided curiosity, she had decided to test this boon, and had found herself bearing the child of Surya while still an unmarried woman. The stigma associated with childbirth outside marriage left her with little choice but to abandon the newborn Karna on the bank of the Ganges (where he was rescued by the childless couple Adhiratha and Radha). Kunti entreated Karna to assume his rightful position as her son, the eldest Pandava, and the future king of their people. She argued that it was not right that he had, out of ignorance, chosen to wait upon the sons of Dhritarashtra. Dhritarashtra's sons had snatched the prosperity of the Pandavas away from them through unfair means; the time had come for Arjuna and Karna to unite as the brothers that they really were, and to reclaim their right. In doing so, Karna would be obeying the wishes of his mother, and thereby fulfilling the highest of his duties. Kunti then promised Karna the status and respect that he had craved all his life:

कर्णं शोभिष्यसे नूनं पञ्चभिभ्रीतृभिर्वृतः
वेदैः परिवृतो ब्रह्मा यथा वेदांगपञ्चमैः
V.143.11

Oh Karna, you will doubtless shine in much glory, surrounded by your five brothers, just as Brahma (the creator) himself shines, surrounded by the gods, when attending the sacrificial fire.

And in the distance Karna also heard the voice of Surya, confirming Kunti's words and also affirming that great good would come of Karna's following his mother's advice.

Most men would succumb easily to the cocktail of emotional blackmail and strategic gain that Karna was given. But he remained unwavering in his loyalty to the Kauravas. Politely but firmly, he reminded Kunti that she had deprived him of the status and prestige of being a Kshatriya by abandoning him at birth; although she had not fulfilled her duty to him as a mother, she had few qualms in asking him to fulfil the responsibilities of a son and obey her commands. He, however, was not in a position to follow her wishes for two reasons. First, if he now joined the mighty Pandavas on the eve of the battle (who had Arjuna on their side, and Lord Krishna as his charioteer), claiming to be their brother, he would be the subject of accusations and ridicule that he had switched sides at the last minute out of cowardice.

Second, his presence was crucial to the Kauravas, who believed that Karna's prowess and skill could help them take on their almost invincible foe. The sons of Duryodhana had given Karna their affection and respect, and had also given him world recognition and recompense. He intended to return the favour by continuing to fight on their side, to his death if necessary. Karna offered a strong moral argument:

मया प्लवेन संग्रामं तितीर्षन्ति दुरत्ययम्
अपारे पारकामा ये त्यजेयम् तानहं कथम्
V.144.14

They [Dhritarashtra's sons] are relying on me, exactly as they might rely on a ship that will help them navigate a rough and dangerous sea. They depend on me to overcome the great difficulties that they are facing today. How can I possibly abandon them in their time of need?

The friendship of the Kauravas with Karna would not go in vain: Karna intended to fight on their behalf, willingly forsaking his life if necessary.

In committing to this path, Karna had renounced potential victory and glory. His sacrifice, however, went one step further. While all the codes of loyalty and honour dictated that Karna could not forsake his friends in their hour of need, he could also not completely disregard the concerns of Kunti, his birth mother. He thus promised her that she would always have five sons. Even though all the Pandava brothers could potentially be slain by Karna, he would reserve his might for Arjuna. Either Arjuna would die at Karna's hand, or Karna himself would attain glory by being slain by Arjuna in the war. Karna had thus not only abandoned his real family, a very powerful alliance with Arjuna (and Krishna) that would make victory certain, and the promise of kingship, but he had embraced an even greater probability of defeat and death by tying his hands and promising Kunti the survival of five sons. He stood by his promise to the very end, resisting other attempts, including one by Krishna in the middle of the war, to win him over.

4.3.2. Shalya's betrayal and loyalty

The Pandavas were not the only side that hoped to trigger defection from the other party; the Kauravas attempted similar strategies of offering carrots to the friends of the Pandavas, hoping to tempt them to their own side. An important illustrative attempt can be found in Duryodhana's devious attempt to win over Shalya, an ally of the Pandavas.

Shalya was an uncle of the Pandavas. He and his massive force were moving with speed and determination to the aid of his nephews, who had requested his assistance. Duryodhana, on hearing of Shalya's plans and progress, had pavilions of great luxury and decadence erected to serve as rest-houses for his journey. There, Shalya and his men were waited upon as gods. Shalya was delighted with this hospitality, which he believed was being showered upon him by his nephew, Yudhishthira, and partook of it without hesitation. At this point, Duryodhana revealed himself to be Shalya's generous host, and Shalya in return offered to grant him a wish, even though the two were on opposite sides. Duryodhana asked Shalya to serve as the leader of his army. Shalya agreed. He told Duryodhana that he must pay his promised visit to Yudhishthira, but would return speedily.

On meeting Yudhishthira, Shalya told him of all that had transpired. Yudhishthira requested him to act on behalf of the Pandavas in the following way. The time would come when Shalya would be asked to serve as charioteer for Karna, Arjuna's supreme foe. At this point, Shalya should do all he could to demoralize Karna, and thereby facilitate his defeat and the victory of the Pandavas. Shalya agreed to this, and promised Yudhishthira the following:

तस्याहं कुरुशार्दूल प्रतीपमहितं वचः
ध्रुवं संकथयिष्यामि योध्दुकामस्य संयुगे
यथा स हतदर्पश्च हततेजाश्च पाण्डव
भविष्यति सुखं हन्तु सत्यमेतद् ब्रवीमि ते
V.8.30, 31

Oh noble king of the Kuru clan, when Karna plans his battle with Arjuna, I will give contrary and damaging advice. This will destroy his pride and confidence, and he will be easily slain in battle. In this I speak the truth.

Shalya kept his word to Yudhishthira. He was asked to drive Karna's carriage, and while doing so, he constantly worked to demoralize Karna and did everything in his power to disrupt his concentration. Even as Karna faced the battle with Arjuna that he had prepared for much of his life, and a battle that would be unto death for one of them, he found his own charioteer repeatedly questioning his prowess, comparing it with and belittling it against the power of the enemy, and also pointing to his lowly birth. For example, in the run-up to the battle, Shalya advised 'the son of a charioteer' that Karna's challenging Arjuna would be tantamount to a jackal challenging a lion, a foolish child poking a king cobra in its hole with a stick, a rabbit goading an elephant, a sparrow competing with an eagle in the art of flying, a frog croaking at a thundercloud, and a dog snarling from the precincts of the house at a tiger roaming freely outside.

Karna, understandably, did not take well to these insults, but he responded with dignity. For example, he admitted that he was well aware of Arjuna's ability to vanquish both men and gods, and yet he was going to fight him. He had also seen through Shalya's ruse in befriending Duryodhana and serving as Karna's charioteer.

अप्रियो य: परुषो निष्ठुरो हि क्षुद्र: क्षेप्ता क्षमिणश्चाक्षमावान्
हन्यामहं तद्दृशानां श्तानि क्षमाम्यहं क्षमया कालयोगात्
अवोचस्त्वं पाण्डवार्थे प्रियाणि प्रघर्षयन् मां मूढवत्पापकर्मन्
मय्याजैवे जिह्नगतिर्हितस्त्वं मित्रद्रोही सप्तपदं हि मित्रम्
VIII.29. 20, 21

Dislikeable, cruel, unkind, mean-minded and unforgiving individuals (like you) are wont to criticize forgiving and kind individuals (like me). I could destroy hundreds of such individuals, but time and fate lead me to follow the path of forgiveness at this hour.

You have spoken unkind words to me, you nefarious fool, and have spoken words of praise towards Arjuna only to undermine me (and my morale). Walking seven steps together establishes a friendship, but your malicious and cunning thinking make you a treacherous betrayer of friends.

Karna went on to remind Shalya of the dark and dire times that Duryodhana was facing on the battlefield. As his loyal friend, Karna was doing everything in his power to help his cause. But Shalya, even though he had professed loyalty to Duryodhana, was doing everything to undermine his victory. Karna thus stated: Every syllable of the word 'friend' is embodied in who I am, while every syllable of the word 'enemy' manifests itself in you.

Shalya's perfidious behaviour towards those he publicly claimed to serve, the Kauravas, has received considerable condemnation from commentators. Gurcharan Das, for example, writes that despite his many excesses (which Krishna recounts mercilessly at the time of Karna's death, thereby persuading Arjuna to fire his arrow at a vulnerable Karna), 'Karna is remembered for his friendship and loyalty and Shalya is remembered as "the enemy with the face of a friend"... when Gandhari surveys the corpses on the Kurukshetra battlefield at the end of the war, Shalya's tongue is being eaten by birds.'[27] While Das is right on the question of morality—Shalya's treachery was indeed reprehensible, especially when contrasted with Karna's extreme loyalty and heroism—a different perspective emerges when we examine Shalya's behaviour in terms of coalitions.

Shalya's actions derive mainly, and perhaps even solely, from his desire to assist the Pandavas. Karna is a formidable opponent for Arjuna, and his defeat is seen to be virtually impossible. When he is asked by Yudhishthira to pursue the Pandava cause by serving as Karna's charioteer, his treachery towards Karna is extreme, but so is his loyalty towards his real allies and friends. In fact, from the perspective of the Pandavas and Shalya himself, he has never defected from the original bloc at all; he has simply used access to the Kauravas to further promulgate their cause. And Shalya's loyalty to the Pandavas— which requires him to play his deceitful game with Duryodhana and Karna—is far from costless. When Karna is killed in the war, the mantle of leadership passes on to Shalya. He fights from the Kaurava side with courage and

[27] Das 2009.

valour—against his own kinsmen this time—and dies in the war. Shalya's underlying loyalty to the Pandavas thus costs him his life, and also requires him to pay the difficult moral price of being judged a traitor to Karna, and further battle with the Pandavas from the side of the enemy. Seen from this perspective, Shalya comes out looking pretty strong as fundamentally a Pandava loyalist (for whom destroying the Kauravas' chief weapon—Karna—justified all means, including treachery towards Karna and subsequent leadership of the Kaurava army). Duryodhana emerges as a somewhat naïve optimist, who foolishly came to believe that his hospitality would win over the brother of the second wife of Pandu, Madri, and that an issue-based coalition would trump the familial loyalty of the Pandava bloc.

4.3.3. Ashwasena and Karna: A failed coalition

Recall the story of the prince of snakes, Ashwasena, who sought an alliance with Karna at the time of the war, even as Karna and Arjuna were engaged in ferocious battle. We discussed this story in Chapter 2 with reference to the use of the strict distributive strategy. The story is also important, however, in shedding light on the limited benefits that issue-based coalitions yield in the Mahabharata.

To recap, Ashwasena's mother was killed by Arjuna when the Pandavas set fire to the Khandava forest. Driven by the desire to avenge his mother's death, Ashwasena entered Karna's quiver (unknown to Karna), and, having wrapped himself around Karna's arrow, reinforced the powerful Nagaastra weapon that Karna fired at Arjuna. The arrow, however, was inaccurate in its aim, and Karna, despite having received due warning from Shalya that the arrow needed to be realigned, firmly refused to correct his original aim. The arrow thus missed its target; with Ashwasena's labours, it was able to knock off the diadem that adorned Arjuna's head, but did no real damage to Arjuna himself. At this point, Ashwasena slithered back to Karna's carriage, and sought an alliance with him.

Ashwasena then urged Karna to fire a weapon again, this time with the knowledge that the mighty snake would be wrapped around it; the snake would thus help in slaying their common enemy. A dialogue between Karna and Ashwasena ensued:

स एवमुक्तो युधि सूतपुत्रस्तमब्रवीत को भवानुग्ररूपः
नागोसब्रवीद् विध्दिकृतागसं मां पार्थेन मातुर्वधजातवैरम्
VIII.90.46 (Gita Press Edition)

Hearing him speak thus, Karna asked the snake of such powerful and ferocious form who he really was. The snake replied, 'I am one who has suffered a grave injustice from Arjuna. He is my enemy because he killed my mother.'

What Ashwasena effectively proposed was an issue-based coalition, which was to be united by the single, brave, and immediate cause of destroying their common enemy, Arjuna. Karna, however, turned down the snake's offer on two grounds: Karna did not desire a victory in the battle that was won on the strength of others, and in any case he would not shoot the same arrow twice. Karna preferred to fight his battle with Arjuna, and, assuring Ashwasena of his own intent and ability to destroy Arjuna, advised him to go on his way. Ashwasena was angered and distraught:

इत्येवमुक्तो युधि नागराज: कर्णेन रोषादसहंस्तस्य वाक्यम्
स्वयं प्रायात् पार्थवधाय राजन् कृत्वा स्वरूपं विजिघांसुरुग्र:
VIII.90.49 (Gita Press Edition)

On hearing such a disappointing reply on the battlefield from Karna, the prince of snakes could not tolerate the insult. Revealing his true and most ferocious form, he decided to attack and kill Arjuna all by himself.

Assuming the shape of an arrow, the snake moved as a blaze of fire and ferocity in the sky. Krishna warned Arjuna of Ashwasena's vengeful intent towards him, and counselled him to slay the snake immediately. Arjuna's arrow struck Ashwasena with flawless accuracy, and the prince of snakes fell to the ground, his body broken into a thousand pieces.

Karna's refusal to accept Ashwasena's offer of an issue-based alliance not only cost the snake his life, but also proved fatal for Karna. Together, Ashwasena and Karna could have defeated Arjuna in battle; Karna alone, and under the curse of Parashurama, found himself vulnerable and unable to defend himself. By the end of the day, both Ashwasena and Karna were killed by Arjuna's hand.

4.3.4. Insights for negotiation

The stories in this section strongly support the arguments made in Section 4.1 regarding the preference of Indian negotiators to balance rather than band-wagon, and also to prefer blocs over issue-based alliances. It offers a third additional insight regarding the importance of an honour code, which was discussed with reference to the stories of Section 4.2. Finally, we also observe a limited but potentially interesting insight into formal versus informal coalitions.

First, all three stories reinforce the preference of the protagonists for bloc-type coalitions, the tendency to reject issue-based coalitions, and the failure of issue-based coalitions when they are attempted at all. Karna's refusal to change sides, even when his birth mother tries to persuade him through the use of both moral and strategic arguments, is an example of his steadfast commitment to the Kaurava bloc. Shalya's attempts to constantly demoralize Karna—even though he had professed loyalty to Duryodhana—are an example of his commitment to use all means necessary to support the Pandavas, with whom he was originally allied. In contrast, Duryodhana's attempt to form an issue-based coalition with Shalya by showering him with unsurpassed hospitality comes at a very heavy price: although Shalya honours his promise of leading the Kaurava army, he does so only after destroying Karna (not only the most formidable warrior on the Kaurava side but also Duryodhana's most loyal friend). In any case, issue-based coalitions are seldom the norm. For instance, Ashwasena's proposal for a pragmatic coalition—focused on the single issue of destroying Arjuna, the mortal enemy of both Karna and Ashwasena—is rejected by Karna. Both Ashwasena and Karna thus end up fighting Arjuna independently, and both get killed as a result.

Second, we also find evidence of the preference of protagonists for opting for balancing rather than bandwagoning, even in wartime. We see this most strongly in Karna's case, when he is presented with strong incentives for bandwagoning. Kunti reveals to him that the Pandavas are his brothers, and points out that an alliance between Arjuna and Karna would allow the duo to achieve remarkable feats and ensure their invincibility. Besides, the Pandavas will welcome their eldest brother and install him as the king. The sun god further confirms that Kunti's proposed course of action will work to Karna's advantage. Later on in the epic, Karna is approached by Lord Krishna and urged to switch sides. Karna himself indicates that he has foresight that the Pandavas will win the war; the balance of power will sooner or later fall heavily on the side of the Pandavas. Nonetheless, Karna prefers to balance against his brothers, who have (ignorant of his real identity) derided and insulted him in the past, and stays unwavering in his allegiance to the Kauravas, who have supported him in his time of need and whose debt he intends to pay with his death.

Third, akin to the stories of Section 4.2, we find the recurrence of honour codes of heroism. We see this strongly in Karna's rejection of a host of pay-offs (which range from maternal blessing and reuniting with his long-lost family to glory through an invincible alliance with Arjuna and kingship after the Pandava victory), and his persistent loyalty to Duryodhana. Here the code seems to be driven by the debt of gratitude.[28] Interestingly, Shalya—usually

---

[28] Note that our tragic hero is making quite a different trade-off from one that was made by another tragic hero—Achilles. Achilles had the choice of a short life of renown or a long one of obscurity. He chose the former. In Karna's case, he is making a choice between glory and almost certain death and defeat (if he stays with the Kauravas) versus glory and a prosperous and happy life (if he switches to the side of the Pandavas). The source of glory by fighting on the side of the Kauravas derives from being a loyal soldier; the source of glory by fighting on the side of the Pandavas derives from fighting on the side of Dharma, the gods, and his own family. Karna, bound by his honour code, chooses the former.

We are grateful to Sir Geoffrey Lloyd for a valuable discussion in Darwin College on the different cultures of heroism in ancient times.

regarded as the opposite of Karna, that is, the treacherous Shalya versus the loyal Karna—also has an honour code, where his loyalty to his original alliance with the Pandavas subsumes all subsequent promises, and the end of helping to destroy Arjuna's arch-enemy justifies all means.

Finally, the story of Shalya offers us a small but potentially interesting insight into the importance that is attached to informal versus formal alliances. Shalya's bond to the Pandavas is not treaty-based; it derives from kinship and affection for his nephews. In contrast, his agreement with Duryodhana is *relatively* more formal, being based on a notion of diffused reciprocity: in return for Duryodhana's hospitality, he offers him a boon, which Duryodhana chooses to be Shalya's acceptance of leadership of the Kaurava army. This relatively formal alliance, however, is not held to be sacred by Shalya; in fact, Shalya uses his new-found closeness to the Kauravas to win a massive advantage for the Pandavas, his informal but closer allies. Even though he later fights on behalf of the Kauravas, his primary purpose of inflicting unparalleled damage to Kaurava strength and morale via Karna's death is fulfilled. In this case, then, the informal alliance effectively trumps the formal one.

4.4. COALITIONS IN POST-WAR AND RELATED STORIES

Coalition activity does not cease in the aftermath of the war, and we have a plethora of stories related to the central plot in which we see dynamic coalition activity. In this section, we discuss one post-war story involving a key protagonist and two related stories.

4.4.1. Yudhishthira's negotiation with Indra on the entry into heaven

After the Pandavas had won the war, and rebuilt and reigned in the kingdom for 36 years, old age came to afflict them, and the death of their kinsmen (especially Lord Krishna's ascent to heaven) hit them hard. Yudhishthira decided that the time had come for them to renounce their worldly possessions and to make their final journey; the other brothers and Draupadi agreed. The brothers and Draupadi thus made arrangements for their succession and the governance of the kingdom, and began their voyage, performing many austerities and pursuing the path of Yoga. They were initially followed by their people, who tried to persuade them to return to the kingdom. But

gradually their subjects returned to Hastinapur, and the Pandavas and Draupadi proceeded on their own with only a stray dog to accompany them. As the
journey progressed, each member of the Pandava party in turn fell lifeless to
the ground, their deaths being retribution for their individual sins (such as
arrogance, vanity, partiality, and gluttony, among others). Yudhishthira was
the sole member of the Pandava clan to survive the long and arduous journey,
with just the faithful mongrel to keep him company. As the journey reached its
end, Indra arrived in his chariot to bear Yudhishthira to heaven, and instructed him to mount the carriage.

Yudhishthira was distraught at the prospect of reaching heaven without the
company of his brothers and his wife. He thus entreated Indra to allow his
kinsmen to accompany him in the ascent. Indra reassured Yudhishthira that
the other four Pandava brothers and Draupadi, having cast off their earthly
bodies, had already reached heaven, and were awaiting his arrival. Yudhishthira then asked that the dog, who had shown him such long-lasting
devotion, should be allowed to ascend to heaven with him. Indra, however,
refused, claiming that there was no place in heaven for dogs, and referred to
religious rituals that seemed to suggest that sacrifices that dogs observed would
be rendered unsuccessful. Indra argued that Yudhishthira, by abandoning the
dog and entering heaven on his own, would be committing no unkindness.
But Yudhishthira stood firm:

भक्त्यागं प्राहुरत्यंतपापं तुल्यं लोके ब्रह्मवध्याकृतेन
तस्मात्राहं जातु कथंचनादद्य त्यक्ष्याम्येनं स्वसुखार्थी महेन्द्र
XVII.3.11

*It has been said that abandoning him who is devoted to one is a great sin, which
equals the sin of killing a Brahmin. Hence for my own happiness today, there is no
way that I will abandon this dog.*

Indra attempted to persuade Yudhishthira three times to abandon the dog,
offering him moral justification and tempting rewards for pursuing such a
course of action. For instance, he pointed out that Yudhishthira had renounced all material things and attachments; he had even left his dead
brothers on the wayside and carried on with his journey. Why, then, was he
so adamant in refusing to abandon the dog? Yudhishthira responded: 'There
can be neither friendship nor enmity between the living and the dead. When
Krishna and my brothers died, there was nothing that I could do to bring them
back to life. Hence I abandoned them, but I stood firmly by them throughout
their lives. I have no doubt that to abandon a creature who is devoted to one is
as reprehensible as frightening someone who seeks one's protection, killing a
woman, robbing a Brahmin, or injuring a friend.' No amount of argumentation and reasoning by Indra could sway Yudhishthira's mind: he chose to stay
united with his loyal and mute friend, rather than reunite with his family in
heaven and bask in eternal happiness.

At this point, the stray dog was transformed, revealing itself to be Dharma, who had put Yudhishthira to his final test. And Yudhishthira, the son of Dharma, had excelled. Dharma recalled other instances of Yudhishthira's generosity and virtue, and then stated:

अयं श्वा भक्त इत्येकं त्यक्तो देवरथस्त्वया
तस्मात् स्वर्गे न तुल्यः कश्चिदस्ति नराधिप
XVII.3.20

Once again, believing, 'This dog is devoted to me,' you have refused the celestial chariot of Indra that would have taken you to heaven. This proves that there is no king comparable to you in heaven (in nobility and virtue).

Yudhishthira was duly rewarded with the place of a celestial in heaven. The story is a very strong illustration of the virtue that the Mahabharata attaches to coalition loyalty, and the rewards that such loyalty generates.

4.4.2. Rama and Sugriva

Dark times had fallen on Lord Rama, an avatar of Vishnu and the key protagonist of the Ramayana (an epic in its own right, but one whose story also forms a part of the Mahabharata). His stepmother plotted, and successfully persuaded the ageing king to send Rama—the firstborn and also the true and worthy heir to the throne—into exile, and crown her own son, Bharata, as the regent. Rama obeyed, and his devoted wife and brother, Sita and Lakshmana, accompanied him into exile. Whilst in exile, Sita was abducted by the powerful demon king Ravana. Rama's need for reliable allies was great if Ravana's massive military force was to be defeated and the rescue operation was to be successful. As Rama and Lakshmana launched into their search for Sita, they befriended a Gandharva, and in return were given some valuable information that would assist their coalition formation. The Gandharva advised the two brothers to go to the lake of Pampa and to meet Sugriva and his four counsellors. 'Recount to him the cause of your sorrow. He will empathize with your plight, and he will give you assistance.'

Sugriva's position was indeed akin to Rama's. As a result of a fraternal feud, Sugriva's brother Bali had appropriated the throne and also Sugriva's wife, and had banished Sugriva from the kingdom. Rama was persuaded of Sugriva's innocence, and agreed to assist him by killing Vali, thereby reinstating him as king and also reuniting him with his wife. In return, Sugriva promised Rama the backing of his security intelligence and army, which would be tasked with locating Sita's whereabouts and then fighting alongside Rama and Lakshmana. Both sides kept their sides of the bargain.

इत्युक्त्वा समयं कृत्वा विश्वास्य च परस्परम्
अभ्येत्य सर्वे किष्किन्धाम् तस्थुर्युध्दाभिकांक्षिण:
III.264.15

In this way promising each other their mutual trust, they all went to Kishkindha town with the intention to fight a battle.

Vali was a fierce opponent, but one who could not escape the prowess and skill of Rama. Sugriva's fortunes were duly restored, and he came to Rama's assistance, first by sending out his spies and securing news of Sita, and then by inflicting extreme and devastating losses on Ravana's demonic armies. The alliance served both parties well, and fulfilled the goals that both Rama and Sugriva had started out with. The alliance, moreover, did not end with the war. Particularly important was the personal alliance that was formed between Rama and Hanuman. Hanuman was one of Sugriva's counsellors, who had accompanied the overthrown king into exile. Hanuman was a supremely intelligent and mighty monkey god, believed by many to be an incarnation of Lord Shiva. His contribution to the war effort was consistently vital, and at several stages proved the key to securing victory over Ravana. Both Rama and Hanuman are worshipped across India even today, and the long-lasting—indeed eternal—alliance between the two provides the subject of many inspirational songs and hymns.

This story is interesting for two reasons. First, at least parts of the alliance outlive the original purpose, for example through the long-lasting friendship between Rama and Hanuman. Second, although Rama's need for allies and an army is urgent and great, he does not take the easy route of trying to secure an alliance with Vali—a powerful king who is already in power—and instead seeks the friendship of the exiled and dethroned Sugriva. In other words, Rama clearly avoids the path of bandwagoning. While there may be a strategic logic to his choice about which we could speculate (for instance, Rama's friendship would be more valued by the weak and downtrodden, and rewarded with complete loyalty), there is a strong moral content to his choice. The Gandharva who has advised Rama of the virtue of an alliance with Sugriva suggests empathy to be a uniting cause. But there is something even bigger than empathy at work. When Vali taunts Sugriva for attempting to battle with him, and offers him the chance to escape with his life, Sugriva addresses him, but does so with the intent of informing Rama of the real situation and his resulting plight:

हृतदारस्य मे राजन्हृराज्यस्य च त्वया
किं नु जीवितसामर्थ्यमिति विध्दि समागतम्
III.264.29

Oh King, you have robbed me of my kingdom and my wife. Under these conditions, where can I find the will or strength to live? This has been my thought and I am here to court my death—assume that this is the reason why I am here today.

It appears that Rama is morally persuaded by Sugriva's cause, and thus chooses to help him over Vali.

4.4.3. The gods plan the downfall of Nahusha

Nahusha was a king who, through the performance of many austerities and penances, had acquired great power. With his increasing power came much hubris. He drove away the king of the gods—Indra—and usurped his throne, took to insulting the wisest and noblest sages by forcing them to draw his carriage, and perpetrated many acts of wickedness. His reign attracted much resentment, from the gods and sages alike.

The gods knew that some action was necessary. Individually, however, even the gods feared Nahusha, for his power derived from a boon that he had received from Brahma: any man or god who came within Nahusha's sight would also become subject to his control. Thus Brihaspati reported to Indra, who had gone into hiding:

तेजोहरं दृष्टिविषं सुघोरं मा त्वं पश्येन्नहुषं वै कदाचित्
देवाश्च सर्वे नहुषं भयार्ता न पश्यन्तो गूढरूपाश्चरन्ति
V.16.26

His eyes are full of poison and he consumes the energy of all those who look him in the eye. The gods are terrified of him, and they move around only in secret and avoid gazing on him.

But through collective and coordinated action (that is, through a coalition), they would stand a chance.

The coalition that they came up with to defeat Nahusha was a product of different agendas and trade-offs logrolled together. Together, the gods would fight and make specific gains that each valued individually. Indra would regain his kingdom in heaven. In return for their assistance, Indra would grant the gods their own dominions. Thus Kubera acquired sovereignty over the Yakshas and wealth, Yama acquired sovereignty over the underworld, and Varuna acquired sovereignty over the seas. Agni, the fire god, was promised a share in all sacrifices. The details of these trade-offs appear in the shlokas below.

त्वं चेद्राजन्नहुषं पराजयेस्तद्वै वयं भागमहाम शक्र
इन्द्रोसब्रवीद्भवतुभवान्नपां पतिर्यम: कुबेरश्च महाभिषेकम्
सम्प्राप्नुवन्त्वद्य सहैव तेन रिपुं जयामो नहुषं घोरदृष्टिम्
तत: शक्रं ज्वलनोसप्याह भागं प्रयच्छ मह्यं तव साह्यं करिष्ये
तमाह शक्रो भविताग्ने तवापि ऐन्द्राग्न्यो वै भाग एको महाक्रतौ
V.16.30, 31, 32

[All the gods addressed Indra as follows:] Oh Indra, if you are ready to defeat King Nahusha with our assistance, then we should also be allowed to share the benefits of the yagya [or fire-sacrifice]. Indra replied, Lord Varuna, may you be the master

of water. May Yama and Kubera also take up their positions (and establish their sovereignty over the domains of death and wealth). Together, our coalition of the gods will secure victory over Nahusha of the terrible gaze. Then Agni said to Indra, please allow me a share in the fire-sacrifice, I will also help in the effort. Indra agreed, stating that Indra and Agni together will have a joint share of the great sacrifice.

This coalition, at face value, is an issue-specific coalition, created to defeat Nahusha. In fact, it shows the classic logrolling that underpins a bloc-type coalition: the defeat of Nahusha was the primary purpose only for Indra, whereas the other gods, by supporting this cause, derived individual-specific gains. It is also worth bearing in mind that in the great wars of the past, and when facing great and terrible dangers, the gods had always allied together on one side (putting any internal bickering aside), while the demons grouped together on the other side. Hence, in terms of longer-lasting commitments too, this coalition was a bloc of like-minded parties.[29]

4.4.4. Insights for negotiation

The three stories in this section illustrate three interesting themes: a dominant tendency against bandwagoning (even if this means that one would end up with weak allies); a strong resistance to defection (even if offered tempting alternatives); and a willingness to engage in logrolling and trade-offs to keep the coalition united (which is usually a characteristic of bloc-type coalitions).

The first insight—resistance to bandwagoning and standing by weaker allies—is illustrated most powerfully in the first two stories, and at least weakly in the third. Yudhishthira shows himself willing to renounce even the eternal joy afforded by heaven, and thereby flout the advice of Indra himself. Instead, he prefers to stand by the stray dog that has accompanied him on his journey. Similarly, at no point is Rama tempted to join forces with Vali, the powerful monkey-king who sits on the throne and has the vast armies whose help Rama must secure to rescue his wife. Instead, he throws in his lot with the banished Sugriva, despite the fact that Sugriva has little by way of wealth or military capacity to offer Rama. This coalition strategy of allying with the weak, and resisting bandwagoning, is well rewarded in both cases. In the third case, while we do not see evidence of allying with the weak, we also do not see evidence of bandwagoning. For instance, neither the gods nor the sages are tempted to join forces with Nahusha. We are told that until they hatch their plans to facilitate

---

[29] As it turned out, Indra and his allies did not actually need to put their plan into action after all, for the two sages—Agastya and Bhrigu—formed a coalition of their own, and defeated Nahusha with a curse whereby he was transformed into a snake and fell to the earth.

his downfall they live in fear of him, but they certainly do not consider allying with him.

Second, the first two stories also illustrate the reluctance of protagonists to defect from a coalition. Yudhishthira, despite all the moral arguments that he is offered by Indra as well as some very tempting carrots, refuses to abandon the stray dog that he regards as his faithful ally. Rama is admittedly not made any counter-offers to trigger defection by Vali; but the fact that Vali already has a title and standing army does not tempt Rama at any point to change sides, switching from Sugriva to Vali. Both Yudhishthira and Vali reap considerable benefit from their loyalty to their allies.

Third, the latter two stories demonstrate the importance of logrolling in coalition formation and maintenance. Sugriva and Rama have different individual goals to pursue, even though each empathizes with the plight of the other as kings in exile. They engage in issue linkage, however, through the logrolling of their particular concerns into the agenda of the coalition, as is the practice with bloc-type coalitions. The gods similarly agree to ally with Indra in order to help him regain his kingdom from Nahusha, but in return secure several other gains from Indra that are specifically valuable to each of them as individuals with different interests.

4.5. CONDITIONS FOR EXCEPTIONS

The previous sections illustrate the proclivity of protagonists in the Mahabharata to avoid bandwagons and prefer balances, and form bloc-type rather than issue-based coalitions that involve a good deal of logrolling of agendas. Only one of the stories sheds any light on the preference for formal versus informal coalitions, and indirectly suggests that formal alliances are trumped by informal ones (hence, although Shalya has agreed to assist Duryodhana in the war, he continues to act in ways to advantage the Pandavas with whom he is directly related). In this section, we explore instances of deviation from the norm in the stories discussed earlier in this chapter, and also present a new story, which offers a significant case that represents the exception. Deviations from the norm may be expected to show a preference for issue-based coalitions, bandwagons, and formal agreements.

4.5.1. Evidence of deviations from the norm, Sections 4.2–4.4

Deviations from the norm that take the shape of either bandwagoning or a reliance on formal alliances are minimal in the previous stories. In fact, we see a very strong tendency to balance and no examples of bandwagoning in the previous nine stories. The evidence is less clear on formal versus informal coalitions: this does not usually crop up as an issue either way, except for a weak suggestion towards a formal coalition failing in one case. We do find some interesting examples, however, of attempts at forming issue-based coalitions. The main part of this subsection thus focuses on this particular deviation.

Three of the nine stories discussed in the previous sections offer illustrations of issue-based coalitions that were attempted. In all three cases, the attempts fared badly. In Section 4.2.3, we encountered the story of how both Duryodhana and Arjuna approached Lord Krishna to secure his help in the impending war. Arjuna and Krishna were related by the bonds of family and friendship, and a like-mindedness that transcended specific issues. Here lay the roots of a classic bloc-type coalition. In contrast, Duryodhana had been repeatedly reprimanded by Krishna in the past for his many extreme and reprehensible actions. When Duryodhana chose the vast armies of Krishna, he made a pragmatic choice that underpins all issue-based coalitions; Arjuna, when he chose Krishna—even though he had vowed not to engage in any direct combat (and in spite of the fact that the Pandava army was small compared with the Kaurava numbers)—simply chose a trusted friend to now also serve as an ally, and created a bloc. The Arjuna–Krishna bloc worked to the tremendous advantage of the Pandavas: Krishna's presence on the Pandava side was a major cause for their victory. In contrast, Duryodhana's pragmatic crisis diplomacy procured him a large force, but not even the mightiest army could match the might of Krishna.

The attempt to establish another issue-based coalition was discussed in Section 4.3.2. Shalya had always been on the side of the Pandavas, united with them by blood as well as by sympathy for their cause. Duryodhana offered Shalya inordinate hospitality, and asked for Shalya's support in the war. While Shalya agreed to this on paper, he remained committed to helping the Pandavas. The result of this issue-specific coalition was that Duryodhana placed a loyal Pandava—and a traitor to the Kauravas—at the heart of the Kaurava strategic effort. Shalya inflicted heavy damage on the Kaurava prospects for victory in his role as Karna's charioteer. In other words, Duryodhana's issue-based coalition with Shalya generated heavy costs for the Kaurava side.

The third story in which we saw an issue-specific coalition being attempted concerned the unfortunate snake prince Ashwasena, as discussed in Section 4.33. Despite the fact that both Ashwasena and Karna shared the same paramount cause—the destruction of Arjuna—Karna's refusal to embrace this focused and powerful coalition, which Ashwasena had proposed, resulted not only in the failure of their shared goal, but the deaths of both Karna and Ashwasena when each tried to tackle Arjuna on his own.

What the episodes discussed indicate is not only that issue-specific coalitions are infrequently attempted (in contrast to bloc-type coalitions) but also that they generate costs in the few instances when they are attempted. We also see a consistent tendency for characters to balance, and no exceptions are available for bandwagoning in the stories discussed. Neither carrots nor sticks are able to persuade the heroes or villains to bandwagon. In fact, a broader point is evident: switching sides and coalition defection are particularly frowned upon. Finally, we do not see much attention being paid to the formality versus informality of coalitions. There is only one instance, Duryodhana's coalition with Shalya, which suggests some formal reciprocity as an underlying basis for the agreement. Having incurred Duryodhana's debt, Shalya seems to feel obliged to offer him a generous boon, and Duryodhana in turn believes in the credibility of such an offer. This formal coalition ultimately fails, however, and the Pandavas' familial alliance with Shalya trumps his promise to Duryodhana.

4.5.2. An issue-based alliance between the gods and demons

The gods and demons had for aeons constituted two warring blocs. But the quest for Amrita—the drink of immortality—provided an unprecedented cause for unity between these eternal enemies. The ocean would have to be churned to draw out this nectar, and this mammoth task required the gods and demons to join forces. The effort was the result of celestial advice. Balancing behaviour, at least towards the achievement of this goal, would have to be put on hold. This alliance represented the epitome of an issue-based coalition: not only was it focused on a single cause, but it also demonstrated flexibility in the choice of allies for the pursuit of the goal. The gods and demons thus came together. The ocean agreed to the extraction of the nectar in return for his share of it. The gods and demons then sought the permission of the king of tortoises to place the churning staff on his back, to which he agreed. They used an enchanted mountain—Mandara—as the churning staff, and the king of snakes—Vasuki—as the rope with which the churning staff would be turned. The demons held Vasuki by his hood and the gods held him by his tail, and through their joint efforts emerged many wondrous beings and objects from the sea. These included the unleashing of the most dreadful and potent of poisons—Kalakuta—which Shiva consumed to save all three worlds. And then, finally, emerged the much sought-after Amrita.

At first glance, the alliance between the gods and demons seemed to have generated success to mutual advantage. In fact, the quest was far from over, for each side coveted the precious potion solely for itself, and attempted to ensure that the other side would not be able to acquire it. Knowing the intentions of the demons, Vishnu sent the beautiful Maya—literally, the power of illusion—to bewitch them. Spellbound by her charms, the demons surrendered the nectar to her. But soon afterwards, a ferocious battle ensued between the two sides. Vishnu now took the shape of his incarnation—Mohini—a dancer and an enchantress, and once again acquired possession of nectar on behalf of the gods. The gods now speedily drank the life-reinforcing potion, and were able to return to battle with heightened power,[30] and were further assisted in their war efforts by Vishnu. The alliance thus proved to be very temporary, with disastrous consequences for the demons:

तदागतं ज्वलितहुताशनप्रभं भयंकरं करिकरबाहुरच्युत:
मुमोच वै चपलवदुग्रवेगवन्महाप्रभं परनगरावदारणम्
I.17.21

Vishnu's powerful discus blazed as fire itself, and was equipped with the strength to devastate huge cities belonging to the enemy. With arms that were as large and as strong as elephant trunks, and with tremendous speed, Lord Vishnu launched this forceful chakra upon the demons.

ततो मही लवणजलं च सागरं महासुरा: प्रविविशुरर्दिता:सुरै:
वियद्गतं ज्वलितहुताशनप्रभं सुदर्शनं परिकुपितं निशाम्य च
I.17.28

Thus troubled by the gods, and witnessing the discus of fire targeting them with ferocity and speed, the greatest demons sought refuge in the underworld and in the salty sea.

The gods won the battle and, having consumed the nectar, they entrusted the remainder to Vishnu, safely stowed away from the reach of the demons. The coalition had not only disintegrated, but it had produced highly unequal gains and resulted in great loss to one side (leaving it considerably worse off compared with its pre-coalition position).

4.5.3. Insights for negotiation

The stories discussed in this section together illustrate the limited utility of issue-based coalitions, and indeed the losses that they might generate. Formation of blocs remains the dominant behaviour pattern, and defection from a coalition (which in some cultures may well be hailed as a sign of pragmatism and flexibility) is frowned upon.

---

[30] Only one demon—Rahu—was able to disguise himself and partake of the drink in the company of the gods. But his ruse was discovered, and Vishnu slashed his body in half with his discus.

The stories have little to say about formal versus informal coalitions, except for the limited insights offered by the story of Shalya. Here, a relatively formalized issue-based coalition is trumped by intrinsic bloc loyalty.

Examples of bandwagoning behaviour are hard to come by. The story of Amrita provides one of the few examples of an issue-based coalition in the Mahabharata, and also an instance when the dominant strategy of balancing is abandoned. It shows us that if the prize of collective action is overwhelmingly high (in this case, it is immortality), even long-standing enemies, who have constantly tried to sway the balance of power in their favour, may converge to form an issue-based coalition. But the chances of being double-crossed by one's new-found allies are high in such a situation. In this case, the demons ended up with the sucker's payoff, while the gods rendered themselves doubly indestructible by securing immortality for themselves and also depriving the demons (their sworn enemies but erstwhile allies) of it. The positions, however, could just as easily have been reversed: the demons had been just as intent upon securing their advantage over the gods, but were outwitted. Issue-based coalitions may thus emerge, but the dominant behaviour patterns of balancing and abiding by underlying bloc loyalties will be difficult to escape for either side. To do well out of such a coalition would require constant vigilance (given the likelihood of being double-crossed) and guile (to outsmart the other side).

4.6. COALITION STRATEGIES OF A RISING INDIA

In this section, we investigate the coalition behaviour of a rising India, focusing specifically on two regimes that show us particularly important variations across each other and over time—trade and the nuclear non-proliferation regime. We conduct this analysis in light of the lessons derived from the Mahabharata, and examine the persistence of continuities in India's coalition behaviour as well as the changes that have emerged as India's power has risen. Before doing so, we provide a recap of the main insights of the Mahabharata concerning coalition behaviour.

1. Bandwagoning is the strategy that is avoided at almost all costs, with heroes and villains alike showing a tendency to prefer balancing, even if this means that the only alternative available to them will be to ally with very weak parties.
2. Coalitions are mainly of the bloc type, bound by strong ideational links (and an appeal to familial bonds, Dharma, loyalty, and other such values), and transcend specific issue areas.

3. When issue-based coalitions are attempted (infrequently in comparison with bloc-type coalitions), they are usually a costly enterprise and generate poor returns.

4. Defections are rare, often regarded as a violation of an honour code. This, along with the inclination for bloc-type coalitions, contributes to considerable coalition stability (and, by implication, some negotiation inflexibility).

5. Interesting distinctions are drawn between categories of allies, which seem to depend on pre-existing friendships and familial loyalties. It is noteworthy that familial bonds do not necessarily or consistently trump those of friendship.

6. The negotiations of the Mahabharata do not tell us much directly about the importance attached to the formality or informality of coalitions. One story suggested that when choosing between a relatively recent and formal coalition versus a longer-standing but unstated understanding with an informal ally, the latter will prevail. The other insights, relating to categories of friendships and the honour code indirectly, reinforce the idea that older bloc-type alliances are likely to prove more reliable than newly formalized coalitions.

4.6.1. International trade

On issues relating to international trade, India historically displayed considerable leadership and activism in coalition formation and maintenance. In the early years of the GATT, it banded together with other developing countries, and lobbied hard—with a high degree of consistency—for their joint cause of developing country exceptionalism. In 1954, the Indian delegate to the GATT made the case for special treatment for developing countries; in 1960, the Indian delegate S. T. Swaminathan similarly argued: 'We feel that the contracting parties have, in the past, not been able to sufficiently come to grips with the problems of expanding the trade of less developed countries... It would, in our view, be a thousand pities if the concentration of pressures from imports on certain limited sectors of production in particular countries leads to a general reversal of the efforts to expand international trade and, in particular, exports from the less-developed countries.'[31] India was a leading member of the Informal Group of Developing Countries in the GATT,[32] and also participated actively in the UN system via the G77. It was

---

[31] GATT, L/1229, 20 June 1960.

[32] Evidence of this activism can be found at Stanford's GATT Digital library, see <http://gatt.stanford.edu>, under the search terms of 'Minutes of the Informal Group of Developing Countries'. India was an active part of this group, and the archive generates 611 minuted

instrumental, along with other allies from the developing world, in securing the establishment of the UNCTAD, and then began to push for the New International Economic Order in the 1970s. All these coalitions were bloc-type coalitions, which brought together a group of developing countries and often transcended issue areas. They showed differing degrees of formalization, with formality/informality representing less a conscious strategic choice by India or its allies and more a function of the particular institution that the coalition worked in. The UN and the UNCTAD, for instance, were much more amenable to group diplomacy, and hence India's participation in a more formal coalition that took the shape of the G77. In contrast, the GATT emphasized its member-driven nature and did not recognize group diplomacy, leading to the emergence of informal coalitions.[33] All these coalitions represented attempts by the South to balance the economic dominance of the North, in terms of both process and outcomes.

In the Uruguay Round and the run-up to it, India's coalition strategy and mettle were put to the test. India was a founding and leading member of the G10 coalition—a traditional bloc-type coalition—which attempted to resist the inclusion of the new issues of TRIPS, TRIMs, and services under the umbrella of the GATT. India and its allies opposed the launch of a new round in the first instance, and further argued that no new issues were to be included in any GATT negotiations until the long-standing concerns of developing countries on tariffs and non-tariff barriers to trade were addressed. With hindsight, the chances of success of the G10 coalition were low at the outset and diminished rapidly, even in the pre-negotiation phase of the Uruguay Round (1982–6). The coalition comprised solely developing countries, and its agenda was directly opposed to that of the US (and powerful interest groups within the US). Amidst this polarized standoff, a combination of developed and developing countries began an exploratory exercise to investigate the implications of including the new issues, particularly services, in the GATT. The consultative process eventually crystallized into an issue-based coalition—the Café au Lait group (so-called because it was led by Colombia and Switzerland)—which combined developed and developing countries (and expanded rapidly in membership), and was particularly influential in setting the agenda for the Uruguay Round. The G10 were invited to join this consultative process, but declined, firmly adhering to their position of resistance. As the Uruguay Round progressed, most of the members of the coalition were bought off through bilateral pressures and side payments. Only India resisted these pressures and temptations, continuing to toe the coalition's hard line, until it ended up completely isolated in the endgame.

reports of the group. India was also involved in the collective submissions by 'A Group of Less Developed Countries' through the 1960s, available in the Stanford GATT Archive.

[33] Narlikar 2003.

As a result, it found itself in a position that was considerably worse than it would have been had it shown greater flexibility earlier on in the game.[34] Rajiv Kumar has thus argued, 'India responded as a coalition player and as part of its objective of retaining the leadership role, rather than acting on its own self-perceived or even attributable national concerns.'[35] The G10 was not just a classic bloc-type coalition uniting a group of developing countries, but it was one that served effectively as an attempt to balance, first against the US and subsequently against the dominant coalition that came to comprise the over-whelming majority of the contracting parties to the GATT.

With the creation of the WTO and India's own programme of economic liberalization well under way, Indian negotiators had more cause to support at least certain aspects of trade liberalization. Its stakes in the regime were higher, so we could reasonably expect to see India more willing to bandwagon with the dominant and developed powers (especially if they were also pushing for an agenda of trade liberalization). Given the diversified interests of India's growing economy, and also the relatively greater ability of issue-based coali-tions to make concessions, we could perhaps also reasonably suppose that Indian negotiators would decrease their proclivity to create and maintain blocs. In fact, this was not the case. In 1996, India took the lead in establishing a coalition called the Like Minded Group of Developing Countries (LMG),[36] which resisted the inclusion of a new set of issues, the so-called Singapore Issues (which covered competition policy, government procurement, trade and investment, and trade facilitation). The coalition also argued that devel-oping countries had not secured the expected gains of the Uruguay Round agreements but had had to endure the costs of their implementation; this imbalance needed to be corrected before any new negotiations could take place. The coalition became particularly important in the pre-negotiation phase of the Doha Development Agenda, when it took a firm line against the launch of a new round. In both its membership structure and agenda of resistance, the coalition showed considerable resemblance to the G10. It also showed a similar trajectory to the G10: under duress or under temptation (or a mix of both), all the coalition members gradually defected. India, however, resisted several tempting bilateral offers until it found itself isolated—again—in the endgame at the Doha Ministerial of 2001, and was left with little choice but to cave in.[37] Not only did India help in the creation

---

[34] See Narlikar 2003 on the history of bargaining coalitions in the GATT, particularly the Uruguay Round; and Narlikar and Odell 2006 for India's tendency to end up isolated through its rigid adherence to the collective position.

[35] Kumar 1995, p. 166.

[36] The original members of the LMG were Cuba, Egypt, India, Indonesia, Malaysia, Pakistan, Tanzania, and Uganda. By 1999, the Dominican Republic, Honduras, and Zimbabwe had also joined the coalition.

[37] Narlikar and Odell 2006.

of a bloc-type coalition, but it persisted single-handedly in a heroic effort to stand up against the growing majority outside, when all its allies had band-wagoned with the North. It attracted considerable opprobrium for its role in blocking consensus, and it also found itself in a very poor bargaining position to make any demands when all its allies had jumped ship. The consensus reached was, as a result, not on terms favourable to India. The insights of the Mahabharata certainly resonate here: India as a leader of the LMG showed a strong resistance to bandwagoning, a firm adherence to the collective agenda even at high cost to itself, and a preference for bloc-type rather than issue-based coalitions.

These tendencies have persisted, and perhaps become even more pro-nounced, as India's power has risen. This is somewhat surprising: given India's deeper enmeshment in the global economy, along with the status that it has acquired in the WTO, we might expect India's behaviour to change towards more flexible issue-based coalitions, and at least an avoidance of balancing against the established powers. But India continues to lead coalitions that comprise developing countries, as illustrated in Table 4.1. Its participation in coalitions involving developed countries is limited (an example of this is W52 Sponsors on Geographical Indications), and it does not invest comparable levels of leadership in these coalitions. Its adherence to coalitions involving other developing countries resembles its coalition behaviour in the past, and thus many of the coalitions retain important features of bloc-type coalitions— and also signal balancing rather than bandwagoning behaviour.

That said, there are also some differences between India's coalition behav-iour during the Doha Developed Agenda negotiations versus the days of the GATT and the early years of the WTO. The most notable difference is that these coalitions are 'strong coalitions', that is, coalitions that are able to adhere to their collective positions, and do not collapse in the endgame. The G20 and G33 on agriculture stand out in this regard.[38] Both coalitions were formed at the Cancun Ministerial of 2003 and solely comprise developing countries. The G20 seeks greater access to the agricultural markets of the developed world, while the G33 seeks to protect the agricultural markets of developing coun-tries. Both have displayed great resilience, and resistance to defection and collapse. India, along with other leading members, has played an important role in creating these coalitions, whose strengths lie in several factors. First, growth in the size of the economies of the leading members contributes to the influence that the coalition can exercise. Second, India in particular (along with Brazil) has the ability, and has shown the willingness, to bear responsi-bility towards such coalitions, which includes the costs of sustaining the coalition's unity through information sharing and allowing some free-riding for smaller members. In standing up to the positions taken by the EU and the

---

[38] Narlikar and Tussie 2004; Narlikar 2012.

US on agriculture, these are very much balancing coalitions. And while they are issue specific to the extent that they are focused on agriculture, they retain their fundamental bloc-type nature in bringing together a heterogeneous group of countries, engaging in a logrolling of the individual agendas, and appealing strongly to a shared developmental agenda and a shared identity of members as developing countries. The strength of the coalition comes at a price: these strong blocs find it difficult to make concessions for two reasons: (a) coalition allies may see any attempts by the leaders to initiate concessions as a sign of potential defection; and (b) the outside parties (in this case, the EU and the US) can interpret concessions as a sign of weakness, especially if they are aware of potential divisions within the coalition. Hence, though they are a source of empowerment for their members—the rising powers, including India, as well as smaller countries—their rather limited flexibility and inability to make concessions contribute to making negotiations more deadlock-prone.[39]

It is also important to note that India's adherence to these coalitions is not cost free. Besides the costs associated with the operation of the coalition, for example, information sharing and allowing some free-riding, there are also reputational costs, depending on how 'disruptive' a coalition is seen to be and also the extent to which the hard-line positions of a coalition come to be associated with the leadership of one country. India has willingly borne these costs, often in the face of considerable criticism from multiple sources. In the July 2008 negotiations, when Brazil suggested a compromise with the US on agriculture, the G20's collapse looked imminent. It was averted through India's proactive diplomacy, which ensured that Brazil and other members of the G20 did not offer to make independent concessions to the US and the EU, and maintained the collective position of the coalition. While India was successful in maintaining the coalition, the result was that no concessions could be offered by the coalition or its individual members. Deadlock resulted, the blame for which was placed squarely on India, amidst much international condemnation.

India's coalition behaviour in international trade today thus adds up to the following: India continues to lead coalitions of developing countries, as was its practice in the GATT. These balancing blocs indicate a differentiated notion of responsibility that India bears towards certain groups of countries, and stands at variance with its more reserved notion of international responsibility. These coalitions are a source of empowerment for India and its allies, but they also exacerbate the likelihood of deadlock and thereby also make India susceptible to international opprobrium. India, nonetheless, continues to show commitment to its coalitions. India's strict distributive strategy (as discussed in

---

[39] Narlikar 2009; Kahler 2013.

Chapter 2), proclivity to moralistic framing (Chapter 3), and coalition activism in balancing bloc-type coalitions perversely contribute to stalemate in an organization that India has every interest in sustaining and reinforcing.

It is worth bearing in mind that India's coalitions with other developing countries are not restricted to the WTO. We have seen India form alliances with other rising powers, with the BRICS forum providing the most obvious example, but also the BASIC grouping in climate change negotiations, and IBSA on various areas of economic cooperation between the democratic rising powers. Several of the statements of these groupings continue to emphasize a bloc-type agenda, laden with traditional demands based on developing countries' exceptionalism. For example, the IBSA Statement of 2008 flagged up a fairly traditional bloc-type agenda, which included the call for the reform of various institutions of global governance, attached considerable importance to South–South Cooperation, and emphasized the urgency of reaching Millennium Development Goals (through several means, including the developed countries increasing their financial flows to the developing world).[40] India not only associated itself with the G77 statement on the UN Report on Globalization and Interdependence, but spoke with considerable eloquence on the vulnerabilities of developing countries and the limited gains that had accrued to them from globalization: 'If globalization is to succeed, it must be fair, and benefit the whole of humanity. Developmental considerations must be at its core.'[41] On other economic issues, for instance the reform of the IMF, it has worked closely with other rising powers as part of the BRICS group. In the climate change negotiations, too, we see India adhering to a similar Southern solidarity. The Special Envoy to the PM, in a media briefing, stated the following:

> In terms of the developing country positions, you will find that much of the positions that we have taken on major issues are the same. Otherwise, how do we come up with G77 plus China submissions? . . . All those are the result precisely of that kind of coordination and consultation. In all the multilateral negotiations that we have, our effort is to try and see whether we can mobilise a consensus position amongst the G77 and China because our interests on certainly the broad issues are very much similar. There may be specific issues by the way where our perspectives may be somewhat different. But on the broad issues, the broad approach, I think we are more or less on the same pitch.[42]

More recently, India's role in the BRICS grouping reinforces the story of an attempt at balancing, or at least the avoidance of bandwagoning, with the established powers. In 2012, at the BRICS Summit in New Delhi, the idea of a BRICS Development Bank was proposed. Although the 2013 BRICS summit

---

[40] IBSA Summit Statement 2008.   [41] Natchippan 2008.   [42] Saran 2009.

in Durban did not live up to the hype that had been created around the launch of the new bank, the leaders of the five countries did come up with a statement emphasizing their commitment to a new structure and also the establishment of a 'Contingent Reserve Arrangement' which 'would have a positive precautionary effect, help BRICS countries forestall short-term liquidity pressures, provide mutual support and further strengthen financial stability'.[43] India has also worked closely with the BRICS countries in attempting to modify governance mechanisms and leadership of the international organizations. Of course, not all elements of the relationship between India and the other rising powers are cooperative. India's relationship with China is probably the most difficult in the BRICS group, and both Brazil and India are aware that they are unlikely to receive the support of China and Russia in their bid for a permanent seat on the UN Security Council. Further, all the BRICS countries are involved in a competitive scramble for resources in Africa. And for all the criticisms that they have voiced over the leadership positions of major international organizations, their record of coordinating amongst themselves to put up a joint candidate has been poor. But overall, most of these coalitions, despite the variations in membership as well as competitive elements in the different relationships, appeal to the concerns of developing countries, and suggest the persistence of a bloc-type mentality in a rising India's international negotiations, and balancing efforts against the established powers or the North.

Trade, in other words, is far from unique in terms of India's continued adherence to blocs and balances, even as the country's has risen and it has acquired positions of importance and influence in major multilateral negotiations.

4.6.2. Nuclear non-proliferation

While the international trade regime shows us that India's proclivity for forming balancing blocs persists even as it has acquired a position of increasing importance in the WTO, thereby reinforcing the lessons of the Mahabharata, the nuclear non-proliferation regime offers us some important and different insights into India's coalition behaviour. As discussed in the previous chapters, the NPT is one regime that has been significantly altered to accommodate India. The Indo–US deal on civilian energy cooperation was the necessary precursor to this regime revision (or overhaul or indeed breakdown, depending on how one regards the special waiver for India to which the Nuclear Suppliers Group agreed). After all, the India that was wont to

---

[43] BRICS 2013.

complain of the 'nuclear apartheid' represented by the regime, and fought for the collective rights of non-nuclear weapons states, would have found it very difficult to go it alone and to enter into a special relationship with the US, as the rising India has done. Something has indeed changed, but the significance of this change is perhaps less clear-cut than some mainstream accounts suggest.

Some observers have hailed India's closer relations with the US as a replacement of India's ideology-driven foreign policy with one driven by pragmatism and realism. C. Raja Mohan thus writes, 'As a nuclear power India becomes stronger economically and acquires greater confidence in pursuing its manifest destiny on the global stage, the *moralpolitik* that overwhelmed the public discourse for decades has given some space to *realpolitik*.'[44] While Mohan regards the turn to the US as an exercise in realpolitik, a brief engagement with International Relations (IR) theory would suggest a Constructivist account working at least as persuasively: the attempt by the US to engage with India has triggered a process of socialization, which has led to the transition of the US and India from 'estranged democracies' to 'natural allies'. In coalition terms, then, we could take this argument a step further, to posit that a rising India, as it receives more recognition from the established powers (particularly the US), will switch away from balances to bandwagons, from ideological bloc-type coalitions to issue-specific ones, and will embrace formal alliances more readily than it has ever done before.

A closer inspection reveals India's engagement with the US is at best an exception to the overwhelming predominance—in the Mahabharata, and indeed in recent times across multiple regimes—of the formation of balancing blocs by Indian negotiators. First, it is important to bear in mind that even when India was facing tremendous pressure in the aftermath of the tests, Indian negotiators showed little sign of caving in to the Clinton administration's demands that it sign the NPT and the CTBT. Recall further just how fiercely the deal was contested domestically, as highlighted in the previous chapter. Writing about the process in 2006, Stephen Cohen noted, 'it seems that opposition is stronger, and deeper on the Indian side, even though New Delhi has more to gain than the United States. It is curious that some elements of India's small but feisty strategic community cannot accept "yes" for an answer . . . '.[45] The deal was ultimately approved by the Indian Parliament, but only after a no-confidence vote that the government survived with considerable difficulty (the government's majority was narrow, with 275 in favour and 256 against). Politicians of different political persuasions found common ground in their suspicion of the US (and indeed the West) and their

---

[44] Mohan 2006.   [45] S. Cohen 2006.

opposition to the deal, and carried a substantial popular opinion with them. A good deal of the opposition stemmed from the concern that India, by cosying up to the US, was surrendering its sovereignty and autonomy.

No matter how much gusto with which the India and the US declare each other to be 'natural allies' and 'strategic partners', the bilateral deal is not an alliance. Nor is it seen within India as an initial step towards building an alliance with the US or other established powers. It has also not contributed towards deepening US-India relations in other issue areas, such as trade or climate change.[46] A rising India may refrain somewhat from using the moralizing language of non-alignment, as it was accustomed to do in the Cold War era, and may offer some strategic and pragmatic reasoning at least as partial justification (as argued particularly in the last chapter). But its actions suggest little evidence of bandwagoning with the established powers. The report *NonAlignment 2.0* is illustrative of both the changes that are taking place and also the persistent and important continuities. The report, in keeping with Raja Mohan's argument, uses the language of strategic pragmatism to argue that 'Coalitions will be a lot more contingent and fluid, and will need artful management.'[47] But the fact that the entire argument of the report is framed in terms of a revised non-alignment is strongly indicative of pervasive continuities.

4.7. CONCLUSION

Recall the theoretical insights with which we began this chapter. Realism suggested that as states grew in power they would move from bandwagoning to balancing, while Constructivism suggested that a rising power could be socialized from balancing to bandwagoning. India's behaviour shows quite a different trajectory, however, with balancing coalitions remaining the dominant form even as its power has risen. This balancing is reinforced by the tendency to form bloc-type coalitions, often with other developing countries, whose heterogeneous membership is often united by a shared idea or identity. We do see some strategic pragmatism in coalition formation; but the fact that the US–India nuclear deal remains just that (and no more than that), and also that India's bloc-type balances persist in other issue areas, together suggest that old habits die hard. Overall, balancing

---

[46] A small illustration of how deep-rooted and wide-ranging the differences between the two countries still are can be found in a report for the US Congress by the Congressional Research Service, authored by Kronstadt et al. 2011.

[47] Khilnani et al. 2012.

coalitions continue to dominate India's negotiation behaviour even as its power rises, defections are rare, and blocs with other developing countries remain more the norm than the exception. And while this behaviour is inconsistent with the theory, it is perfectly consistent with the examples of negotiations that we have analysed from the Mahabharata. In fact, most of the examples from the Mahabharata illustrate not only that balancing and bloc-type coalitions are the dominant types, but also that issue-based coalitions result in almost certain failures, while bandwagoning is rarely even attempted (see Table 4.2).

What this chapter indicates, then, is that India's coalition strategy is unlikely to change, even if the occasional language of strategic pragmatism might suggest otherwise. Bloc-type balances are deeply rooted in India's negotiating culture, as are values that frown upon coalition defection and assert the importance of backing allies even if they are weak. Importantly, this does not translate into a crude dichotomy between realpolitik and moralpolitik, or interests and ideas. Rather, it suggests how interests are defined in the first place and then justified. It also does not preclude occasional measures akin to India's 'strategic partnership' with the US, especially when facing extreme conditions and when the pay-offs are particularly high. But if the past and present are anything to go by, then it is likely that at least in the near future, such strategic partnerships with the established powers will be carefully defined and limited, and will form at best exceptions to the norm of balancing blocs.

Recall that there is little new about balancing coalitions and bloc-type coalitions in India's history, so should there be reason for concern now? Our answer is a probable yes, for the following reason. While India constituted and led similar coalitions in the past, it did not enjoy a comparable clout in the first 50 years of its independence. The coalitions that it leads today enjoy more power than ever before, partly because of India's own increased influence as a growth market (along with the parallel increase in the influence of other leaders of such coalitions, such as Brazil), and partly because of India's ability to offer more side payments to allies to preserve the cohesion of the coalition. While such coalitions are a valuable mechanism for preserving pluralism and diversity in the international system, both balancing coalitions and bloc-type coalitions are fundamentally blocking coalitions that are also deadlock inducing. There is a real risk that such coalitions, especially if combined with the effects of India's distributive strategy and moralistic framing, may put further sand in the wheels of the multilateral modes of global governance.

Table 4.1 Coalitions Involving India in the Doha Development Agenda

Coalition	Timing	Membership	Agenda
G20	Formed at the Cancun Ministerial Conference 2003; continues to date.	Original signatories: Argentina, Bolivia, Brazil, Chile, China, Colombia, Costa Rica, Cuba, Ecuador, El Salvador, Guatemala, India, Mexico, Pakistan, Paraguay, Peru, Philippines, South Africa, Thailand and Venezuela.	Opening up of the agricultural markets of developed countries.
G33	Proposal in July 2003; coalition crystallizes at Cancun Ministerial 2003; continues to date.	Antigua and Barbuda, Barbados, Belize, Benin, Botswana, China, Congo, Côte d'Ivoire, Cuba, Dominican Republic, Grenada, Guyana, Haiti, Honduras, India, Indonesia, Jamaica, Kenya, Korea, Mauritius, Madagascar, Mongolia, Mozambique, Nicaragua, Nigeria, Pakistan, Panama, Peru, Philippines, St Kitts and Nevis, St Lucia, St Vincent and the Grenadines, Senegal, Sri Lanka, Suriname, Tanzania, Trinidad and Tobago, Turkey, Uganda, Venezuela, Zambia, Zimbabwe (actually 42 members)	Strategic Product and Special Safeguard Mechanism for developing countries
NAMA-11	Formed just before the Hong Kong Ministerial, 2005; continues to date.	Argentina, Brazil, Egypt, India, Indonesia, Namibia, Philippines, South Africa, Tunisia, Venezuela	Seeks flexibilities to limit market opening for industrial goods.
'W 52' Sponsors	Formed in July 2008 in the run-up to the July Package Negotiations.	Albania, Angola, Antigua and Barbuda, Austria, Barbados, Belgium, Belize, Benin, Botswana, Brazil, Bulgaria, Burkina Faso, Burundi, Côte d'Ivoire, Cameroon, Cape Verde, Central African Republic, Chad, China, Colombia, Congo, Croatia, Cuba, Cyprus, Czech Republic, Democratic Republic of the Congo, Denmark, Djibouti, Dominica, Dominican Republic, Ecuador, Egypt, Estonia, European Union (formerly EC), Fiji, Finland, Former Yugoslav Republic of Macedonia, France, Gabon, Gambia, Georgia, Germany, Ghana, Greece, Grenada, Guinea, Guinea Bissau, Guyana, Haiti, Hungary, Iceland, India, Indonesia, Ireland, Italy, Jamaica, Kenya, Kyrgyz Republic, Latvia, Lesotho, Liechtenstein, Lithuania, Luxembourg, Madagascar, Malawi, Mali, Malta, Mauritania, Mauritius, Moldova, Morocco, Mozambique, Namibia, Netherlands, Niger, Nigeria, Pakistan, Papua New Guinea, Peru, Poland, Portugal, Romania, Rwanda, Saint Kitts and Nevis, Saint Lucia, Saint Vincent and the Grenadines, Senegal, Sierra Leone, Slovak Republic, Slovenia, Solomon Islands, South Africa, Spain, Sri Lanka, Suriname, Swaziland, Sweden, Switzerland, Tanzania, Thailand, Togo, Tonga, Trinidad and Tobago, Tunisia, Turkey, Uganda, United Kingdom, Zambia, Zimbabwe	Sponsors of TN/C/W/52, a proposal for 'modalities' in negotiations on geographical indications (the multilateral register for wines and spirits, and extending the higher level of protection beyond wines and spirits) and 'disclosure' (patent applicants to disclose the origin of genetic resources and traditional knowledge used in the inventions).

Sources: <http://www.wto.org>; Narlikar and Tussie 2004.

Table 4.2 Success and Failure of Coalition Strategy

	Episode	Coalition strategy	Coalition strategy
		- Balancing - Bloc type	- Bandwagoning - Issue based
1.	Karna–Duryodhana	- Balancing—successful (Duryodhana secured a loyal ally against the Pandavas) - Bloc type—success (the coalition transcends issue areas and survives till the bitter end)	- Bandwagoning—not attempted - Issue based—not attempted
2.	Pandavas rescue Duryodhana	- Balancing—not attempted - Bloc type—successful (family loyalty constitutes Yudhishthira's honour code and he is ultimately rewarded for it, even though he incurs short-term losses by surrendering a potential strategic advantage)	- Bandwagoning—not attempted - Issue based—not attempted
3.	and Duryodhana and Duryodhana	- Balancing—not attempted - Bloc type—Success for Arjuna	- Bandwagoning—not attempted - Issue based—failure for Duryodhana
4.	Karna refuses to switch sides	- Balancing—partial success (Karna chooses the wrong side, but dies a hero, renowned for his bravery and loyalty) - Bloc type—partial success (same as above)—bloc united by ties of friendship rather than family	- Bandwagoning—not attempted - Issue based—not attempted
5.	Shalya's betrayal and loyalty	- Balancing—success - Bloc type—success (united by familial bond, Shalya helps the Pandavas) - Informal coalition (i.e. with family)—successful	- Bandwagoning—not attempted - Issue based—failure for Duryodhana (given Shalya's deception) - Formal coalition—failure (family loyalty trumped the agreement with Duryodhana)
6.	Karna–Ashwasena	- Balancing—failure - Bloc type—not attempted	- Bandwagoning—not attempted Issue based—failure (Ashwasena and

(*continued*)

Table 4.2 Continued

Episode	Coalition strategy - Balancing - Bloc type	Coalition strategy - Bandwagoning - Issue based
		Karnla are both killed because of Karna's refusal to form the proposed coalition)
7. Yudhishthira and the dog	- Balancing/resistance to bandwagoning—successful - Bloc type—successful (along with strong resistance to defection)	- Bandwagoning—not attempted - Issue based—not attempted
8. Rama and Sugriva	- Balancing/resistance to bandwagoning—successful - Bloc type—successful	- Bandwagoning—not attempted - Issue based—not attempted
9. The gods and Nahusha	- Resistance to bandwagoning—successful - Bloc type—successful	- Bandwagoning—not attempted - Issue based—not attempted
10. Gods and demons ally over Amrita	- Balancing—not attempted - Bloc type—not attempted	Bandwagoning—not attempted (though balancing put on hold) Issue based—partial success (success for the gods but failure for the demons)
	Balancing/bandwagoning avoidance: 8 attempted (6 successes, 2 partial success, 1 failure, 2 not attempted)	Bandwagoning—not attempted: 10 Issue based: 4 attempted (1 partial success, 3 failures, 6 not attempted)
	Bloc type: 8 attempted (7 successes, 1 partial success, 0 failures, 2 not attempted)	

REFERENCES

Advani, L. K. 2008. Speech of Leader of the Opposition in the Lok Sabha and Bharatiya Janata Party Leader L. K. Advani in the Lok Sabha on the Motion of Confidence in the Council of Ministers. 21 July. In Avtar Singh Bhasin ed., *India's Foreign Relations Documents—2008*. New Delhi: Public Diplomacy Division, Ministry of External Affairs.

BRICS. 2013. Statement by BRICS Leaders on the Establishment of the BRICS-Led Development Bank Durban, South Africa. 27 March. Accessed at <http://www.brics.utoronto.ca/docs/130327-brics-bank.html> on 30 March 2013.

Cohen, Raymond. 2004. *Negotiating across Cultures: International Communication in an Interdependent World*. Washington DC: United States Institute of Peace Press (first edition, 1991).

Cohen, Stephen. 2001. *India: Emerging Power*. Washington DC: Brookings Institution.

Cohen, Stephen. 2006. A Deal Too Far? Washington DC: Brookings Institution. February. Accessed at <http://www.brookings.edu/views/papers/cohens/20060228. pdf> on 9 August 2012.

Das, Gurcharan. 2009. *The Difficulty of Being Good*. New Delhi: Allen Lane.

GATT. 1960. Statement by Mr. S.T. Swaminathan at the Meeting of the CONTRACT-ING PARTIES on 31 May. L/1229, 20 June 1960.

Hurrell, Andrew. 2006. Hegemony, Liberalism and Global Order: What Space for Would-be Great Powers. *International Affairs*, 82:1, January, 1–19.

IBSA Statement. 2008 Delhi Summit Declaration of the 3rd Summit of the India-Brazil-South Africa (IBSA) Dialogue Forum. New Delhi. 15 October. In Avtar Singh Bhasin ed., *India's Foreign Relations Documents—2008*. New Delhi: Public Diplomacy Division, Ministry of External Affairs.

Kahler, Miles. 2013. Rising Powers and Global Governance: Negotiating Change in a Global Status Quo. *International Affairs*. 89:3, May, pp. 711–29.

Khilnani, Sunil, Rajiv Kumar, Pratap Bhanu Mehta, Prakash Menon, Nandan Nilekani, Srinath Raghavan, Shyam Saran, and Siddharth Varadarajan. 2012. *Non Alignment 2.0: A Foreign and Strategic Policy for India in the Twenty-First Century*. New Delhi: Centre for Policy Research. Accessed at <http://www.cprindia.org/sites/default/files/NonAlignment%202.0_1.pdf> on 16 August 2013.

Kronstadt Alan K., Paul K. Kerr, Michael F. Martin, and Bruce Vaughn. 2011. India: Domestic Issues, Strategic Dynamics, and U.S. Relations, Congressional Research Service, CRS Report for Congress, Prepared for Members and Committees of Congress. September. Accessed at <http://www.crs.gov> on 16 August 2013.

Kumar, Rajiv. 1995. The Walk Away from Leadership: India. In Diana Tussie and David Glover eds., *Developing Countries in World Trade*. Boulder, CO: Lynne Rienner.

Kux, Dennis. 1992. *Estranged Democracies: India and the United States, 1941–91*. London: Sage Publications.

Malone, David. 2011. *Does the Elephant Dance?* Oxford: Oxford University Press.

Mehta, Pratap Bhanu. 2009. Still under Nehru's Shadow? The Absence of Foreign Policy Frameworks in India. *India Review*, 8:3, July, 209–33.

Mohan, C. Raja. 2006. *Impossible Allies: Nuclear India, United States and the Global Order*. New Delhi: India Research Press.

Narlikar, Amrita. 2003. *International Trade and Developing Countries: Bargaining Coalitions in the GATT and WTO*. London: Routledge.

Narlikar, Amrita and John Odell. 2006. The Strict Distributive Strategy for a Bargaining Coalition: The Like Minded Group in the World Trade Organization. In John Odell (edited), *Negotiating Trade: Developing Countries in the WTO and NAFTA*. Cambridge: Cambridge University Press.

Narlikar, Amrita. 2009. A Theory of Bargaining Coalitions in the WTO. In Amrita Narlikar and Brendan Vickers eds., *Leadership and Change in the Multilateral Trading System*. Dordrecht: Martinus Nijhoff.

Narlikar, Amrita ed. 2011. Small States in Multilateral Economic Negotiations. Special Centenary Issue. *The Round Table: Commonwealth Journal of International Affairs*, 100:413, April.

Narlikar, Amrita. 2012. Collective Agency, Systemic Consequences: Bargaining Coalitions in the WTO. In Amrita Narlikar, Martin Daunton, and Robert Stern eds., *The Oxford Handbook on the WTO*. Oxford: Oxford University Press.

Narlikar, Amrita and Diana Tussie. 2004. The G20 at the Cancun Ministerial: Developing Countries and their Evolving Coalitions. *The World Economy*, 27:7, July, 947–66.

Natchippan, Sudarasana. 2008. Statement by Member of Parliament and Member of the Indian Delegation to the United Nations Dr E. M. Sudarsana Natchippan on Agenda Item 51—Globalization and Interdependence at the Second Committee of the UNGA. New York. 29 October. In Avtar Singh Bhasin ed., *India's Foreign Relations Documents—2008*. New Delhi: Public Diplomacy Division, Ministry of External Affairs.

Saran, Shyam. 2009. Media Briefing by Special Envoy of Prime Minister on Climate Change Shyam Saran.Pittsburg, September 24. In Avtar Singh Bhasin ed., *India's Foreign Relations Documents—2009*. New Delhi: Public Diplomacy Division, Ministry of External Affairs.

Singh, Jaswant. 2012. NAM in Tehran. Project Syndicate11 September. Accessed at <http://www.project-syndicate.org/commentary/nam-in-tehran-by-jaswant-singh> on 4 January 2013.

Tellis, Ashley. 2012. Can India Revive Non-Alignment? *Yale Global Online*. 28 August. Accessed at <http://yaleglobal.yale.edu/content/can-india-revive-nonalignment> on 4 January 2013.

Walt, Stephen. 1987. *The Origins of Alliances*. Ithaca: Cornell University Press.

5

Time

The Long Shadow of the Past and the Future

Different negotiating cultures hold different conceptions of time. These differences can be a source of misunderstanding and deadlock, but they can also be used strategically to one's advantage and the other's disadvantage. In this chapter, we investigate how the notion of time has affected India's negotiation behaviour in the past, and how it continues to affect the bargaining process and outcomes that involve a rising India.

This chapter, in parallel with the last three, proceeds in seven parts. First, we offer a theoretical overview of the notion of time in bargaining situations. We also present a brief discussion of how some of these theoretical ideas have been applied to India's negotiation behaviour, and provide our own investigation into how far these findings are reflected in India's traditional bargaining. In Sections 5.2 to 5.5, we draw on episodes of the Mahabharata to investigate how the various protagonists were affected by and used the notion of time in different negotiation settings. Section 5.6 examines the continuities and changes in the negotiation behaviour of a rising India, focusing particularly on the idea of time. Section 5.7 provides the conclusion.

5.1. TIME AS A VARIABLE IN INDIA'S NEGOTIATIONS

Amongst the many differences that exist between different negotiation cultures, perhaps one of the most striking is between the Americans and other more ancient societies, and how they approach time and history as variables in the negotiation process. Raymond Cohen's pioneering study, which draws comparisons and contrasts between the American style of negotiation versus that of older cultures (China, Mexico, Egypt, India, and Japan), distinguishes between 'monochronic' and 'polychronic' contexts of time. Cohen's findings are relevant to our study:

Americans ... are mostly concerned with addressing immediate issues and moving on to new challenges, and they display little interest in (and sometimes little
knowledge of) history. The idea that something that occurred hundreds of years
ago might be relevant to a pressing problem is almost incomprehensible ... In
marked contrast, the representatives of more antique societies possess a pervasive
sense of the past, of the long run. They are likely to harbour enduring memories
of their treatment at the hands of the United States and the West in general. This
preoccupation with history, deeply rooted in the consciousness of ancient civilizations, cannot fail to influence diplomacy. Past humiliations for these societies
(which are highly sensitive to any slight on their reputations) are not consigned to
the archives but continue to nourish present concerns.[1]

Cohen goes on to investigate the applicability of this insight in relation to
different cultures, and provides several examples of 'India's "geologic sense of
time" and ready acceptance of delay'. For example, recounting the experiences
of Walter Bollinger, the United States Agency for International Development
(USAID) director in India in the early 1990s, Cohen writes: 'Indians, with
their 3000-year perspective, are not worried if their procedures do not fit into
the US time frame ... he found himself labouring under a strong sense of
urgency, and was deeply frustrated by Indian bureaucratic politics and their
serene assumption that they had all the time in the world.'[2]

Stephen Cohen's research reinforces this argument and adds to it. He points
to the strong sense of history that pervades Indian negotiators and politicians:
'Despite foreign policy failures and much debate over tactics, the Indian elite
holds fast to a vision of national greatness ... the historical memory of a great
Indian civilization has practical consequences. Indian officials believe they are
representing not just a state but a civilization. Few state-civilizations are
India's equal. Believing that India should be accorded deference and respect
because of its intrinsic civilizational qualities, many Indian diplomats and
strategists are wary of having to depend upon states that do not appreciate
India's special and unique characteristics.'[3] In this historical and civilizational
vision of self-perception, Cohen traces the 'Indian propensity to lecture other
powers, great and small' (as discussed in detail in Chapter 3 of this book). But
it also translates into a very strong sense of the *longue durée*, as was indicated
in the previous quote by the USAID director, and indeed suggested by Stephen
Cohen's own statement: 'India can wait until the rest of the world comes
around to its way of seeing things, or at least acknowledges India's right to do
things "its way."'[4]

How Indian negotiators approach their country's past also affects how they
regard its future, and particularly striking in both Raymond Cohen's and
Stephen Cohen's analyses is the willingness that Indian negotiators display

---

[1] R. Cohen 2004, pp. 35–6.   [2] R. Cohen 2004, p. 180.   [3] S. Cohen 2001, p. 52.
[4] S. Cohen 2001, p. 52.

to accept delays in comparison with their Western counterparts. They offer different mechanisms to explain this willingness. For Raymond Cohen, the primary mechanism relates to the sense of a historical perspective, which is common to many traditional societies: 'in the overall scheme of things, where the individual counts for so little in the face of much greater, inexorable forces, what could be more futile than urgency?'.[5] Negotiators with an eye on the 3,000-year-old history of their civilization are unlikely to be swayed by the pressure of immediate deadlines. Stephen Cohen highlights another mechanism, and attributes the patience of Indian negotiators to the fact that the Indian system is 'agreement averse'. Neither domestic politics nor bureaucratic compulsions can easily corner a negotiator to accept an agreement that is not on India's preferred terms, and 'Indian diplomats do not put their careers at risk by failing to reach an agreement.'[6]

Jeswald Salacuse reinforces the argument about timing. He gives the example of a contract between the state government of Maharashtra and the Dabhol Power Company—a subsidiary of ENRON—that was cancelled in the 1990s on the grounds that it had been concluded in 'unseemly haste'. Efforts to expedite the negotiation process through fast-track procedures were viewed by important segments of the public as an indication of the failure of the government to protect the public interest. In his survey of 12 nationalities, Salacuse found that Indians had the largest percentage of people who considered themselves 'to have a low sensitivity to time'.[7]

Aggregating these findings, we would expect India's negotiating culture to a) involve a deep-rooted sense of history, which would manifest itself most directly through references in speeches but also through other mechanisms (including, as Stephen Cohen has suggested, the seriousness with which India takes its 'global mission', and an expectation that India will be valued for its historically derived 'special and unique characteristics') and b) a readiness to accept delay rather than conclude a seemingly hasty agreement. Both these approaches to time in the negotiation process are likely to make it easier for India to walk away from a negotiation. They also reinforce the tendencies highlighted particularly in Chapters 2 and 3, that is, the use of a strict distributive strategy (that the resistance to the pressures of short-term deadlines reinforces) and the inclination to moralize (that proud historical traditions buttress). In the remainder of this section, we investigate the extent to which these trends were borne out in India's negotiation behaviour in the first few decades after independence.

There is no dearth of speeches by Indian public figures that emphasize their country's historic greatness. Just one powerful illustration is to be found in Jawaharlal Nehru's speech to India's Constituent Assembly, which remains

---

[5] R. Cohen 2004, p. 34.   [6] S. Cohen 2001, p. 85.   [7] Salacuse 2004, p. 3.

alive today not only in the archives consulted by scholars but even as a popular choice for schoolchildren in elocution competitions. The speech is striking in the reference to the historic moment that it marks, as well as indicative of a deep-rooted sense of history and India's place in the world:

> Long years ago we made a tryst with destiny, and now the time comes when we shall redeem our pledge, not wholly or in full measure, but very substantially. At the stroke of the midnight hour, when the world sleeps, India will awake to life and freedom. A moment comes, which comes but rarely in history, when we step out from the old to the new, when an age ends, and when the soul of a nation, long suppressed, finds utterance. It is fitting that at this solemn moment we take the pledge of dedication to the service of India and her people and to the still larger cause of humanity.
>
> At the dawn of history India started on her unending quest, and trackless centuries are filled with her striving and the grandeur of her success and her failures. Through good and ill fortune alike she has never lost sight of that quest or forgotten the ideals which gave her strength. We end today a period of ill fortune and India discovers herself again. The achievement we celebrate today is but a step, an opening of opportunity, to the greater triumphs and achievements that await us . . . We are citizens of a great country, on the verge of bold advance, and we have to live up to that high standard.

The speech is one indication of Nehru's commitment to rooting and justifying India's negotiation behaviour and foreign policy with frequent historical reference. Interestingly, however, in the 1940s, while the appeal to past grandeur as well as relatively recent colonial oppression found frequent mention, India's participation in the agreements establishing the post-war system was not that of a foot-dragger. Even before its independence, it became an original member of the International Monetary Fund and the United Nations. As early as 1948, India took the initiative and called for the use of atomic energy only for peaceful purposes, and the elimination of atomic weapons from national armaments. In the same year, it even solicited UN involvement in its conflict with Pakistan. In 1954, it became the first country to call for an end to all nuclear testing.[8] In the negotiations aimed at establishing the International Trade Organization (ITO), an enterprise that was eventually aborted largely because of the American refusal to ratify the agreement, India played an active role. For example, it participated in the London Conference in 1946 as one of 18 members. It also worked to advance the cause of developing countries. For instance, in cooperation with Australia, Brazil, China, Cuba, and Lebanon, it argued that the ITO allow for a provision whereby underdeveloped countries could use import quotas to promote industrialization. The group was successful in securing these terms in the Havana

---

[8] Weiss 2010; also see <http://www.un.int/india/india_and_the_un_disarm.html>, accessed on 2 April 2013.

Charter via Chapter IV on Economic Development.[9] Its constructive activism in the ITO negotiations also meant that it was active in the negotiations that led to the creation of the GATT. Of the 23 countries that were original signatories to the GATT—the 'interim' regime that came to govern the multilateral trading system for nearly half a century—India was one. Contrary, then, to the arguments presented thus far by Salacuse and others, this behaviour pattern does not suggest that a newly independent India had a negotiating culture that readily accepted delays. However, as we argue below, this willingness to play ball in India's early years of independence was soon replaced by considerable caution in signing international agreements or accepting new responsibilities.

As a new entrant into the international system, still laying claim to its statehood, India's enthusiastic embrace of various multilateral agreements made sense. After all, membership of various multilateral forums helped it establish the legitimacy of this claim and also signalled its willingness to be a fully fledged member of the international community. But this enthusiasm proved to be short lived. In part, this may have been a result of the lesson that India learnt the hard way, when, contrary to Nehru's expectations, the United Nations failed to condemn Pakistani action; not only had India failed to garner the international support that it believed it deserved, but the dispute had become internationalized. Additionally, as the Iron Curtain descended across Europe, the various institutions of multilateralism found themselves deadlocked. The economic institutions, which the Soviet bloc largely stayed out of, had disappointed India: the GATT, for instance, was not seen as an institution sensitive to the special developmental needs of the Third World. And for all the lip service that the Great Powers and the UN bodies paid to disarmament, the nuclear arms race was in full swing between the superpowers, and the number of nuclear weapons states was also growing. The international system was not living up to India's high expectations, and it could therefore be argued that, with the onset of disillusionment, its initial readiness to sign on to new international commitments waned. While still active in various multilateral forums, it showed much greater willingness to contribute to situations of delay and deadlock rather than to accept agreements on unsatisfactory terms.

In the GATT, India's position in the 1950s involved raising the cry for what would be later called Special and Differential Treatment (as discussed in previous chapters). In expressing its pronounced dissatisfaction with the politics and the economics of the GATT, it was joined by other developing countries. It invested a good deal of its diplomatic effort into the creation of the UNCTAD, which was

---

[9] Toye 2003.

formed in 1964, and became a particularly active member through the 1960s and 1970s. Within the GATT, its behaviour was largely obstructionist: in the pre-negotiation phase of the Uruguay Round, for instance, it led the G10 coalition that opposed the launch of the new round. It continued in its activism for global disarmament, a powerful illustration of which was Rajiv Gandhi's 1988 plan for global and universal disarmament to be applied on a non-discriminatory basis. But it refused to agree to any halfway measures that divided the world into nuclear haves and have-nots. It came under a great deal of pressure before the 1995 Review Conference of the NPT (which brought about the indefinite extension of the treaty), but refused to sign the deal. To override Indian objections and almost certain veto, the negotiations over the Comprehensive Test Ban Treaty (CTBT) were moved from the UN Conference on Disarmament (which operates on the basis of consensus) to the UN General Assembly (which operates on the basis of majority voting). The CTBT was approved by a vote of 158 in favour, three against, and five abstentions. India was one of the three countries that voted against the resolution, along with Bhutan and Libya.[10] Effectively, India was showing all the signs of being a country that could not be hectored or hurried into signing a deal. But several of these deals on offer were indeed not on terms hugely favourable to India (at least not in the way India defined its own self-interest); is it not a trifle unfair to dismiss an ability to stand up for oneself as a readiness to accept delay, and to accuse India's negotiators of having 'a geologic sense of time'? This is where the lessons of the Mahabharata and the negotiations of India as a rising power become particularly relevant.

While the examples in the previous paragraph suggest strategic calculation rather than an intrinsic dislike of 'haste' in concluding agreements, a rising India faces quite a different strategic situation in comparison with India in the 1970s, 1980s, or even the mid 1990s. Time as a variable in trade and non-proliferation negotiations for a rising India is discussed in detail in Section 5.6. Suffice it to note at this point, however, that the agreements on offer under the regimes today are certainly on terms more favourable to India than they were 15 or 20 years ago. India stands to gain significantly from at least some of the deals that are under negotiation. If we find a persistent readiness to accept, and indeed contribute to, delays in reaching even those agreements that are largely on terms favourable to India, then the culture-specific hypotheses may have some value-added to offer. Just how these culture-specific notions of time might play out in the negotiation process can be learnt from examples from the Mahabharata, to which we now turn.

---

[10] <http://www.un.org/Depts/ddar/ctbt/ctbt.htm>, accessed on 9 April 2013.

5.2. TIMING AS A VARIABLE IN PRE-WAR NEGOTIATION

References to the nature of time are pervasive throughout the Mahabharata, and the pre-war phase is no different. Exactly how the conception of time affects the negotiation process is illustrated in the stories below.

5.2.1. The terms of exile

Recall the first dice game, when Yudhishthira gambled away not only his kingdom but also the very lives of all the Pandava brothers and Draupadi. The dreadful excesses of the Kauravas, however, attracted powerful ill omens, and the elders of the Kaurava clan were overcome with shame, grief, and fear. At this point, the blind king Dhritarashtra declared the spoils of the rigged dice game as null and void, and returned everything that the Pandavas had lost, including their kingdom as well as their freedom and weapons. Duryodhana and his allies were infuriated and alarmed by this action. Duryodhana pointed out to his father that it was certain and inevitable that the Pandavas, who had been so greatly insulted and humiliated, would return to seek revenge:

आत्तशस्त्रा रथगताः कुपितास्तात पाण्डवाः
निःशेषं वः करिष्यन्ति ऋद्धा ह्याशीविषा यथा
II.66.11

Father, armed with their weapons and riding their chariots, the Pandavas in their fury will destroy your entire family as ferocious and venomous vipers.

The old king, by returning their kingdom, chariots, and weapons to them, had empowered and armed the enemy. Dhritarashtra was persuaded by this argument, and he summoned the Pandavas back to the assembly. To undo his own act of generosity, which had attempted to make amends with the Pandavas, he allowed Duryodhana and his associates to propose another round of the dice game.

For the second round of the dice game, the Kauravas again proposed high stakes: there was to be only one round, and the losers were to renounce all their worldly possession and go into exile in the forest as ascetics, for 12 years. Further:

त्रयोदशं च सजने अज्ञाताः परिवत्सरं
ज्ञाताश्च पुनरन्यानि वने वर्षाणि द्वादश
II.67.10

The thirteenth year must be spent incognito while residing in an inhabited town. If the identities are discovered, then you will have to endure another 12 years of exile in the forest.

The onlookers in the assembly shuddered in fear for the Pandavas, for all knew that the dice game was rigged again. Exactly as the Kauravas had anticipated, Yudhishthira would not be able to turn down the invitation, not only because of his excessive love of gambling, but because he genuinely believed that no noble king could turn down a challenge. He accepted the challenge, lost the game, duly accepted the terms of exile, surrendered the kingdom, and left with his brothers and wife to lead a life of severe austerity in the forest for 12 years.

In relation to our study, both the Kaurava offer and the Pandava acceptance of it are interesting. The first dice game involved several stakes, all of which Yudhishthira lost, and the final outcome was that the Pandavas were enslaved by the Kauravas, having lost everything. This was a harsh outcome, but it provided closure for both sides. Interestingly, the second dice game did not replicate these terms. Instead, it engineered an outcome that would not produce closure but delay. From the Kaurava perspective, this was a sub-optimal outcome, as it meant a near certainty of the return of the Pandavas within a maximum period of 25 years, even more infuriated and even more desirous of vengeance. From the Pandava perspective, this outcome was better than the one proposed in the previous dice game, but it was far from ideal. They did not, for example, try to negotiate the terms of the agreement by trying to reduce the number of years in exile, or to alter the proviso relating to the 13th year. The social and divine reaction to the stake of the second dice game was also one of apparent acceptance. Even the Kaurava elders did not intervene to secure kinder terms for the Pandavas. Delay appears to have been an acceptable outcome for the winners, the losers, and all third parties.

5.2.2. The timing of revenge

In exile, the Pandavas faced a bleak life of hardship and austerity for 12 years. Early on in the exile, the revered sage Markandeya visited them in their humble but pleasant abode in the forest. He reminded Yudhishthira that even the mighty Lord Rama—an incarnation of Lord Vishnu who was invincible in battle—had endured exile (in accordance with the wishes of his step-mother which his father could not deny). Yudhishthira should resist choosing the path of might and reclaiming the throne, even though he had the prowess to do so, for such a path would be an unrighteous one. In virtue and morality, Yudhishthira was matchless; he would now be well served by adhering to the prescribed terms of the exile.

यथाप्रतिज्ञं च महानुभाव कृच्छ्रं वने वासमिमं निरुष्य
ततः श्रियं तेजसा स्वेन दीप्तामादास्यसे पार्थिव कौरवेभ्यः
III.26.17

Oh noble king, in keeping with your word, you will complete this difficult exile, after which you will reclaim your glorious prosperity with your power.

In other words, it was important that Yudhishthira and the other Pandavas serve the time they were due to serve; only after this would justice be restored. But the hardships were difficult indeed to endure, and the pain and humiliation of the Pandavas at the hands of the Kauravas hung heavily on the minds of Yudhishthira's brothers and Draupadi. Draupadi and Bhima in particular thus implored and goaded him into taking swift and decisive action against the Kauravas.

Draupadi bitterly reminded Yudhishthira of the public humiliation to which the Kauravas had subjected her, and also of the condition to which all of Yudhishthira's brothers and Yudhishthira himself had been reduced. Backing her argument up with reference to historical example and philosophical teachings, she argued that the time for forbearance was over. In the rich and sharp debate that ensued, Draupadi advanced a philosophy of action rather than one of forbearance and waiting. She argued that whether there be success or there be failure, one should not despair because success depends on many different factors. If even one of the necessary elements is missing, success may prove elusive. But importantly, if no effort is made, then there is no possibility of success at all. Therefore action is supreme, and inaction is folly.

Bhima joined in the debate at this point, and offered strong support for Draupadi's arguments. He laid the blame for the Pandavas' plight squarely on Yudhishthira's participation in the rigged dice game; he must fight (and also allow his brothers to fight) to reclaim their lost kingdom and respect. The Kauravas had seized their kingdom not through virtue but through deceit in a dice game; it was Yudhishthira's moral duty to regain it.

Yudhishthira addressed the arguments presented by Draupadi and Bhima with his characteristic patience, counterargument, and historical reference. While he offered a detailed interpretation of what he believed to constitute virtuous behaviour, his bottom line is particularly interesting. Yudhishthira accepted the blame that Bhima placed on him, and admitted that the pain and humiliation that his brothers and Draupadi felt were paramount in his heart as well. But he had agreed to the terms on which the dice game was played, which included the terms of exile. It was impossible to violate those terms now. Instead, he urged that the Pandavas wait for the right time to arrive, when they would seek revenge and retribution:

न त्वद्य शक्यं भरतप्रवीर कृत्वा यदुक्तं कुरुवीरमध्ये
कालं प्रतीक्षस्व सुखोदयस्य पक्तिं फलानामिव बीजवाप:
III.35.18

Oh brave of the Bharata clan, having taken a vow in the Kaurava assembly, it is not possible [for me to agree to an attack now]. Just as a farmer sows his seed and awaits patiently for the appropriate time to harvest his fruit, so also you should wait for our time to come.

Yudhishthira was not objecting in principle to the revenge that his brother and wife sought, but to its timing. Delayed justice was acceptable to Yudhishthira, whereas justice sought in haste and in violation of one's word was not.

5.2.3. The killing of Shishupala

Shishupala was born in the line of the King of Chedi, and was related to Krishna. At the time of his birth, a divine forecast was made: he would enjoy a life of affluence and power, but was destined to be killed by Lord Krishna. Shishupala's mother, who was also Krishna's aunt, entreated him to grant her a boon and pardon the wrongdoings of her son. Krishna duly promised her the following:

अपराधशतं क्षाम्यं मया ह्यस्य पितृष्वसः
पुत्रस्य ते वधार्हाणां मा त्वं शोके मनः कृथाः
II.40.22

Even if your son deserves death at my hands for his sins, I will forgive him one hundred offences. Therefore, do not grieve.

Shishupala indeed grew up to become a strong and great king, but his entire being was marked by arrogance and intemperance. True to the prophecy, and in keeping with Krishna's foresight, he committed many acts of gratuitous and senseless violence and cruelty. These included preying upon the innocent and vulnerable, disrupting religious rituals, and attempting to destroy Krishna's prosperous hometown Dwarka by setting fire to it. Each one of his offences would have been deemed deserving of the death penalty at the time, but was duly forgiven by Krishna. The final act came when Shishupala arrived in the Kaurava assembly, brimming over with violence in words and actions, and launched into a litany of remarkably brutal and fierce insults to the elders, including Krishna. This rant, challenging the honour of everyone present, turned out to be his hundredth offence, and he was slain by Krishna's discus with the following words:

दत्तं मया याचितं च तानि पूर्णानि पार्थिवाः
अधुना वधयिष्यामि पश्यतां वो महीक्षिताम्
II.45.24 (Gita Press edition)

My promise to his mother is now fulfilled (for he has now committed 100 sins). Now, oh monarchs, I will slay him before your eyes.

Shishupala's excesses were extreme and numerous, but Krishna resisted the temptation to punish him for his wickedness for many years. Of particular relevance to us is Krishna's promise to Shishupala's mother, which delayed the comeuppance that Shishupala well deserved. Krishna's actions were consistently measured, and displayed patience and restraint, even when Shishupala's offences directly affected Krishna's own kinsmen and people. It is worth recalling that Krishna's boon to Shishupala's mother was a limited one: he did not agree to withhold punishment indefinitely nor did he exercise pre-emptive punishment, but he effectively delayed the inevitable.

5.2.4. Insights for negotiation

The three stories discussed in this section together illustrate the acceptability of delay in the negotiation process. In fact, it is even regarded as a virtue. Lord Krishna showed no haste in teaching the malevolent Shishupala a lesson, and was able to alert the royal assembly to the extreme patience he had exercised before he finally killed his cousin. Markandeya cautioned Yudhishthira against seeking immediate revenge, and advised him to abide by the terms of the exile (long though those years would be) and then reclaim the throne. Yudhishthira too, as the highly moral son of Dharma, refused to be swayed by Draupadi's bitter entreaties or Bhima's angry jibes, which argued for an immediate reprisal against the Kauravas. Even when the terms of the exile were negotiated, neither the Pandavas nor the Kaurava elders who sympathized with their cause attempted to shorten the period of exile. Interestingly, even the Kauravas chose the suboptimal route of delay in the second dice game by sending the Pandavas into exile (from which their return was likely along with their determination for vengeance), rather than the easier route of servitude for the Pandavas (from which their return was highly unlikely) that the first dice game had provided. Both heroes and villains thus show a preference for delay, and a suspicion of quick and immediate solutions.

Second, the importance of referring to the past (not always or necessarily one's own) is evident in the second and third episodes. For example, Markandeya refers to the suffering of Lord Rama in exile, and the exercise of restraint on his part in order to abide by the wishes of his father, and uses this historical/mythical example to reinforce his argument that Yudhishthira should also wait to fulfil his promise and serve the terms of the exile before avenging his family's humiliation and ill treatment at the hands of the Kauravas. Krishna also makes historical reference, although to a more recent past, when he reminds the assembly of the 99 times that he has forgiven Shishupala's grave offences. In neither instance is the particular event treated as discrete, but rather as one of a long and continuous chain of events.

Third, it is evident from at least the latter two stories that not only is haste firmly avoided, but that there is also a particular notion of time wherein a certain hour is regarded as the appropriate moment for completing an action. Hence, in the second episode, Markandeya assures Yudhishthira that his time will come when he will destroy the Kaurava army; Yudhishthira too, when offering counterarguments to Bhima and Draupadi, emphasizes that the right time to reap the seeds they are sowing will come, and that time is not the present. Krishna's willingness to forgive Shishupala 99 heinous crimes represents not just a delay in punishment for the arrogant king, but also a wait for the right time when comeuppance may be legitimately delivered.

5.3. THE CONCEPT OF TIME IN WARTIME NEGOTIATIONS

Even when caught up in the dire conditions of war, the protagonists of the Mahabharata show ready recourse to appeal to historical/mythical glory and show a preference for delay rather than closure (even if this involves prolonged suffering). We give one illustration of the former and two of the latter.

5.3.1. Bhishma's prolonged suffering and delayed death

Recall from Chapter 2 the story of Bhishma, who took the vow of abstinence out of duty to his father, and was rewarded for his selflessness with the boon that the hour of his death would be of his own choosing. This rendered Bhishma invincible, and he was a formidable asset to the Kaurava side. He served as the first Kaurava commander-in-chief in the war, and wreaked devastation on the Pandava army: Yudhishthira compared him to the god of death—Yama—himself in the battlefield. Further, Bhishma's energies and martial prowess showed no signs of abating, and it became obvious to the Pandavas that they had no chance of winning the war as long as their grandsire lived. Taking advantage of Bhishma's intrinsic affection for them, the Pandavas and Krishna entreated him on the evening of the ninth day of the war to advise them on how they might secure victory in the war.

Bhishma admitted that his indestructible might meant that the Pandavas would not emerge as victors as long as he was fighting against them. Then he revealed the way in which the Pandavas could overpower him: only an arrow from Arjuna's celestial bow—the Gandiva—could prove fatal, and this only under the condition that Bhishma chose not to defend himself and counterattack. These conditions could only be met in a unique situation: namely, that Arjuna would have to shoot at Bhishma while using Shikhandi as a shield. Shikhandi had been born a woman but had transformed into a man. The chivalrous and noble Bhishma would never do battle with a woman, and Shikhandi's birth as a woman would thus prevent Bhishma from raining his arrows upon him (or to defend himself from Arjuna if Arjuna were to use Shikhandi as a shield).

On the tenth day of the war, after much debate on the morality of taking this terrible course of action, the Pandavas decided to follow Bhishma's suggested plan. Arjuna accordingly shot at Bhishma while standing behind Shikhandi, and Bhishma, exactly as expected, immediately ceased his counter-attack. All the Pandava generals now surrounded Bhishma and launched a full-scale multi-pronged attack, using different weapons against him. The only arrows that could pierce Bhishma's body through his armour were those shot by Arjuna, and they came in their thousands. Bhishma knew in his heart that arrows of such precision and aggression could not belong to Shikhandi, and could only in fact be fired from Arjuna's bow.

नाशयन्तीव मे प्राणान्यमदूता इवाहिताः
गदापरिघसंस्पर्षा नेमे बाणाः शिखण्डिनः
VI.114.59

Akin to the messenger of the god of death, Yama, these arrows are destroying my very breath. Their touch is akin to the blow of a mace or an iron rod; they cannot belong to Shikhandi.

By the time the sun had set, Bhishma's body was pierced with Arjuna's countless arrows, and he finally fell from his chariot. However, his body failed to touch the ground, and remained suspended on the arrows that had penetrated his body. The great warrior Bhishma thus now lay on what was effectively a bed of arrows.

When this tragic event was taking place, the sun was still in the southern hemisphere, which was considered to be an inauspicious hour for death. A great commotion now arose amongst men and gods as to why Bhishma had willingly accepted this inauspicious time to serve as the hour of his death. A celestial voice was heard that raised the same question, to which Bhishma, the son of the river goddess Ganga, replied from his bed of arrows:

स्थितोस्मीति च गांगेयस्तच्छुत्वा वाक्यमब्रवीत्
धारायामास च प्राणान्यतितोसपि हि भूतले
उत्तरायणमन्विच्छन्भीष्मः कुरुपितामहः
VI.114.89

I am still alive. The grandsire of the Kurus, even after having fallen, will not draw his last breath just yet, but wait for the auspicious hour when the sun has moved into the northern hemisphere.

And ever true to his word, Bhishma chose to wait on his torturous bed of arrows for some six months, rather than choose the easier path of immediate death with less suffering.

Bhishma's choice provides us with a powerful illustration of how readily delay is embraced even under very difficult and painful circumstances. In fact, delay is almost to be expected; no one is surprised by Bhishma's decision to prolong his suffering in order that his hour of death is an auspicious one. The only time when everyone expresses surprise is when they think (mistakenly) that Bhishma's death will be immediate and at an unfavourable time.

5.3.2. The killing of Jayadratha

Following the fall of Bhishma in battle, Dronacharya took over as command-er-in-chief of the Kaurava army. The Pandavas already seemed to have gained the upper hand, however, and in the first two days, despite Drona's skill and experience, failed to generate many Kaurava successes. Facing pressure from Duryodhana, on the 13th day of the war, Dronacharya designed a military formation in the shape of a mighty impenetrable wheel, called the Chakra-vyuha. Only Arjuna had the training to unlock this wheel formation to take on the Kaurava forces, and also subsequently exit from it. Aware of this, the Kauravas had pre-emptively diverted Arjuna by engaging him in another combat. Under the circumstances, the remaining four Pandava brothers found themselves with little choice but to rely on Abhimanyu—Arjuna's teenaged son—who had the knowledge of breaking into the wheel formation but lacked the critical knowledge to exit from it. The Pandava brothers assured Abhimanyu and each other that they would follow in close proximity behind the young warrior with all their armed forces, and would destroy the wheel formation in its entirety, thereby rendering exit from it redundant. But things did not go according to their plan.

Abhimanyu entered the wheel formation as agreed. But before the Pandava army could follow him into this potentially dangerous trap, the Kaurava forces closed in swiftly behind him. Leading the Kaurava forces in this closure strategy was Jayadratha, the brother-in-law of Duryodhana, intent upon inflicting revenge on the Pandavas for a past encounter in which he had received a thorough and humiliating defeat. Abhimanyu was thus trapped inside the wheel formation, with no army to back him up. He fought single-handedly with all the great Kaurava warriors, including all their greatest generals (Karna, Dronacharya, Kripacharya, Ashwatthama, and Duryodhana himself), who were waiting inside the wheel formation. Abhimanyu impressed and astonished the powerful and illustrious Kaurava warriors with his bravery and skill, and many accomplished Kauravas were slain at this young hero's hands. But in a battle of one against so very many, he was eventually killed.

When Arjuna returned, he learnt from his grief-stricken kinsmen about the dreadful way in which his son had been killed (one—and that a child—against so many seasoned warriors). His brothers explained their failure to protect Abhimanyu by appealing to Jayadratha's history: Jayadratha had performed many austerities and thereby obtained a boon from Lord Shiva that on one day in a major battle, he would prevail upon and defeat all the Pandava brothers (except for Arjuna). The brothers had come very close to breaking through the wheel formation as they followed closely on Abhimanyu's heels, but Jaya-dratha's entry into the battle at that stage had completely destroyed the advantage that the Pandavas had secured, and the tide had turned in favour of the Kauravas.

Arjuna held Jayadratha directly responsible for having blocked the entry of the Pandava army into the wheel formation, and thereby having prevented even the semblance of a fair fight. Enraged, he thus swore that even a coalition of all the gods, demons, birds, snakes, sages, or indeed any other creatures that existed, would not be able to protect Jayadratha from his wrath. And he vowed:

यद्यस्मिन्नहते पापे सूर्योऽस्तमुपयास्यति
इहैव सम्प्रवेष्टाहं ज्वलितम् जातवेदसम्
VII.51.37

If the sun sets before I have killed that sinful Jayadratha, I will at this very spot enter a blazing fire (and end my life).

When Krishna came to know of Arjuna's oath, he was furious. He reprimanded Arjuna severely:

असंमन्त्र्य मया सार्धमतिभारोसयमुद्यतः
कथं नु सर्वलोकस्य नावहास्या भवेमहि
VII.53.3

You did not seek my advice before publicly proclaiming your vow [to kill Jayadratha]. Your rash and thoughtless action has exposed us to becoming the laughing stock of one and all.

Krishna then advised Arjuna that he had set himself a task that would be very difficult to accomplish. Krishna's spies had informed him that Jayadratha, having also acquired the knowledge of Arjuna's intent, had sought and secured the protection of Duryodhana. Access to Jayadratha would now be nearly impossible within the time frame to which Arjuna was publicly committed.

Ultimately, Arjuna did manage to kill Jayadratha, but in very large measure thanks to the repeated (and often divine) intervention by Krishna. The story is important because of the reaction that Arjuna's commitment to an immediate and inflexible deadline elicits from Krishna. Interestingly, Arjuna's behaviour is not regarded as an action of heroism or of any other praiseworthy virtue. Even Krishna—himself a very powerful god and an incarnation of Vishnu— finds such a deadline unrealistic, and reprimands Arjuna severely for his foolhardy haste. Although Krishna is finally able to help Arjuna accomplish his goal within the deadline, it is obvious from the text that this is not behaviour that should be commended, emulated, or encouraged.

5.3.3. Shalya is persuaded to become a charioteer by Duryodhana

On the 17th day of the war, and after he had already served for one day as commander-in-chief of the Kaurava army, Karna requested Duryodhana to secure a particularly accomplished charioteer for him. The source of the request was Karna's belief that while his own martial skills surpassed those of Arjuna, his arch-enemy had a strategic advantage, because his charioteer was Lord Krishna himself. Duryodhana duly approached Shalya, who he believed had defected to the Kaurava side (see Chapter 4), as the ideal candidate. Not only did Shalya belong to the class of distinguished charioteers (Maharathi), but his expertise in Ashwavidya (the knowledge of handling horses) could potentially be a great asset to Karna were he to agree to the role.

Shalya was infuriated by Duryodhana's request, which he beheld as a gross insult: how dare Duryodhana ask him—a charioteer of distinction and greatness—to serve Karna, who was of lowly birth. It is possible that Shalya's rage was feigned, and served as a ruse to conceal the original plan that he had hatched with Yudhishthira, that is, to demoralize Karna. But, his rage feigned or not, Shalya was poised to stage a walkout from the Kaurava camp. At this point, Duryodhana did everything in his power to pander to Shalya's ego. He was able to pacify him substantially by comparing him with Lord Krishna. He argued as follows:

पार्थस्य समरे कृष्णो यथाभीशुवरग्रहः
तेन युक्तो रणे पार्थो रक्ष्यमाणश्च पार्थिव
यानि कर्माणि कुरुतेप्रत्यक्षाणि तथैव ते
VIII.23.12

Just as Lord Krishna himself has taken up the reins of Arjuna's chariot in the battlefield, so also should you take up the reins of Karna's war chariot. You are witness to Arjuna's many brave deeds, which he is accomplishing due to the protection that Krishna gives him as his charioteer (and by implication, you could give the same protection to the Kauravas' most worthy warrior).

He ultimately argued that Shalya's competence exceeded Krishna's because of Shalya's ability to handle horses. With Shalya clearly now giving the appearance of being swayed by the argument, Duryodhana decided to reinforce the case by giving him an elaborate story that drew on glorious historical example.

Duryodhana recounted a story that the great sage Markandeya had narrated to his father. Three demons, of dreadful prowess and ambition, performed arduous penance and austerities, and were given a boon by Brahma that granted them three flying cities (Tripura). The boon gave them not just reign over the three cities but also ensured that the demons became almost indestructible. They could only be destroyed by a single arrow that seared through all three of them; this in turn could only be achieved in one moment, which would occur after 1,000 years when their three cities would be aligned. The malevolence of the demons grew with the granting of the boon, and they tormented the gods, humans, and creatures of the underworld alike. All living things then pleaded with Lord Shiva—the destroyer—to come to their rescue for only Shiva had the fierce energy and skill to take on this demonic trinity.

Shiva agreed to accept the mission; but to achieve success in this difficult task, even Mahadeva—the greatest god of the gods—needed some help. He required a chariot that was built with the elements and energies of all three worlds, and his shaft was made of the power of Vishnu, fire, the sun, and the moon; the gods themselves took the shape of the horses that drew the chariot; the holy texts became the retinue of warriors to guard the chariot; the year and the seasons became the bow that Shiva would use; and Shiva's own shadow was the string of the bow. These enchantments were many, but none of them would serve their purpose without the aid of a worthy charioteer to guide Shiva's chariot; so Shiva requested a charioteer who was superior even to himself. The gods thus chose Brahma, as in the Hindu Trinity Brahma was (arguably) superior to even the greatest god of the gods—Shiva—for he was the creator. The task was successful: the demons were destroyed and the world was saved.

Having narrated this story in much detail, Duryodhana urged Shalya to take on the same role of responsibility and superiority as had been accepted by the creator of the universe. Thus comparing Shalya to Brahma and Shiva to Karna, Duryodhana urged Shalya in the following words:

रथिनाभ्यधिको वीर: कर्तव्यो रथसारथि:
तस्मात्त्वं पुरुषव्याघ्र नियच्छ तुरगान्युधि
VIII.25.2

Only one who is even more accomplished than the warrior himself should be appointed as charioteer. Therefore, you lionheart, please take up this role and keep Karna's horses in control.

With this powerful narrative and appealing comparison, Shalya now declared himself convinced, and agreed to take on this role. The story is a useful illustration of how effectively protagonists made use of references to historical and mythical traditions, and thereby secured their preferred outcomes in a bargaining game. Importantly, this particular negotiation between Duryodhana and Shalya was taking place in the midst of a war. Duryodhana found it necessary to engage in detailed historical and mythical reference to strengthen his case and to persuade Shalya, even though this was just prior to battle recommencing, when most leaders would have preferred to recuperate their energies and discuss specific strategies.

5.3.4. Insights for negotiation

The first two stories in this section reinforce the lessons of the stories offered in Section 5.2: delay in a negotiation is seldom problematic, whereas swift solutions are almost always seen in terms of haste, and are frowned upon.

Neither Bhishma himself nor his many kinsmen and well-wishers give a second thought to the extreme suffering to which he subjects himself by prolonging his own death; in contrast, even a heavenly voice speaks up in astonishment when it appears that Bhishma has fallen to his death, and has allowed this to occur at an inauspicious hour. Krishna, with his divine powers, has control over many events, but even he is exasperated by the immediacy of the deadline that Arjuna has set himself for killing Jayadratha.

The third episode also indirectly illustrates the absence of haste: painstaking detail and planning were used to finally destroy the demonic trinity of Tripura, and special attention was given to ensuring that all the planning converged at the appointed moment (i.e. the only moment when the three demons would be aligned and vulnerable to Shiva's one shaft). But the main insight of the story for our purposes has to do with the importance that both Duryodhana and Shalya attach to historical/mythical example. Shalya shows reluctance and anger at being asked to serve as Karna's charioteer; and while Duryodhana's flattering comparisons between him and Krishna help, the detailed interpretation of a mythical/historical past and the application of the analogy between Shalya and Brahma sway him decisively towards Duryodhana's plan.

Bhishma's story also reinforces the additional insight that was offered by Section 5.2, that is, the importance accorded to the auspicious/inauspicious nature of the hour. In other words, if faced with a favourable agreement, but one whose timing is regarded as somehow unsuitable, delay will be favoured even at the cost of foregoing the favourable terms of the agreement.

5.4. CONCEPTUALIZATION OF TIME IN POST-WAR AND RELATED STORIES

5.4.1. Arjuna loses his powers

Towards the end of the Mahabharata, Krishna ascended to heaven, and entrusted Arjuna with the responsibility of protecting his people, the Yadavas of Dwarka. But internecine strife and moral decline struck the Yadavas hard and deep, and in a drunken brawl, almost all the men of Krishna's clan fell upon each other in senseless violence, and died. On hearing of these events, Arjuna, in accordance with his promise to Krishna, rushed to the rescue and attempted the evacuation of the women and children from the city. This evacuation effort was especially important because it had been prophesied that Dwarka would soon be submerged into the sea. The residents of Dwarka, thus accompanied by the brave Arjuna, began their slow march towards the Pandava city of Indraprastha as refugees. But during this journey, they were attacked by a group of violent marauders. Arjuna's powers, completely and unexpectedly, failed him; he found himself unable even to string his bow. All his divine weapons failed to make their appearance when he called for them, and he rapidly ran out of arrows. Arjuna was devastated at his own inability to protect the defenceless people of his dearest friend, and was heartbroken at having failed to fulfil Krishna's last wish.

A broken man, inconsolable in his grief, the once heroic Arjuna therefore approached the sage Vyasa for his advice. Vyasa counselled Arjuna to abandon his sorrow, and reassured him that he had fulfilled his duty despite the adverse outcome. Krishna had the power to alter the course of the universe, but he had allowed these events to transpire in accordance with the diktats of time. Vyasa reminded Arjuna that time—Kala—was at the root of everything.

कालमूलमिदं सर्वं जगद्बीजं धनंजय
काल एव समादत्ते पुनरेव यदृच्छया
स एव बलवान्भूत्वा पुनर्भवति दुर्बल:
XVI.9.33, 34

Time is the root of all things and the seed of the universe, Arjuna. It is time that gives in plenitude and also takes everything away at its own will. He who was once mighty can thus be rendered weak.

कृतकृत्यानि चास्त्राणि गतान्यद्य यथागतम्
पुनरेष्यन्ति ते हस्तं यदा कालो भविष्यति
XVI.9.35

Your weapons have accomplished their purpose, and that is why just as they had appeared to you, now they have departed from your hands. When the time is right again, they will once again come into your possession.

The story emphasizes the overriding importance attached to time and timing in Indian philosophy. Self-imposed deadlines or those imposed by others are meaningless against the inexorable forces of time. It is one's duty to wait for the appropriate moment for all decisions and actions, and haste is futile.

5.4.2. The debate over death and time

After the war was over, Bhishma still lay on his bed of arrows awaiting the optimal hour of death. Yudhishthira approached him, ridden with sorrow and guilt, given his own part in the war. In his sermon to Yudhishthira, Bhishma emphasized that Yudhishthira was not a free agent. Rather, he was an instrument of the all-powerful and invisible force of time. As was his usual practice, the grandsire then consoled Yudhishthira by referring to an ancient debate this time between an old woman, a huntsman, a snake, Death, and Time.

An old and kind woman lived with her only son. When her son was suddenly killed by a snakebite, a huntsman, who was in the vicinity, caught the snake, and having trapped it, brought it before the old woman. Pronouncing the snake as evil for having killed a child, he offered to kill the snake in a manner that suited the grieving mother's wishes. The kind woman, however, thought that as killing the snake would not restore the life of her child, such violence was best avoided. In any case, she argued that the death of her son was predestined, and the snake could not be blamed for it. The huntsman, however, insisted that the snake deserved to die, not only for his wicked act of killing the woman's child, but also because of the many deaths that he would cause in the future. The old woman's repeated objections to this course of action fell upon deaf ears.

At this point, the snake, which was in great pain and fear, spoke in a human voice with much difficulty. 'I am not a free agent. It was Death who sent me to perform this act. I did not bite him out of anger or to satisfy my own wish.' The debate continued for some time, with the huntsman still refusing to absolve the snake of his responsibility in causing the boy's death, and the snake defending his innocence and placing the blame on Death himself. At this point, Death entered the debate, and argued that neither he nor the snake were free agents. Both were subject to the will of Time:

विवशौ कालवशगावावां तदिष्टकारिणौ
नावां दोषेण गन्तव्यौ यदि सम्यक्प्रपश्यसि
XIII.1.58

We are both helpless as we are under the control of Kala (Time) and can only obey his orders. If you consider the matter carefully, you will not blame either of us.

In fact, as Death argued, everything was under the control of Time: the sun, moon, water, wind, Indra, fire, the skies, the earth, all the elements, emotions and the lack of emotions, all were created by Time, and it is Time again that destroys them.

Time now arrived on the scene to defend his own case. He argued that neither the snake, nor Death, nor Time himself were responsible for the boy's death. Rather, it was Karma—the previous actions of the boy in this life and in previous lives—that had caused him to die. Note that while both Death and Time—personified and worshipped as gods—were present to defend their cases, Karma as a separate entity was absent, because it represents the fruits of previous actions that accrue differently to each individual.[11] Ultimately, the snake was released, and the woman, the huntsman, Death, and Time went their own ways, satisfied by the idea that none of them was directly responsible

[11] Death and Time are forces external to the individual, which allows their personification as independent entities; while Karma is internal to the individual, and determined by his/her own past actions.

for the boy's death. Rather, it was his own Karma that had transpired events to take the shape that they had.

While Time had defended himself, and blamed the boy's actions in the past as responsible for his death, Bhishma in fact offered an important interpretation: Time was far from guiltless; it was Time that inspired individuals to act in the way that they did. In other words, it was Time that determined Karma. Bhishma thus concluded with the following words of wisdom, which absolved both Yudhishthira and Duryodhana of the terrible consequences of the war:

न तु त्वया कृतं पार्थ नापि दुर्योधनेन वै
कालेन तत्कृतं विद्धि विहता येन पार्थिवाः
XIII.1.75

Neither you, nor Duryodhana, nor Arjuna are to be blamed for your actions; it was Time that caused you to act in the ways that you did, and caused the destruction of many monarchs.

The story reveals the overriding importance that Bhishma ends up ultimately attaching to Time. It is also noteworthy that the debate between the characters of Bhishma's story is detailed and prolonged, with no one ultimately accepting responsibility for the death of the boy. Recall our discussion in Chapter 3 on the moralizing and verbosity demonstrated in debates in the Mahabharata. This story is a classic example of both features.

5.4.3. Chirakarin and Gautama

Bhishma's sermon to Yudhishthira from his deathbed included many references to the Hindu view of time. When Yudhishthira asked him whether one should act speedily or with delay, Bhishma told him the story of Chirakarin and Gautama.

Sage Gautama, as a result of a misunderstanding with his wife, in a fit of anger commanded his son to kill her. Having thus issued the command, he left for the forest to continue his meditation. Gautama's son was Chirakarin, thus named and subject to frequent ridicule by short-sighted and shallow-minded people for his characteristic tendency to ponder long and hard before taking any decision or action. His proclivity to deliberate and consider all matters with great care was often mistaken for idleness. Chirakarin accepted his father's instruction in the first instance, but immediately after Gautama's departure, his characteristically deliberate and thoughtful nature led him to consider seriously the morality of the dreadful act that he had been asked to perform. What followed was a careful consideration of the meaning of fatherhood, motherhood, the duties of parents towards their children and vice versa, the different moral standards applied to men versus women, and so forth. Ultimately, Chirakarin decided that he would not fulfil his father's wish for three reasons: his mother was innocent and had been wrongly accused by his father, she deserved protection as a woman, and above all she was exempt from such grievous punishment because she was his mother, and therefore was deserving of the highest possible respect.

In the meantime, the sage Gautama began to regret his harsh and cruel instruction. Killing a woman was a grievous sin, and ordering the killing of his own wife doubly so. The burden of this sin would be immense, as would the burden on Chirakarin's soul if he conducted this act of matricide. Besides, it was also becoming clear to Gautama that he had misjudged and wrongly accused his blameless wife. As he returned home, he desperately hoped that his son had exercised his trademark caution, and had delayed taking any action.

When Gautama discovered that Chirakarin had not carried out his order and his wife still lived, he was overjoyed. He blessed his son, extolled the virtues of careful consideration in different aspects of one's life, and commended him for his quality to deliberate long and hard before taking any action:

चिरेण मित्रं बध्नीयाच्चिरेण च कृतं त्यजेत्
चिरेण हि कृतं मित्रं चिरं धारणमर्हति
XII.258.66

One should enter into a friendship only after long and careful reflection. Friendships based on such thoughtful deliberation also last for a long time.

एवं सर्वेषु कार्येषु विमृश्य पुरुषस्ततः
चिरेण निश्चयं कृत्वा चिरं न परितप्तते
XII.258.70

Thus all tasks should be executed after very careful and long consideration. This ensures that an individual who performs all tasks in such a manner will be saved from having to repent over them.

Caution and consideration must be reserved not only for actions that might produce adverse consequences for other individuals, but also positive actions such as the building of friendships and alliances. Bhishma uses the moral of this story to strongly argue that haste makes waste. Even inaction (something that the Bhagwad Gita proscribes) is superior to action that is taken in haste.[12]

5.4.4. Insights for negotiation

The stories in this section reinforce some of the insights of the previous sections, and also offer two new ones.

First, that time is an inexorable force, beyond the control of men, is borne out strongly in the first two stories in this section. In the first story, not all of Arjuna's noble intentions and heroic skills can avert the inevitable loss of his

---

[12] Recall, for instance, the second shloka in Chapter 3, Section 3.3.1.

powers at a time when his need is great (recall also a somewhat similar and terrible inevitability that Karna faced, when his chariot wheel sank into the ground, and all his knowledge and skills deserted him at the hour of his death, as discussed in Chapter 3). In the second story, Bhishma's interpretation tells us that Time is the real culprit, responsible for taking the life of the boy. This moment was predetermined, inevitable, and unavoidable; under such circumstances, human attempts to set deadlines for themselves lose their meaning.

The second story offers us an important additional insight. It reminds us that the notion of Karma—the long history of one's past actions extending back into previous lives—is inextricably linked to a long and continuous notion of time. And given how far-reaching the consequences of even one's smallest actions are likely to go, it is hardly surprising that individuals err on the side of caution in the Mahabharata.

The third story reinforces the lessons of the previous sections in a very explicit way. Chirakarin's caution and slowness of action are rewarded, whereas speedy action would have brought nothing but death, grief, and repentance.

5.5. EXCEPTIONS TO THE NORM

In this section, we investigate exceptions to the dominant norm that we might find in the episodes discussed in previous sections. We also present one episode that illustrates the exception in detail, and then provide a discussion of the insights that these exceptions offer us.

5.5.1. Evidence of negotiations using immediate deadlines, Sections 5.2–5.4

The episodes discussed in the previous sections offer us a few examples of negotiators in the Mahabharata pushing for immediate action and setting themselves and their counterparts very short deadlines. But the main message that results from these stories is that action thus taken generates high costs and low return, and that the wise avoid the path of haste. Three stories are particularly relevant from this perspective: Gautama's instruction to Chirakarin, Arjuna's vow to kill Jayadratha within a tightly defined time limit, and Draupadi and Bhima's debate with Yudhishthira about seeking revenge on the Kauravas.

We see the potential costs of hasty action in the case of the sage Gautama, whose readiness to pronounce immediate death on his innocent wife would have brought certain grief and regret on the whole family, were it not for the caution and restrain exercised by his son. We also see that Krishna admonishes Arjuna severely for his impetuous vow to avenge the death of his son by killing Jayadratha within a set time limit of 24 hours. Krishna regards this vow as foolhardy, and forewarns Arjuna that he has jeopardized the credibility of the Pandavas by swearing to this unrealistic deadline. Ultimately, it is only as a result of Krishna's exceptional help that Arjuna is able to fulfil his pledge. In neither instance is the inclination to work with tight deadlines (imposed externally by Gautama on Chirakarin, and self-imposed by Arjuna) commended; if anything, it is frowned upon, and readers are dissuaded from following these examples.

In their debate with Yudhishthira, Draupadi and Bhima offer powerful arguments in favour of a philosophy of action that is immediate, and where reprisal is swift. Yudhishthira does not dispute that the Kauravas deserve their comeuppance, given the havoc and misery that they have wreaked on the lives of the Pandavas. He also does not completely omit the strategic argument when debating with Bhishma: attacking the Kauravas from the Pandavas' position in exile will result in certain defeat of the Pandavas, whereas declaring war after full preparation will secure a well-deserved victory. But this is not his central argument. Instead, the argument that Yudhishthira focuses on the most has to do with the appropriateness of the time when action should be taken against the Kauravas. As the most moral of all the heroes of the Mahabharata, it is not surprising that Yudhishthira opts for the righteous path of first fulfilling the terms of the exile that he had agreed to (on behalf of the Pandavas) and then mounting a full-scale revenge on the Kauravas after having done the promised duty. Yudhishthira is not alone in arguing for delayed action over immediate action; the great sage Markandeya has counselled him that a postponed counter-attack would be the correct course of action, whereas the temptation to use force at this point would not befit Yudhishthira's historically noble conduct. And indeed, when the Pandavas do eventually embark upon the course of war, one of the many reasons why they are seen as having right on their side is because they have served the terms of their exile and shown great patience.

Thus far, therefore, the exceptions that we have come across are all consistently represented in the text as mistakes; an excessive concern with deadlines leads to regret, whereas allowing things to run their course or patiently waiting for the appropriate time are strategies that are rewarded.

5.5.2. Ashwatthama's haste in seeking revenge

Recall the stories of the unfortunate and misguided Ashwatthama, which we discussed in Chapters 2 and 3. Of particular relevance to us now is the one in Chapter 3, Section 3.3.3. Ashwatthama, inconsolable in his grief and rage at the devious and deceitful manner of the killing of his father (Dronacharya), friends, and allies at the hands of the Pandavas, announced his decision to attack the sleeping and unaware camp of the enemy. The hours of the night were reserved for sleep, and battle was forbidden; Ashwatthama's planned course of action thus violated the ethical and legal codes of war. Kripacharya and Kritavarma were alarmed to hear of Ashwatthama's intent, and they debated with Ashwatthama on the morality of this plan of action. Unable to persuade him to change his mind, Kripacharya then tried to persuade Ashwatthama to at least delay his attack on the Pandavas to the morning. In doing so, Ashwatthama would be pursuing the honourable path, rather than incurring the ignominy that would come with an attack on a sleeping foe. Kripacharya promised him that if he were to hold off his attack until the next morning, he would have both Kripa and Kritavarma fighting by his side:

अनुयास्यावहे त्वाम् तु प्रभाते सहितावुभौ
अद्य रात्रौ विश्रमस्व विमुक्तकवचध्वजः
X.4.2

We will together follow you into battle tomorrow morning. Remove your armour, unfurl your flag, and rest tonight.

Kripacharya reminded Ashwatthama of his capabilities, which were so great that even Indra could not defeat him. He had no reason to attack the sleeping Pandava camp at night in violation of the laws of war. Together, the next morning, the three of them would march into the battlefield and wreak unprecedented havoc and destruction, thereby attaining immense happiness and glory. Therefore Ashwatthama should avoid haste and rest through the night, in preparation for the battle the next day.

The bargain was clear: if Ashwatthama launched his attack in the stealth of the night, he would have to fight alone; and he would attract universal condemnation for a morally reprehensible and cowardly act. If he launched his attack the following morning, he would be accompanied by the two mighty Kaurava warriors, Kripacharya and Kritavarma, and the attack would bring Ashwatthama not only success but glory. Vengeance would be achieved in both cases, but with shame and dishonour in the first case, and success and glory in the second. A small amount of patience would thus reap many fruits. But Ashwatthama insisted that reprisal be immediate and swift, and refused to wait the passage of the night to take action. He argued that the Pandavas benefited from the protection of Lord Krishna and Arjuna, and therefore would be invincible in the morning in a fair fight. Besides, there lived no man who could control Ashwatthama's grief and wrath, given the news that he had received of the destruction of his friends and the victory of the Pandavas. The tumult in his heart made sleep impossible for him. Only the immediate destruction of the Pandavas would give him peace.

अहं तु कदनं कृत्वा शत्रूणामद्य सौप्तिके
ततो विश्रमिता चैव स्वप्ता च विगतज्वरः
X.4.33

Having slaughtered the enemy in their sleep, I will finally rest, and sleep a feverless and untroubled sleep.

Thus determined to avenge the death of his friends, and to punish the Pandavas for the wicked ways in which they had slaughtered many of the Kaurava greats, including Dronacharya, Ashwatthama rode out to the Kaurava camp that night. Inside the camp he was unstoppable, and single-handedly he destroyed almost all the unprepared Pandava warriors (except for the Pandava brothers, Lord Krishna, and Draupadi). This instant gratification, however, came at a very high price, which we discussed in detail in Chapter 2. On discovering the carnage that Ashwatthama had brought upon her family, Draupadi too demanded vengeance. Ashwatthama was deprived of all his powers and weapons. Krishna further placed a dreadful curse upon him that deprived him of the ease of death, and destined him to 3,000 years of extreme loneliness and suffering.

This story—a significant exception to the norm of patience that we see in the Mahabharata—reveals a powerful lesson that reinforces the merit of the rule of caution and delay. Ashwatthama's impatience came at a terrible price, whereas even a small delay, as advised by Kripacharya, could have brought success and glory.

5.5.3. Insights for negotiation

Exceptions to the dominant norms are limited. The few cases discussed in this section that suggest deviations from the norm of caution and delay occur rarely, and they lead to poor outcomes. In contrast, patience and willingness to delay decisions/actions are almost consistently rewarded.

In the few and limited exceptions available to us, while we see the adverse consequences of tying oneself to immediate and tight deadlines, we do not see any exceptions to the general tendency to appeal to the past, either one's own or a more distant one (real or mythical). Hence, even in his impatience, Ashwatthama is careful to recite the many misdeeds of the Pandavas in the war, against which his own actions should be measured. Draupadi and Bhima, even while urging Yudhishthira on the course of speedy and urgent action, justify their positions by referring to historical examples (that is, timing, as discussed in this chapter) and philosophical reasoning (that is, moralistic framing, as discussed in Chapter 3). Yudhishthira, when justifying his preference to wait, also uses similar devices. Even Arjuna's reckless vow is justified by referring to Jayadratha's recent misconduct in relation to the killing of Abhimanyu.

5.6. TIME AND INDIA'S NEGOTIATIONS AS A RISING POWER

The stories discussed in the previous sections of this chapter reinforce the findings of existing scholarship regarding how Indian negotiators view time, and also offer two new insights. We provide a brief recap of these here, then investigate how these insights map out in relation to India's negotiation behaviour as a rising power.

1. Reinforcing the findings of previous scholarship on the subject, all the stories emphasize the risks of hasty action, and accepting immediate and urgent deadlines is often regarded as foolhardy behaviour. Swift decisions and speedy actions are usually followed by repentance and regret (see Table 5.1 for a distribution of the success rates of speedy action versus delay).

2. Emphasizing the findings of other authors, episodes in the Mahabharata also reveal the importance that protagonists attach to historical reference for justifying and explaining their actions.

3. Related to the previous two findings is an interesting additional insight: no event seems to be regarded as discrete. Rather, mythical and historical memories run deep, and every event is seen as part of a long chain of events that often go far back in time. This reinforces the relative imperviousness of negotiators to time constraints.

4. Time or Kala is presented as an inexorable force, matched only by the notion of Karma, in determining the course of events. Unlike Karma, however, where the scope for human action is considerable (recall, for example, the discussion on the Bhagwad Gita in Chapter 3), Kala allows little room for human manoeuvre. This translates only partly into a fatalistic world view, in that negotiators do not push to reach an agreement on the grounds that a decision will be made when the right moment arrives. But this also means that negotiators will—in contrast to a fatalistic world view—be able to resist agreements and block consensus if they do not believe that the timing is right, or if they believe that their opponent is hurrying them into an agreement because of his/her own time constraints. Both tendencies, even while opposed to each other, will tend to make for an agreement-averse system.

5. Related to the last point about the force of Kala is the idea that appears across many stories that a certain hour in the future will be appropriate and auspicious over all others. This relates to the idea of 'muhurta' in Indian philosophy. Just how literally it is sometimes interpreted in international politics was seen in 1947, when India's independence was scheduled for 15 August, but astrologers predicted the 14th to be the auspicious day for the occasion. As a compromise, Nehru settled for the

midnight hour of the night of 14 August and the morning of the 15th.[13]
While this example involved some formal reference to astrology, we see
this idea of the appropriate hour playing out on an informal and
frequent basis in the stories (e.g. in Yudhishthira's case it is not astrology
that leads him to wait, but his own word that the Pandavas will abide by
the terms of the exile; the appropriate hour will thus arrive only after
their promise is fulfilled). In principle, the auspicious hour may well be
immediate. But in practice, at least in the stories of the Mahabharata
discussed here, the auspicious or suitable hour is always one that requires
patient waiting (e.g. in the case of Yudhishthira's plan to reclaim the lost
glory and honour of the Pandavas, or in the case of the wounded
Bhishma's choice of the hour of his death). And whether delayed or
immediate, it is always something that must be considered; it is a force
that is external to the negotiation and works independently of any
artificially set deadlines.

5.6.1. India's notion of time and international trade negotiations

After the initial flurry of joining various multilateral organizations and signing
multilateral agreements, independent India began to show traits of caution
and delay in international trade akin to those that we see in the stories of the
Mahabharata.

India was an original signatory to the GATT, and as discussed in Section 5.1,
it played an active part in the negotiations over the Havana Charter. By 1954, its
caution towards the regime was becoming clear. Sir Raghavan Pillai led the
charge, highlighting the cause of what would later become known as Special and
Differential Treatment: 'All that the underdeveloped countries ask is that, in the
name of reducing barriers to international trade, they should not be denied the
fullest opportunity to develop their economy and to choose and decide for
themselves the most appropriate measures for the purpose.'[14] This translated
into a demand that developing countries be allowed the use of Quantitative
Restrictions (which went beyond what was already provided for in the GATT
for countries facing severe Balance of Payments difficulties), and further that
they be allowed flexibility on tariff bindings. Fundamental to the ideas enunciated by Sir Raghavan was that the same pace of trade liberalization could not be
applied by the developed and developing worlds, and that India and other
developing countries needed longer periods for implementation of the rules.
Implied in the critique of the GATT was that developing countries could not be
bound by the same commitments or deadlines as the developed world.

---

[13] Jack 2008.   [14] GATT 1954.

This caution increased in the following decades. In the middle of the Tokyo Round, the chief Indian negotiator had the following to say about agricultural trade liberalization: 'As we all know, world stocks of grains continue to be at precariously low levels and our small world remains dependant by and large on current harvests. This is hardly a healthy situation for promoting trade when there are serious apprehensions about continued supplies at least in some parts of the world.'[15] Once again, when even some of the worst culprits of agricultural protectionism were beginning to consider some minimal liberalization of agricultural markets, India argued that this was not the appropriate time to pursue such a strategy.

In the run-up to the Uruguay Round, and through much of the round itself, India's delaying tactics persisted. India's position in the early to mid 1980s was that there was no question of launching a new round until there was a clear commitment on the part of the developed economies to provide a standstill and rollback on various grey-area measures (including the so-called 'Voluntary Export Restraints'). Through its various coalition strategies and hard bargaining, India was able to delay the launch of the round but not stop it. After the round was launched in 1986, India tried hard to delay agreement. Just one example of the reluctance to help close a deal can be found in India's response to other countries' attempts to secure an 'early harvest' in 1987. Ambassador S. P. Shukla stated India's opposition to this strategy as follows: 'For some time now we have been hearing refrains on the theme of an "early harvest" in the Uruguay Round... This single undertaking was itself a balanced package catering to the interests of all participants. A selective approach, picking only certain elements for inclusion in an "early harvest" would seriously disturb that balance.'[16] In fact, as was discussed in the last chapter, India was the last country in the developing world to finally give up its opposition to the Uruguay Round.

This behaviour pattern has continued as India's power has risen in the WTO. If anything, we see these tendencies even further enhanced in spite of the fact that it has benefited considerably from the opportunities offered by the regime (evidenced in its growing trade shares as well as its constant presence in small-group consensus-building meetings of the organization). The WTO constitutes a regime that India now has clear incentives to foster and sustain. Nonetheless, as the leading member of the Like Minded Group, India had opposed the launch of a new round; while many different countries could see potential for agenda-setting in a new round of trade negotiations, India saw little gain to be made from a new round until the costs of implementation of the Uruguay Round had been met. As different members of the coalition were bought off (Chapter 4), India ended up isolated in the endgame

[15] GATT 1976.   [16] GATT 1987.

and had to give in. The Doha Developed Agenda (DDA) was launched in 2001, with only grudging acceptance from India. At the Cancun Ministerial in 2003, India led the coalition of the G20, which stood up to the attempt by the EU and the US to hurry through a deal on agriculture, and it also worked hard to resist a deal that included the Singapore Issues (opposed by a great majority of developing countries). India's commerce minister, Arun Jaitley, made a strongly worded speech at the conference, some of which resonated with the speeches made by former Indian representatives (going as far back as Pillai's speech in the 1950s) in its emphasis on Special and Differential Treatment: 'Given the differences in levels of development and the ability of countries to assume obligations, it is imperative to ensure that equal rules to do not apply to unequal players . . . The multilateral trading system has to acknowledge that developing countries *cannot afford to travel at the same speed* as developed countries to achieve gains.'[17]

As the negotiations have plodded along, several countries have contributed to the recurrence of deadlock of the DDA.[18] It would be wrong to hold India solely responsible for the problems encountered by the regime, but India's readiness to walk away from a deal is certainly a contributing factor (especially given the size of its large and growing economy). In 2006, as attempts were being made to break the deadlock, Indian negotiators were reported as saying that 'no deal is better than a bad deal'. India's commerce secretary is reported to have said, 'This is the only round of talks where we will have a development dimension. We may not get a development round at the WTO again in the future. So even if it takes another three years to reach an agreement, that is better than agreeing to something unsuitable.'[19] While this position is understandable, given the history of distrust that has been building up in the WTO, of particular note and interest is the willingness of the Indian negotiator to publicly commit to the acceptability of a delayed outcome. It stands out in contrast to the games often played by other states, which emphasize urgent deadlines, and even by the Director General of the WTO, Pascal Lamy, who repeatedly emphasized the critical nature of immediate deadlines. Just how much Indian negotiators resent being pressured into signing agreements with immediate deadlines is evident from the concerns expressed by a former Indian ambassador, B. L. Das: 'This is not the first slow down at WTO negotiations but every downturn like this has resulted in damages to developing countries. After a downturn like this everybody is anxious to get results. So rather than developed countries making changes, the developing countries are the ones making concessions. So what I fear is that the current downturn will again force us to make concessions. We have to be careful that we are not put under pressure that we are forced into doing certain actions to break this

---

[17] WTO 2003 (our emphasis).   [18] Narlikar 2010.   [19] Samaraweera 2006.

deadlock.'[20] The quotes by both negotiators are a telling illustration of the importance attached to a particular reading of past negotiations, the extent to which landmarks in the negotiation process are regarded as constituting a long series of events (past, present, and future), and also the suspicion with which negotiations under the pressure of deadlines are viewed.

The closest that the Doha negotiations came to an agreement was in July 2008. As discussed in previous chapters, India received a good deal of the blame for the deadlock that occurred in this phase of the negotiations. Of relevance to this chapter was the explicit reference by the Indian minister of commerce and industry, Kamal Nath, of his willingness to walk away from a deal: 'Do we give developed countries the unfettered right to continue subsidizing and then dumping those subsidies on us jeopardizing lives of billions? The position of developed counties is utterly self-righteous: they have enjoyed their SSG (and want to continue it) but our SSM must be subject to all sorts of shackles and restraints. This self-righteousness will not do. *If it means no deal, so be it*.'[21] Note the historical reference made in this quote to the agricultural protectionism of the developed countries, which is used to strengthen the legitimacy of India's position. Note further the unequivocal willingness to walk away from the negotiation, which reinforces the argument made in other scholars about the low sensitivity to time constraints in India's negotiating culture. The hero's welcome that Nath received on his return from Geneva illustrates that the strategy of contributing to deadlock (conceptualized in this instance as delay) went down well with the Indian public.[22] These negotiation strategies, and also the positive reactions they generated domestically, are important, especially because India stood very much to gain from the package deal that was under discussion in aggregate terms.

It is worth pointing out that these themes are not restricted to India's negotiations with the West, nor are they specific to trade. A good example of the former is the attempt by the BRICS countries to go beyond their usual criticisms of the leadership positions of international organizations, and advance a joint candidate for the position of Director General of the WTO. Even at the high-profile BRICS Summit in March 2013, when the pressure on the group to demonstrate some results was high, India agreed with the BRICS countries that the position should be occupied by someone from a developing country, but refused to commit to either the Brazilian candidate or the other candidates from the developing world.[23] India's characteristic caution on this issue continued at the time of writing (April 2013, and not far from the completion date of the selection process, which was scheduled for the end of May).

An example of another issue area where we see some of the same themes being played out is climate change. Shyam Saran, special envoy to the

---

[20] Samaraweera 2006.   [21] WTO 2008 (our emphasis).   [22] Lakshmi 2008.
[23] Bhaumik 2013.

prime minister on climate change, provided an eloquent defence of India's position. In particular, he referred to 'history and equity being on our side', and emphasized the historical roots of the problem that lay in the developed world: 'Climate change is taking place not as a result of current GHG emissions but as a result of cumulative accumulation of greenhouse gases in the global atmospheric space, as a result of anthropogenic activity, mainly fossil-fuel based industrial activity over the past 200 years. True, current emissions are adding to this accumulation on an incremental basis. But looked at in a comprehensive perspective, the total stock of GHG in the atmosphere, in particular CO_2 emissions, is almost entirely the responsibility of developed, industrialized countries.'[24] And when Prime Minister Manmohan Singh highlighted the National Action Plan on Climate Change that the Indian government was voluntarily implementing, he placed green policies within India's historical context: 'India has a *civilizational legacy* which treats Nature as a source of nurture and not as a dark force to be conquered and harnessed to human endeavour.[25] There is a high value placed in our culture to the concept of living in harmony with Nature, recognizing the delicate threads of common

[24] Saran 2008, p. 350.
[25] Our emphasis. The claim, in general, is a fair one, and borne out in many classical Sanskrit writings. But it would be remiss on our part not to at least briefly mention the story of the burning of the Khandava forest by Arjuna and Krishna. The god of fire—Agni—appeared before Arjuna and Krishna, and asked them to satiate his hunger by burning the Khandava forest to ashes (destroying not just the trees but also all the numerous creatures that lived there in harmony). Thus far, he had been unable to do so because of Indra's friendship with the Takshaka—the king of snakes—who resided in the forest. Only warriors with the level of accomplishment of Arjuna and Krishna could perform this task. To assist them in this endeavour, and also as a reward, Agni would help them secure divine and invincible weapons, including the Gandiva bow for Arjuna with its limitless arrows, and the discus for Krishna that never missed its target and always returned to the hand of the owner. Arjuna and Krishna agreed to this bargain, and burnt the forest, and its inhabitants, to the ground. Not even Indra, accompanied by many other gods and divine creatures, was able to stop this carnage. Very few creatures survived this onslaught; the survivors included Ashwasena—the snake prince—who later returned to Kurukshetra to seek revenge on Arjuna. The Pandavas were thus guilty of great environmental damage, which can only be understood in terms of the necessity of the bargain that they had struck with the fire god to procure the weapons that would later help them win the war. The story is very much the exception. But it also points to the trade-offs that the Indian government makes between environmental protection and economic development, and how it enunciates them in key negotiations. Hence, even though the Indian government had developed its National Action Plan on climate change, the prime minister emphasized that 'Our position has been made very clear . . . India cannot, by any stretch of the imagination, be regarded as a major polluter of greenhouse gases . . . Our contribution to global emissions is less than 4 per cent. On per capita basis it is among the lowest—an average of 1.2 tonnes . . . For us the topmost priority is development.' Singh 2008b, p. 344. Shyam Saran's statement echoes this sentiment, and goes a step further in indicating the delay that will necessarily be involved before developing countries can assume the same burden as developed countries: 'Let me also emphasize at this point that ability to adapt to climate change is also linked to the level of development. Richer and more advanced states are better equipped to cope with climate change than are poorer countries. Therefore, development is the best form of adaptation, even if development in a developing country results, in the foreseeable future, to an increase in its GHG emissions.' Saran 2008.

destiny that hold our universe together. *The time has come for us to draw deep from this tradition* and launch India and its billion people on a path of ecologically sustainable development.'[26]

The first four of the five insights, deriving from the Mahabharata and summarized in the early part of this section, have relevance for the bargaining behaviour of a rising India in the international trade regime, as well as other areas of 'low politics' (the fifth insight—waiting for an auspicious or favourable moment—does not show up directly in the examples discussed). Indian negotiators reveal a deep consciousness of the history of their country, including relevant interpretations of past wrongs and injustices. Key landmark moments are seldom regarded as discrete events (or even as an endgame when agreement seems plausible), and almost always as part of a long series of negotiations. Delay is acceptable, indeed even desirable, if the choice is between delay or a swift agreement that might be regarded as hasty. Indian negotiators are thus better able to accept deadlock as the result of a negotiation, in contrast to some Western negotiators, at least in issues of 'low politics'.

5.6.2. India's notion of time and the nuclear non-proliferation regime

While the previous section provides us with several examples of deadlocks that India has contributed to thanks to its long and deep sense of history and its willingness to accept delays, the one area in which we might be able to find the exception to this pattern is the nuclear non-proliferation regime. Recall from the discussion in Section 5.1 that independent India was in no hurry to sign up to many of the agreements of the non-proliferation regime (including the NPT and the CTBT). But India as a rising power has shown an arguably different pattern: the 123 agreement on civilian nuclear energy cooperation, negotiated with the US, is perhaps an illustration of how India will sign on the dotted line quickly if the agreement is framed very much on its own terms. As Chapter 2 argued, insofar as the agreement and subsequent waiver from the Nuclear Suppliers Group secure India de facto status as a legitimate nuclear weapons state (NWS), the agreement is strongly in its favour. The agreement was concluded within a relatively short time period: the talks began in July 2005 and the agreement passed the Indian Parliament's no-confidence motion in August 2008; the NSG waiver was granted in September in the same year; the US Congress approved the legislation in October 2008; the agreement was completed and signed by both parties on 10 October 2008. Compare this flurry of activity with India's decades of criticism of the discriminatory NPT regime

---

[26] Singh 2008a, p. 341 (our emphasis).

from the perspective of the nuclear have-nots, and we seem to see an important exception, where India did not use its characteristic tactics discussed in previous sections. A closer inspection reveals, however, that such an interpretation is a somewhat partial one.

First, the agreement between the US and India was the product of exceptional circumstances, which had much to do with the fact that it was built on strong leadership provided by top political echelons in both countries. Stephen Cohen rightly argues that 'this was from the start, a top-down exercise. As negotiations dragged on, both sides were aware that a comprehensive nuclear agreement would come as a surprise—unpleasant in some cases—in both countries . . .'[27] The extent to which the political leadership in both countries remained committed to the deal makes it unrepresentative of almost all other agreements that India signs, which necessarily involve different levels of the bureaucracies of relevant ministries.

Second, Stephen Cohen also points out that the idea of a compromise with India—a 'halfway house'—went back at least 20 years, even though it was dismissed as unrealistic by both sides at the time. But this means that the gestation period of such an idea was considerably longer than the short three years when the talks were actually taking place. A thawing, indeed warming, of relations between the two countries went back to the Clinton administration, after it had recovered from the shock of Pokhran II.[28] Strobe Talbott has commented on the long game that Indian negotiators were playing even after the 1998 tests, which showed little sign of haste: 'By weathering the storm of US disapproval—by outlasting and outtalking the Americans in the marathon of diplomacy spurred by the test, in short by *not* compromising—the Indians would prove their resolve and resilience, thereby giving a boost to their national self-esteem and self-confidence.'[29]

Third, even though the agreement facilitated the negotiation of a very attractive package for India, particularly the de facto recognition and legitimacy it came to receive from key players (a seemingly impossible achievement given that the NPT disallows the creation of any new NWS), domestic Indian opposition to it was very high. Recall that Stephen Cohen had noted in 2006 when the talks were still on: 'it seems that opposition is stronger, and deeper on the Indian side, even though New Delhi has more to gain than the United States. It is curious that some elements of India's small but feisty strategic community cannot accept "yes" for an answer, and still do not comprehend the historic shift in American policy, nor understand that this agreement is part of a larger adjustment in America's vision of India, one that conforms closely to historical Indian views.'[30]

---

[27] S. Cohen 2006.
[28] S. Cohen 2006. For a first-hand account of this early diplomacy, see Talbott 2004.
[29] Talbott 2004, p. 5.   [30] S. Cohen 2006.

The no-confidence motion against the government in 2008 shows us just how deep-rooted the opposition was, which brought together some unlikely bedfellows from the political right and left (including the Congress government's own leftist allies that had helped it constitute the coalition government). While these political parties differed in the fundamental reasons driving their opposition, the hasty process whereby the deal was done came under challenge and critique from both sides.

L. K. Advani, the leader of the opposition in the Lok Sabha at the time and also the leader of the BJP, accused the prime minister of serious inadequacy in following the due process that the PM himself had established. For example, he had constituted the Joint UPA–Left Committee, presided over by a senior minister, Pranab Mukherjee. Advani argued that the 'senior-most Minister assured that Committee that you will go to the IAEA with our safeguards only after you had taken their consent. Today we are told that you had said that you would go there and you would go to the NSG, and then come back to them ... even in respect of this Confidence Motion Shri Pranab Mukherjee himself publicly said that before taking a vote of confidence from the House, the Government would not go to the IAEA, and that he was saying that after having spoken to the Prime Minister on phone. This is what he said. And suddenly we found that the draft had been sent there ...' Besides criticizing the prime minister for prematurely approaching the IAEA, he also castigated the prime minister for presuming to give the impression that the agreement was on 'autopilot' and would go through irrespective of the results of the no-confidence motion.[31]

Basu Deb Achariya, the leader of the Communist Party (Marxist) that had withdrawn its support for the Congress-led coalition government, also offered a detailed critique. An important element of this critique was the injudicious and rushed manner in which the government had tried to circumvent due process. Achariya cited the example of the prime minister's assurances 'that all our concerns would be properly addressed ... The assurances went haywire.' Echoing the BJP leader's critique, the CP(M) leader went on to highlight how the Left-UPA Committee—a mechanism established by the prime minister to incorporate and allay concerns about the US–India agreement—fell short on due process: 'When the committee met in the month of June, the Agreement was not shown to the committee. Without showing the text of the Agreement, how can the committee come to any conclusion? The committee was told that it was a classified document. The same day, from the IAEA, it was stated that there was no restriction and the Government can circulate the text.' And akin to the Advani, Achariya also emphasized that the PM had jumped the gun in going to the IAEA: 'On 8th July, in a Press Conference, the hon. External Affairs Minister

---

[31] Lok Sabha Debate 2008, pp. 451–62.

stated that the Government would not go to IAEA before it takes the vote of confidence. The day he made the statement, the Prime Minister announced [*sic*] and the Government went to the IAEA. If this is not betrayal, then what is this? This is not only a betrayal and insult to us but also to the nation.'[32]

Both sets of critiques shared their disapprobation of a process that they believed had been rushed through. While the objections to the agreement were several and many-sided, at least one criticism could have been averted if the process had been more considered and less hasty. The government survived the no-confidence initiative, but barely so.

Finally, even after the signing of the agreement with the US, and the other agreements that have followed to enhance the legitimacy of India as a de facto NWS, India's position on the rules that constitute the non-proliferation regime remains largely unchanged. Its sudden and relatively speedy embrace by the West has not prompted India to change its principle or pace on the issue of the NPT or CTBT, or to lower its longer-term ambitions of universal disarmament to partial disarmament that applies selectively to some countries (even though India itself would potentially continue to enjoy de facto legitimacy under the regime). Strobe Talbott wrote in 2004, 'The Indians' goal will still be Nirvana . . . The bomb is seen as a winner, both politically and geopolitically; it is firmly established as both an indispensable instrument of hard power and a talisman of India's having arrived at a place in the sun that it will never abandon.'[33] These words remain just as valid today as they were in the years preceding the US–India nuclear deal. India was not in a hurry to comply with the regime when it was treated as recalcitrant and even as a pariah; given its negotiating culture as well as its patiently won legitimacy in the non-proliferation regime, it will be in even less of a hurry than before.

A closer inspection thus reveals that even the nuclear non-proliferation case and the recent deal-making with the US constitute, at best, highly qualified exceptions to the approach that India usually takes to time.

5.7. CONCLUSION

In this chapter, we find that the lessons of the Mahabharata reinforce existing scholarship on how the notion of time plays out in negotiations involving India. Major and minor protagonists reveal a strong sense of history, and delay in reaching decisions and agreements is usually lauded as a sign of circumspection and patience. The implication of the latter insight is that haste

---

[32] Lok Sabha Debate 2008, pp. 502–3.   [33] Talbott 2004, pp. 230–1.

generates poor rewards, and the stories of the Mahabharata that we discussed in this chapter fully reinforce this moral.

Besides the two observations on history and delay that we started out with, we also find three additional insights from the Mahabharata: a) no event is viewed as a one-off event but is linked to past experiences and future goals; b) time is regarded as an inexorable force, which also means that negotiators are able to stand firm if they believe that they are being pushed into an agreement for which the timing is not right; and c) certain moments are regarded as particularly favourable for a decision or action. Our analysis with respect to India's bargaining as it rises reinforces four of the five insights.

In both the Mahabharata and modern-day India, any exceptions are limited and qualified, and even minimal deviations from the norm on timing usually turn out to be costly. The case of non-proliferation and the US–India nuclear deal provides an illustration of how it can be regarded as an exception in only a very limited way, and also that this minimal exception (i.e. perception that the deal was rushed through without due regard to the established procedures) generated costs for the government (in the form of vehement opposition to the deal, and the no-confidence motion that the government only narrowly survived).

It is worth noting that in the previous chapters we saw some differentiation in India's behaviour depending on the particular negotiating partner. But on the timing variable, we see a consistency in India's bargaining behaviour across the board, whether it is dealing with developed countries or other developing countries. This chapter thus suggests that neither friends nor foes will easily be able to rush India into making a deal, favourable though the terms might be.

REFERENCES

Bhaumik, Anirban. 2013. India Yet to Decide on Next WTO Chief. *The Deccan Herald.* 1 April. Accessed at <http://www.safpi.org/news/article/2013/india-yet-decide-next-wto-chief> on 3 April 2013.

Cohen, Raymond. 2004. *Negotiating across Cultures: International Communication in an Interdependent World.* Washington DC: United States Institute of Peace Press (second revised edition).

Cohen, Stephen. 2001. *India: Emerging Power.* Washington DC: Brookings Institution.

Cohen, Stephen. 2006. *A Deal too Far?.* Research Paper, Brookings Institution. 26 February. Accessed at <http://www.brookings.edu/research/papers/2006/02/28india-cohen> on 3 April 2013.

GATT. 1954. Speech by Sir N. Raghavan Pillai (India). Delivered in Plenary Session on 9 November 1954. Press Release GATT/185.

Table 5.1 Success and Failure of the Delayed Timing Strategy

	Episode	Timing Willingness to delay	Exception Immediate action/haste
1.	The Terms of Exile	- Duryodhana—successful in short term (gains some legitimacy and also gets rid of the Pandavas for some time) - Yudhishthira—successful (abides by the terms of the exile and then seeks revenge; preferred option to slavery)	- Attempted but nullified (Duryodhana's terms of the first dice game, which could have demobilized the Pandavas immediately and permanently, but nullified by Dhritarashtra) - Draupadi and Bhima—unsuccessful (Yudhishthira is unpersuaded on moral and strategic grounds)
2.	The Timing of Revenge	- Yudhishthira—successful	Not attempted
3.	The Killing of Shishupala	- Krishna shows great patience until Shishupala commits 100th crime—successful	Not attempted
4.	Bhishma's prolonged suffering and delayed death	- Bhishma chooses to delay his death to the auspicious hour—successful	
5.	Killing of Jayadratha	- Lesson on the costs of haste—successful (Krishna chides Arjuna for his foolhardy oath, but then helps him after making him understand the costs of such haste)	- Haste by Arjuna—unsuccessful (is able to fulfil his deadline only through divine intervention)
6.	Shalya	- Historical reference to Shiva—successful (Duryodhana manages to persuade Shalya) - Delayed attack—successful (careful and detailed planning to strike the demons at the right moment)	Not attempted
7.	Arjuna loses his powers	- Lesson that deadlines are meaningless—neither success nor failure (Arjuna begins to understand and accept that time is an inexorable force against which no one can win)	Not attempted
8.	Debate between Death and Time	- Lesson that time is an inexorable force—neither success nor failure (which according to Bhishma trumps even Karma).	Not attempted
9.	Chirakarin and Gautama	- Chirakarin's caution—successful	- Gautama's haste—unsuccessful
10.	Ashwatthama	Not attempted	- Ashwatthama's refusal to wait for his revenge—unsuccessful
		Caution and delayed action: 9 attempted, 7 successes, 2 cannot be ranked as successes or failures (but enhance understanding and acceptance)	Hasty actions: 4 attempted, 0 successes

GATT. 1976. Statement made by the Representative of India. 29 January 1976. Multilateral Trade Negotiations Group, Agriculture Sub-Group on Grains. MTN/GR/W/9. 2 February 1976. Accessed at <http://gatt.stanford.edu> on 3 April 2013.

GATT. 1987. Statement by HE Mr S. P. Shukla, Permanent Representative of India. SR.43/ST/16. 22 December 1987. Accessed at <http://gatt.stanford.edu> on 3 April 2013.

Jack, Ian. 2008. *Great Speeches of the 20th Century*. London: Guardian News and Media Ltd. Accessed at <http://www.guardian.co.uk/greatspeeches/story/0,,2059928,00.html> on 20 April 2013.

Lakshmi, Rama. 2008. Hard line at WTO earns Indian Praise. *Washington Post*. 1 August. Accessed at <http://articles.washingtonpost.com/2008-08-01/world/36775131_1_kamal-nath-trade-talks-indian-industry> on 2 April 2013.

Lok Sabha Debate. 2008. Debate in the Lok Sabha on the Motion of Confidence in the Council of Ministers. 21–22 July. Extracts Relevant to Civil Nuclear Energy Co-operation. In Avatar Singh Bhasin ed., *India's Foreign Relations Documents—2008*. New Delhi: Public Diplomacy Division, Ministry of External Affairs.

Narlikar, Amrita ed. 2010. *Deadlocks in Multilateral Negotiations: Causes and Solutions*. Cambridge: Cambridge University Press.

Salacuse, Jeswald. 2004. The Top Ten Ways in which Culture can Affect your Negotiation. *Ivey Business Journal*, September–October, 1–6.

Samaraweera, Dilshani. 2006. 'India says "No Deal Better than Bad Deal" at WTO'. *The Sunday Times* (Sri Lanka), 41:31, 31 December 2006. Accessed at <http://www.sundaytimes.lk/061231/FinancialTimes/ft318.html> on 2 April 2013.

Saran, Shyam. 2008. Speech of Special Envoy of Prime Minister on Climate Change Shyam Saran on Climate Change: 'Climate Change: Will India's Growth Story Confront a New Constraint.' In Avatar Singh Bhasin ed., *India's Foreign Relations Documents—2008*. New Delhi: Public Diplomacy Division, Ministry of External Affairs.

Singh, Manmohan. 2008a. Remarks of Prime Minister Dr Manmohan Singh While Releasing the National Action Plan on Climate Change. 30 June. In Avatar Singh Bhasin, ed., *India's Foreign Relations Documents—2008*. New Delhi: Public Diplomacy Division, Ministry of External Affairs.

Singh, Manmohan. 2008b. Report on Prime Minister Meeting the Press on board his Special Flight to Sapporo, Japan for the G-8 Outreach Summit. 7 July. In Avatar Singh Bhasin, ed., *India's Foreign Relations Documents—2008*. New Delhi: Public Diplomacy Division, Ministry of External Affairs.

Talbott, Strobe. 2004. *Engaging India: Diplomacy, Democracy, and the Bomb*. Washington DC: Brookings Institution.

Toye, Richard. 2003. Developing Multilateralism: The Havana Charter and the Fight for the International Trade Organization, 1947–1948, *International History Review*, 25:2, 282–305.

Weiss, Leonard. 2010. India and the NPT. *Strategic Analysis*, 34:2, 255–71.

WTO. 2003. Statement by HE Arun Jaitley, Minister for Commerce and Industry, and Law and Justice. WT/MIN (03)/ST/7. 10 September. Accessed at <http://www.wto.org> on 4 April 2013.

WTO. 2008. TNC Meeting, Statement of Shri Kamal Nath, 23 July.

6

———

Conclusion

We began this book with the following question: To what extent is the bargaining behaviour of a rising India today a reflection of the country's cultural traditions? The previous chapters have pointed to some important continuities in India's bargaining behaviour by drawing on examples from the Mahabharata. In this final and concluding chapter, we begin by highlighting the relevance and contribution of this research, summarize its findings, and offer some policy recommendations for those wishing to bargain more effectively with India.

6.1. CONTRIBUTION OF THIS RESEARCH

While the interdisciplinary nature of this book makes it relevant and interesting to readers in different disciplines, we hope, our primary contribution is to debates in two fields: International Relations and Negotiation Studies.

Recall from Chapter 1 a polarized and exciting debate in the field of International Relations, which feeds directly into policy, and revolves around the question of whether India, as it rises, will become a more cooperative negotiating partner for the West.[1] Or will its pathways to power and visions of global order collide and diverge from those espoused by the established powers?[2,3] When we began this project, we thought we had the useful but limited goal of intervening in and navigating through this debate. The argument was meant to go as far, and only as far, as follows. If we noticed few

---

[1] The strongest exponent of this view is Mohan 2003, 2006, 2010. The view also finds support in Malone 2011, who describes India as changing from 'idealist moralizer to often-pragmatic dealmaker', p. 249.

[2] Those taking the more cautious view include S. Cohen 2001; Perkovich 2003; Narlikar 2006; Dormandy 2007; Narlikar 2013.

[3] Note that this debate is a fundamental one in International Relations theory, and extends to various rising powers, with a large proportion of writings focusing on China. Classic examples of each position are Mearsheimer 2006 and Ikenberry 2008.

continuities in the behaviour exhibited by protagonists in classical texts—the Mahabharata offering a well-entrenched cultural representation of the literary tradition in Sanskrit—and that of a rising India, then the first side of the debate would have greater chance of winning. Increasing enmeshment in the international system would facilitate new opportunities for learning and adaptation, and even a redefinition of Indian interests and identity. India thus emerged could potentially and plausibly be a largely system-conforming power. If, on the other hand, we found significant continuities in the negotiation patterns of classical and modern Indian negotiators, then the second side of the debate would more likely prevail. India, as its power increased, would not simply transform into a power whose interests and values would align neatly with those of Western powers. And, at least in some areas, we would expect to see revisionism at work, manifest in a clash of interests and values, and perhaps even of civilizations.

We did indeed find some vital continuities in India's bargaining traditions, which suggested that there are reasons to be cautious in assuming that India, as it rises, will transform into an easy or pliable negotiating partner for the established powers. But as we worked through this book, we began to realize that to conceptualize India simply as occupying one end of the debate or the other is to take far too limited a view. Rather, Indian negotiation behaviour needs to be understood on its own terms, taking into account its historical traditions. Certain aspects of its negotiation behaviour are indeed suggestive of revisionism, and an alternative approach to global order. Others, however, are simply a function of long-established traditions. Lack of awareness of such traditions, for instance the willingness of Indian negotiators to delay agreement or moralize excessively, may ordinarily lead the outside party to assume extreme recalcitrance and revisionism. Knowledge of India's negotiating traditions, however, would lead the outside party to approach the negotiation in a different and possibly more tolerant light. Hence, even though we sit towards the cautionary side of the debate, which recognizes considerable potential for difference and conflict as power balances change, our research emphasizes the vital nuances and complexities (and their implications) of Indian's bargaining behaviour that derive from its deep-rooted cultural traditions.

This leads us to the second field to which this book makes a contribution, Negotiation Analysis. As we discussed in Chapter 1, while this field is rich in interdisciplinary insights and shows a clear theoretical recognition of the importance of cultural variation, it has traditionally been surprisingly Western-centric in its empirical base, with few studies dealing directly with data on non-Western negotiating cultures.[4] The paucity of scholarship becomes even more striking if one wishes to investigate the impact of India's intellectual and

---

[4] Valuable book-length exceptions to this are Faure and Zartman 1993; R. Cohen 2004.

philosophical traditions upon its negotiating culture (in contrast to some interesting and detailed studies that have been conducted on the traditional sources of Chinese and Japanese negotiating cultures).[5] Our book provides one of the few accounts that investigate how some of India's classical traditions live on and influence its modern-day negotiations with the outside world. We provide a summary of our research findings in the next section. But before doing so, we believe it is important for us to reiterate the methodology that underlay this project.

The puzzle of India's negotiation behaviour as a rising power was outlined in Chapter 1, as were also the divisions in the academic and policy community on the matter. Previous studies in the field of Negotiation Analysis had already pointed to the importance of factoring in culture to explain the negotiation patterns of different countries. Our main purpose driving this project was to explore the cultural roots of India's bargaining behaviour. We chose to explore these cultural roots via India's well-embedded literary traditions. We had a very wide range of texts that we could have worked with, but the Mahabharata provided the most obvious choice, given the range and scope of the text itself (and its constant engagement with questions of bargaining at both philosophical and mundane levels), and also the multiple levels at which its traditions and teachings live on in the popular Indian imagination today. Potentially it offered us rich material for exploring the extent to which India's bargaining behaviour today is ingrained in its ancient traditions, and it has not disappointed our expectations.

Importantly, the purpose of the project was to explore continuities between ancient India and modern, rather than establish a causal link. Hence, for example, the claim of the project has never been that Indian negotiators act in a certain way because they have read the Mahabharata. At best, the claim can only be an indirect one, precisely as argued by Myron Weiner, whom we cited in Chapter 1: 'This is not to say that there is a direct causal continuity between past and present. The presence of similarities, however, is enough to make us consider the possibility of similar underlying premises ... derived from deeper, fundamental assumptions concerning the nature of man— assumptions that mark one culture from another ...' In keeping with this logic, the reasoning underpinning this enquiry was that if we observed significant continuities, they would help us establish and identify certain key characteristics in the behaviour of Indian negotiators. An understanding of such traits, which are so deeply entrenched that they become almost hardwired into a negotiating culture, is important for two reasons. First, theoretically, our knowledge is insufficient regarding cultural differences that persist in an era of globalization; a study such as ours helps fill some of the gaps that

---

[5] E.g. Blaker 1977; Faure 1998.

Western-centric assumptions necessarily lead to. In the aforementioned debate in International Relations on the possibilities of socialization, awareness of the roots of such bargaining characteristics can help define the limits and open up the opportunities of interest convergence and/or norm diffusion. Second, from a practical perspective, such knowledge can lessen the scope for misunderstanding and facilitate more effective negotiation. We suggest ways in which such knowledge can be applied in Section 6.3, after providing a summary of the results and their implications in Section 6.2.

6.2. SUMMARY OF FINDINGS

The last four chapters covered four aspects of India's negotiation behaviour: negotiation strategy, framing, coalitions, and timing. In each chapter, we analysed ten episodes from the Mahabharata (pre-war, wartime, post-war and related, and exceptions), and further investigated the behaviour of a rising India in the light of these insights. While drawing on examples of India's bargaining behaviour in different multilateral regimes, we focused systematically on two regimes: international trade and nuclear non-proliferation. Such a focus allowed us comparability across the chapters, and also between areas of low politics and high politics.

Chapter 2 focused on India's negotiation strategy. India's reputation in the first several decades after its independence was that of a prickly negotiator, always ready to play hardball even when bargaining from a position of weakness. Opinion today, however, is divided between those who believe that India's negotiation strategy is changing from strict distributive to integrative as its power rises, and others who maintain that India's negotiation strategy remains, and will remain, fundamentally distributive (irrespective of attempts by the established powers to include it at the high table of international negotiations). In the face of these divisions, the lessons of the Mahabharata offer a useful way of determining how deeply embedded the use of a distributive strategy actually is in India's negotiating culture, and thereby also the relative ease (or not) whereby it might be changed.

The stories in this chapter revealed a strong proclivity of all protagonists— heroes and villains, major characters, and minor characters—to use the distributive strategy as the dominant strategy. Interestingly, negotiations in the Mahabharata are approached often as a binary choice—resist or give in— rather than make use of the full distributive–integrative spectrum that allows more give and take. Integrative strategies are used only occasionally, usually when the individual faces particularly extreme circumstances and is subject to duress, and they do not often generate success. There is a greater likelihood of integrative strategies being used with negotiating partners who are regarded as allies or insiders (suggesting a differentiated view of responsibility towards insiders versus outsiders, with more willingness to bear the costs of free-riding and leadership with the former group), but even friends and allies are not exempt from being subject to some tough bargaining. A further useful insight from the stories is the importance of honour or face, which makes it difficult for individuals to back down after they have taken a particular position.

All these insights were reflected in the negotiation strategy used by India, both in the decades after its independence and even today as a rising power. We focused first on India's role in multilateral trade negotiations, which should have provided us with an 'easy' test case of India's transforming negotiation behaviour: the strict distributive strategy may have made sense in the era when the commitment to goals such as self-sufficiency was high, but it would surely make little sense in a system in which India now has increasing economic stakes (given its enmeshment in the global economy) as well as political stakes (given the recognition that it has come to receive in the WTO as a key player, and its invitations to all small-group consensus-building meetings in the organization). However, the empirical analysis revealed that India's distributive bargaining behaviour has persisted. The middle ground remains elusive, choices are often seen as highly polarized, and a strict adherence to a distributive negotiation strategy (even if it generates costs) is regarded as honourable and heroic rather than quixotic or disruptive.

The second issue area that we focused on was non-proliferation, where India's successful conclusion of the US–India agreement on civilian nuclear energy cooperation may be seen as a turn towards integrative bargaining behaviour. After all, India did agree to make concessions to the US, in return for acquiring de facto recognition by not just the US as a legitimate nuclear weapons state but, as a knock-on effect, by the Nuclear Suppliers Group and the international community at large. As the chapter argued, however, agreeing to make some bilateral concessions, while firmly refusing to get locked into any legally binding multilateral agreements (such as the NPT or the CTBT), in return for what is effectively a rewriting of the entire non-proliferation regime, can hardly be regarded as integrative bargaining. If anything, the case reinforces the lessons of the Mahabharata where negotiators play hardball until all their demands are accepted, and may then decide to make some small concessions thereafter. These limited integrative moves are further structured by a rising India in voluntary terms (such as the voluntary moratorium on testing, or the willingness to take on voluntary emissions restraints in climate change, or the tendency to keep applied tariffs in trade at a low level but ensure that bound rates remain high). While this distinction between bound and voluntary is not obvious in the context of the Mahabharata and represents an added feature of modern Indian diplomacy, the trend itself fits well with the general reluctance of its protagonists to willingly accept costly and binding concessions.

The third chapter investigated the issue of how Indian negotiators frame their demands and counter-demands in international bargaining. Drawing on other writings on this subject, we found that the Indian negotiating style is associated with prolixity and moralization. Neither characteristic has rendered it an easy negotiating partner for the West.

While the Mahabharata strongly reinforces the observations of prolixity and moralization, it also offers us some vital nuances. For example, in Western cultures the tendency to moralize is often associated with 'an element of aggression';[6] attempting to establish the high moral ground is hardly a strategy that one would use with one's friends. But in the Mahabharata, the use of long and detailed moral arguments is extended to friends and foes alike. In fact, both prolixity and moralization show a near universalism in the text, with heroes and villains, elders and juniors, and friends and foes using them liberally across different bargaining situations. Strategic arguments, in contrast, are resorted to infrequently. Interestingly, and perhaps in contrast to Western cultures where excessive moralization is seen as a sign of hostility, in the Mahabharata strategic arguments are made when dealing with particularly difficult, unscrupulous, and somewhat suspect opponents. This suggests that the more adversarial the relationship, the more likely it is that negotiators will combine strategic arguments with the default moral ones. Further, even though moralistic framing generates mixed results in the Mahabharata, negotiators continue to use this as the dominant strategy regardless. This suggests that the framing strategy may be used as a justification of one's behaviour to oneself, or possibly to allied or domestic audiences, rather than purely with intent to persuade the opponent. These insights shed new light on the bargaining behaviour of a rising India.

In the case of India's negotiations over international trade, the prolix and moralistic frame is a strongly dominant one, and shows consistency from the time when India was a relatively marginalized player in the GATT to the present, when it has emerged as an influential member of the WTO. In some of the particularly tough negotiations that have formed a part of the Doha Development Agenda, we do see a slant towards the greater use of more pragmatic and strategic frames, but this is almost always as an addition to the moralistic frame. We also see a differentiation in framing strategy depending on whom India is negotiating with: a prolix appeal to ethics and morals remains strong when dealing with other developing countries and Least Developed Countries (i.e. 'friends'), but pragmatism accompanies moralism when dealing with a disgruntled and demanding North.

On non-proliferation, we find that the appeal to moralism was especially high in the first few decades of independence. It is only when we get to India's

---

[6] Pye 1985, pp. 142–3.

negotiations with the US that we see a significant amount of pragmatism injected into its public justifications of the deal. This has led some analysts to argue that India has abandoned its old Third-Worldist moralism for a new and flexible pragmatism that befits a rising power. Somewhat counter-intuitively, our research suggests otherwise. A rising India that showed increasing resort to strategic arguments and justifications was not showing signs of socialization or an internalization of the language of the West; rather, facing a particularly hostile domestic audience, the government had little choice but to introduce the language of national interest and strategic gain to justify the deal. Indeed, going by the insights of the Mahabharata, it could even be argued that an increasing use of strategic framing suggests Indian perceptions of a more hostile negotiating environment with greater possibilities of confrontation.

Chapter 4 focused on coalition behaviour. As we summarize these findings, it is worth noting that the entire text of the Mahabharata is fundamentally one of coalition loyalty. Even the blackest of villainous characters in the text (such as Jayadratha) cannot be accused of defection or disloyalty. The specific questions that we addressed in this chapter were whether India forms issue-based or bloc-type coalitions, bandwagons or balances, and formal or informal alliances. The focus on three sets of coalition alignments makes this chapter the longest and most complex in the book. The summary below is necessarily a simplification.

India, in the first 50 years or so of its life as an independent and modern state, was actively involved in coalition formation. Most of these coalitions were bloc-type coalitions; negotiators showed a general preference for balancing rather than bandwagoning (with only extreme circumstances producing the occasional short-term bandwagoning behaviour); and while proactive in creating and participating in different types of coalitions, India seemed to steer clear of formal alliances. If a rising India were to show signs of increasing conformity with the West, we would expect to see the following changes in its coalition patterns: flexible issue-based coalitions, willingness to bandwagon with some of the established powers that might help preserve the system in which it has high and growing stakes,[7] and also a willingness to give up the discourse of non-alignment and embrace strategic alliances. A continuity in the old patterns would suggest otherwise. The evidence from the Mahabharata could help us mediate between these two extremes to explore which of these tendencies are well rooted in India's negotiating culture and which might be more susceptible to change.

---

[7] Recall, however, that the theoretical logic underpinning this second prediction is Constructivist; Realism suggests that as states grow in power, they will be under less pressure to bandwagon and have greater ability to balance.

The stories from the Mahabharata reveal the clearest data on the preference for balancing. Bandwagoning is consistently avoided by heroes and villains alike. On bloc-type versus issue-based coalitions, protagonists reveal a strong preference for the former type. Issue-based coalitions are attempted less frequently, and generate poor results. The preference for blocs, along with the low likelihood of defection, means that the coalitions are stable and long-lasting, but also inflexible and deadlock inducing. The data is the least clear on the formal versus informal axis, with only one story providing some indirect suggestions towards a preference for informal coalitions rather than formal alliances.

The preference for balancing is strongly borne out for India as it rises, and shows consistency with the preferences of India in the previous half century as well. It is interesting to note that in maintaining this consistency India defies both Realist and Constructivist logics, but fits well with the patterns illustrated in the Mahabharata. In international trade, for instance, India in the GATT formed coalitions with other developing countries that balanced against the North. It has continued to form coalitions in the WTO predominantly with other developing countries, which serve as important balancing forces against the developed countries, even though they are not explicitly referred to as South versus North coalitions. Blocs also continue to be the norm in the WTO as they were in the Mahabharata: even when focused on specific issues such as agriculture, they continue to bring together a heterogeneous group of developing countries, retain their developmental agenda, and engage in considerable logrolling. India contributes leadership to the maintenance of these coalitions, and even shows a readiness to incur costs for the longer-term collective good. A similar behaviour pattern can be observed in other issue-areas and regimes, including via India's participation in the BRICS group.

The non-proliferation regime, once again, serves as a potential exception. In Chapter 4, we highlighted the change in India's policy from being a warrior against 'nuclear apartheid' to a state that has entered into a special relationship with the US and acquired de facto recognition and legitimacy in the regime. This change is obviously a significant one. But in Chapter 4 we also highlighted reasons why this case might provide the exception to the norm, rather than an emerging trend in India's negotiation behaviour. Recall, therefore, the fact that the process and outcome of the agreement were both hotly contested domestically in India. Further, for all the bonhomie emanating from the two states that hailed each other as 'natural allies', there is little sign from India towards a deepening of the improved relations with the US into a formal, or even informal, alliance. The strategic partnership with the US remains a limited and carefully circumscribed arrangement. Moreover, India's commitment to alternative Third Worldist groupings persists, including those dating back to the Cold War era, such as the Non-Aligned Movement and the G77.

While Chapter 4 highlighted the deep-rooted continuities in India's coalition alignments, it also pointed to the differential impact of India's coalition diplomacy today in comparison with the first half-century after India's independence. This is because the coalitions that India now leads are 'strong' coalitions, which it is better able to sustain with its greater economic clout (in cooperation with other rising powers). These coalitions, while a source of empowerment for India and its allies, contribute to making the system more deadlock prone (especially when they are accompanied by the use of a strict distributive strategy and moralistic framing, as discussed in Chapters 2 and 3).

Chapter 5 studied the final negotiation variable: the conceptualization of time by India, and its impact on the country's bargaining behaviour. We began by noting the observations of other scholars on this subject, which together suggested at least two significant time-specific characteristics of India's negotiating culture: a powerful sense of history that manifests itself in international bargaining in several ways, and a readiness to accept delay in reaching agreement. Together, these features result in a low sensitivity of Indian negotiators to time constraints. While both characteristics were evidenced in the multilateral negotiations of an independent India (bar an initial phase of newly established independence), our task was to investigate if these characteristics are representative of a rising India's negotiations, and the extent to which they derive from India's traditional bargaining culture.

The lessons from the Mahabharata were clear. In story after story, we found the great reluctance of major and minor protagonists to make decisions or take actions in haste. In the few instances that such behaviour did take place, it was deemed to be foolhardy and rash, and generated significant costs. References to history (real or mythical) recur, which are used to justify one's actions and persuade the other party of the legitimacy of one's cause. Events are seldom treated as one-off episodes, but regarded as part of a long chain of events, which means that the pressures associated with endgames are considerably diminished in the Indian case. Time or Kala is often described as an inexorable, all-consuming force, which on some occasions is even seen as trumping Karma (the logic in such instances being that one is driven into a certain situation because of one's past actions, Karma, but those past actions in turn are determined by time, Kala). This translates partly into a fatalistic world view: why push for closure in a negotiation if time has already predetermined the right hour for decisions and actions? But the very important flip side of the same argument is that negotiators will be able to withstand pressures to close deals, and ignore imposed deadlines, if they are not satisfied with the timing or the content of the deal on offer. Both views make for an agreement-averse system. But it is the latter, dynamic and action-oriented, side of the argument that we see frequently in a rising India's readiness to block certain agreements (rather than the fatalistic one). The refrain of 'no deal is better than a bad deal' is rooted here.

As Chapter 5 argued, India's recent negotiations in the WTO reflect all the time-related insights summarized above. References to a history of previous negotiations, and the unfairness of previous deals, are frequently used to explain and justify tactics of delay. Particularly interesting has been the willingness of key Indian negotiators to publicly commit to the acceptability of a delayed outcome in the Doha negotiations, and also signal the willingness to walk away from the negotiation. While Indian negotiators are reviled abroad for their contribution to delaying an agreement, they are lauded as heroes in their own country for showing circumspection, caution, and courage in standing up to pressures to conclude a potentially unsatisfactory deal in a hurry. In other regimes too, we found Indian negotiators show the same caution and the notion of the *longue durée* as they were wont to do in the Mahabharata.

The one possible exception—perhaps even a new trend—that we did have available to us was in the area of non-proliferation. It could perhaps be argued that after decades of fighting the cause of universal disarmament, India showed uncharacteristic haste in signing the deal with the US (negotiations for which began in 2005 and were concluded in 2008). However, on closer examination, we found several caveats against assuming that this case presents even a straightforward exception to the norm, let alone a fundamental change in the approach to time. First, the deal was largely a top-down deal; limited involvement of the various echelons of the bureaucratic establishment made it atypical and unrepresentative of Indian diplomacy. Second, the idea of a 'halfway house' for India had a long gestation period—at least 20 years, according to Stephen Cohen.[8] Recall further the patient and firm diplomacy that India exercised in the aftermath of Pokhran II, and in the face of extreme pressures, which provided an important prelude to the eventual negotiation of the 123 agreement. Third, admittedly, a negotiation process lasting three years to complete such a deal was short. But the severity of domestic criticism that this speedy process attracted shows just how much it was seen as an unacceptable deviation from established practice. Finally, even after having secured a deal on very favourable terms, India's opposition to signing key agreements of the regime remains unchanged. It was in no hurry earlier to sign the NPT or the CTBT, even when the pressures to do so were high, and it is certainly in no such hurry now, after it has gained de facto recognition in the regime.

It is worth noting that the first three variables (negotiation strategy, framing, and coalitions) showed a variation depending on one's own negotiating partner. This was the case in the Mahabharata and was fully reinforced in the case of a rising India. Hence, for example, we saw that though a strict distributive strategy is the norm, integrative moves are used either when one

---

[8] S. Cohen 2006.

has no other alternative left or when one is negotiating with friends. While moralistic framing is universally used, it is combined with strategic framing when dealing with adversaries or particularly difficult opponents. Coalitions are formed readily with smaller and weaker players, in other words developing countries in modern times, but balances are the norm against stronger parties. This variation is important because it suggests that India may be more willing to incur the costs of responsibility and leadership in certain groups than others. Interestingly, however, the time variable occurs with consistency in negotiations with most parties and across most regimes.

Besides offering us insights into the four negotiation variables that we started out with, the Mahabharata also offered us several additional insights. These become especially important if we are to try to understand India's negotiating culture on its own terms, rather than restrict ourselves to the frames that we started out with.

First, we found across several of the chapters (particularly Chapter 2, but also 3 and 4), negotiators in the Mahabharata attached great value to an honour code. The nature of this honour code varies and depends on one's position in society (the Kshatriyas' honour code is different from that of the Brahmins', for instance), and also between individuals (Yudhishthira, in the story in Chapter 4, appealed to the family honour when launching the rescue mission to save Duryodhana, whereas Duryodhana contemplated suicide because he believed that his honour code as a Kshatriya had been violated; also in Chapter 4, we saw that Duryodhana sought victory in the war when he approached Krishna and chose his armies, while Arjuna sought renown and chose Krishna himself). But if negotiation positions are assumed on the grounds of an honour code, it naturally makes a climbdown from these positions rather difficult. Combine these with the use of a distributive strategy, moralistic framing, and a culture that attaches considerable value to coalition loyalty, and we end up with an inflexible but heroic negotiator, who one cannot help but admire despite the fact that he/she contributes to making the system more agreement averse.

Second, we find that the Mahabharata shows us that even though its protagonists are reluctant to make concessions, and all too ready to accept and even cause delays, the occasional voluntary and unilateral concessions on one's own terms are more acceptable. Hence, for instance, Dronacharya's willingness to teach Ekalavya some new skills in archery in Chapter 2, after extracting a terrible price from him; or indeed Karna's unilateral and voluntary promise to Kunti that he would target only Arjuna and spare the other Pandava brothers in Chapter 4; or Bhishma's self-imposed vow of celibacy in Chapter 2, and his promise not to fight Shikhandi in Chapter 5. We see this reflected in modern negotiations too, where India has shown reluctance to accept binding multilateral commitments in various issue areas, but has willingly taken on voluntary commitments (including low applied tariff rates, voluntary emissions restraints in climate change, and a voluntary moratorium on nuclear testing in non-proliferation).

Third, on three of the four variables, we see a clear differentiation in how protagonists behave between those whom they regard as friends versus those whom they see as neutrals or adversaries. Adherence to coalitions, moreover, means that these categories are not fluid or flexible (recall, for instance, Karna's refusal to abandon Duryodhana in the face of many moral and material temptations), notwithstanding modern-day rhetoric about fluid and flexible coalitions. This means that while a rising India is likely to continue to be a valuable and stable ally, it will not be easily won over by countries with which it has traditionally maintained a distance. The case of India's deal with the US is illustrative of this. Bar a few public declarations of support (such as a shared commitment against terrorism), India's partnership with the US on civilian nuclear energy remains just that. It has not evolved into a closer relationship that takes the shape of an alliance.

Fourth, the findings in the four chapters, along with the additional insights presented above, together shed new light on India's notion of responsibility and leadership. A rising India has come under considerable criticism for its reluctance to bear the costs of providing global public goods (such as free trade, climate change mitigation, or nuclear non-proliferation). Xenia Dormandy, for instance, writes, 'the government has been less enthusiastic about participating in burden-sharing mechanisms . . . India's willingness to devote resources to international objectives that do not directly benefit its people in clear and concrete ways is . . . in doubt.'[9] While this is true at the level of global public goods, our research has also illustrated the admirable willingness, even fervour, with which protagonists in the Mahabharata come to the rescue of family, allies, and indeed those whom they deem deserving of help, or if they believe the cause to be worthy of support. Similarly, we find that a rising India, while reluctant to make the concessions necessary to secure the provision of public goods, has been unhesitating in its willingness to provide certain club goods, such as coalition unity (which can be an expensive task as it requires logrolling the agendas of weaker players, allowing free-riding, funding research initiatives, and facilitating side payments to keep weaker players on board). It has also shown itself to be a relatively more willing player in entering into cooperative arrangements with other developing countries. Our research thus suggests that Indian negotiators define their responsibilities rather differently from what their Western counterparts expect of them. What this means is that India cannot be called an irresponsible power on the rise, but a power that believes it owes—and exercises—its responsibility in the provision of small-group club goods rather than global public goods.[10]

---

[9] Dormandy 2007.
[10] Early variants of this argument are to be found in Narlikar 2011 and Narlikar 2013.

6.3. POLICY RECOMMENDATIONS

An important contribution of this book has been to highlight the cultural roots of India's bargaining behaviour. India's continued adherence to distributive bargaining, moralizing, steadfast coalition loyalties, and readiness to cause delay, even as its power rises and its stakes in the system increase, may make little sense without reference to the importance of continuities in its negotiation culture. But if culture is such a dominant variable, which explains India's negotiation behaviour as a rising power, what scope for manoeuvre do outside parties have if they wish to negotiate more effectively with India? The question is an important one for India's negotiating partners seeking to secure deals on better terms for themselves. It is critical for those concerned with the maintenance of multilateral cooperation, which can no longer remain the burden of the declining hegemon and requires the effective and constructive participation and commitment of India (and other rising powers). In this final section, we highlight the implications of this research for facilitating more constructive engagement with India. We also suggest ways in which Indian negotiators can use their negotiation culture to their advantage in various multilateral dealings.

6.3.1. Policy recommendations for India's negotiating partners

The focus of this book has been on a rising India's negotiation behavior in multilateral regimes. India's relations with other developing countries have been relatively smooth in the multilateral context, but the West has historically found India to be a more challenging negotiating partner to work with. The recommendations in this subsection are thus targeted mainly at negotiators representing the established powers.

The first step towards more effective negotiation with India lies in an improved understanding of India's bargaining positions on their own terms, rather than simply a reflection of offers and counter-offers made within a Western frame. Other works have pointed out that cultural variation matters;[11] our book shows just how much it can matter with specific reference to India.

Second, all four variables, both in the Mahabharata as well as modern-day negotiations of India post-independence and as a rising power, reveal that India is not the sort of power that will be easily socialized. Its dominant negotiation strategy is, after all, distributive, and has been consistently so for a very long time. Its tendency to moralize makes it difficult for it to climb

---

[11] R. Cohen 2004; Salacuse 2004.

down from the positions that it adopts. Its loyalty to coalitions involving other developing countries makes it difficult for it to barter concessions that might be seen as a sell-out by its allies. And its profound sense of history and long view of time together make it resistant to urgent deadlines, and give it relative ease (in comparison to some Western cultures) to walk away from a negotiation. Had Western negotiators been aware of these cultural traits in recent negotiations, perhaps they might not have been quite as shocked and surprised by India's role in the Doha negotiations, or by India's refusal to sign the multilateral treaties of the non-proliferation regime (even though considerable effort has been made in both regimes to accommodate and produce buy-in from India). The current strategy to engage India by giving it more voice at the negotiating table will not be enough to persuade it either to accept the demands of the West or to bear an increasing share of the burden of providing international public goods.

Third, awareness of the cultural roots of India's bargaining behaviour would also help Western negotiators recognize that some of the traits that they have long been 'irritated' by do not necessarily signal hostile intent,[12] but are a part of a long-established negotiating tradition in a nation where memories die hard. For example, the tendency to moralize, as the lessons of the Mahabharata revealed, is not restricted to dealing with opponents whom one regards as hostile, but is universally used with friends and foes and serves as a legitimizing device perhaps even to oneself. Similarly, in a culture that frowns upon 'unseemly haste',[13] attempts to rush deals through by pressurizing its negotiators with urgent deadlines are likely to be counterproductive. An understanding of such bargaining traits reduces the possibilities of misperception when negotiating with India.

Fourth, one way in which the West could engage with India on its own terms would be to take its moralizing discourse more seriously, and also to make use of India's willingness to accept the burdens of responsibility and leadership in certain contexts but not in others. Indian negotiators have reiterated privately and publicly that their reluctance to contribute to the provision of certain public goods stems from their fundamental questioning of the value of the public goods on offer. Shyam Saran writes on this with considerable eloquence:

> The activism of India or other emerging countries on certain regional and international issues may not always be aligned with that of the Western countries. This does not make such activism irresponsible, just as lack of enthusiasm for

---

[12] Stephen Cohen, for instance, has written that Western diplomats were for long 'irritated by the style of Indian diplomats. While professional and competent, they seemed compelled to lecture their British or American counterparts on the evils of the cold war, the moral superiority of India's policies, or the greatness of its civilization . . .' S. Cohen 2001, p. 66.
[13] Salacuse 2004.

Western actions on certain issues, which India from its standpoint may consider injudicious, also cannot be criticised as irresponsible conduct . . . The same argument can be made about the global financial and trading systems, which have been put in place and are dominated by the industrialized economies of the West. . . . If the emerging countries have been able to achieve rapid growth in their economies, they have been able to do so despite the constraints imposed on them by the global economic and financial systems rather than because of them. The sub-text here is that since the existing regimes have enabled the emerging economies to develop, they should acquiesce in the rules and regulations set by the Western countries rather than seek to modify or alter them. This is not a valid assumption. There may be rules that emerging economies may find acceptable. There may be others they may want to see modified so as to reflect their interests.[14]

This is a fair point. The West would be well served by engaging directly with such arguments, and ask India which public goods it might be willing to accept the costs for, if not these public goods, and which rules would it be willing to uphold, if not these rules. When India uses the strategy of 'Just say no' and threatens to walk away from a negotiation, it should be asked what alternative agreement India would be willing to abide by that also takes into account the interests of other sets of actors. In fact, as one of us has argued elsewhere, the reform of international organizations could be made conditional on India, and other rising powers, pinpointing what credible and achievable visions of global order they bring to the negotiating table, and how far they are willing to go in sustaining an order reformed along such lines.[15] Such an idea of 'Reform-for-Responsibility', or R4R, would also fit in with an idea that came up in Chapter 3 regarding the link between conceptualization of moral duty and social stratification. In keeping with this link, it would seem reasonable to argue that as rising powers move up the international hierarchy, they might be expected to redefine their responsibilities from the small group to the large, and from club good provision (along with domestic development) to the provision of global public goods.

All that said, alterations in negotiation behaviour by India's negotiating counterparts will ultimately only go so far. India's big bargaining advantage—and also a liability if it wishes to be taken seriously as a potential Great Power—is that it finds it relatively easy to walk away from a negotiation (Chapter 6), and in fact avoid the give and take that underpin integrative bargaining, and instead live with offers made on a take-it-or-leave-it basis (Chapter 2). To really get India to engage in the type of bargaining that the

---

[14] Saran 2012.
[15] This idea is discussed in Narlikar 2013. Such an idea would represent a significant departure from current policy, where regimes such as trade and non-proliferation have been reformed to accommodate India in the hope of producing greater buy-in. Such buy-in has not occurred thus far, which suggests that the alternative strategy may be worth a serious try.

fourth recommendation suggests (e.g. over R4R) will also require some changes from the Indian side.

6.3.2. Policy recommendations for Indian negotiators

This book has illustrated India's negotiation behaviour, the cultural values and practices that underpin it, and also the flak that Indian negotiators have received for it in recent times. While the costs of social opprobrium can be high in an international system that attaches at least some value to norms such as legitimacy, India's resilience to pressures has generated an interesting mix of results. In the GATT, it is true that India often ended up with the 'sucker's payoff' in past negotiations, having defended the coalition's position with much moral eloquence and firm naysaying, then finding itself isolated in the endgame. But in the WTO, as a rising power, it has carved a place for itself at the high table of multilateral negotiations, where it has become a leader of strong coalitions that are a further source of its empowerment. It may not have achieved the goals it would have liked thus far in terms of a trade deal, but it has managed at least to delay an agreement on bad terms. In the non-proliferation regime, India's refusal to compromise has been clearly rewarded with its acceptance and legitimization in the regime as a recognized de facto nuclear weapons state. It could thus be argued that India plays hardball not only because its bargaining culture leads it to act thus, but also because it has not been given clear incentives to alter its behaviour. This is where ideas such as R4R might help in prompting more cooperation from India, when simply offering it more voice and influence in various multilateral forums has not worked. But as some of our findings suggest, this may not be as straightforward as one might think.

Recall from Chapter 2 India's persistent use of the distributive strategy, both by protagonists in the Mahabharata and also by Indian negotiators post-independence and in recent times. One of the insights of the Mahabharata was that Indian negotiators seldom make use of the range of strategy options on the distributive–integrative scale, and instead view the negotiation as a binary choice of resist or surrender. This means that negotiators find it difficult to manage the kind of give and take that the implementation of ideas such as R4R requires. There is admittedly considerable beauty in finding a negotiating culture where not everything can be traded and bargained over. But the existence of such values, especially when they are represented by a country of India's size and potential power, can be particularly detrimental in reaching agreements. The costs that accrue to the system are significant. India's aspirations as a rising power that wants to be taken seriously (e.g. via a permanent seat in the UN Security Council, or more votes in the Bretton Woods institutions) also take a battering, and decrease its credibility as a potential Great Power that can assume responsible leadership. For India to be able to engage successfully and constructively with the established powers, a fundamental change in its mindset may be necessary. The most important change will involve a willingness to engage in a genuine give and take, and thereby find creative solutions based on integrative bargaining. But negotiating mindsets and cultures are seldom easy to rewrite, so we suggest four additional, more feasible strategies whereby India could garner an advantage in its negotiations in the short and medium term.

First, it is not just India's negotiating counterparts who could benefit from learning about the cultural sources of India's negotiation behaviour; more self-awareness by Indian negotiators on this will make them more effective in signalling their intent and deal-breakers to outside parties. A good example of this is the time variable, where India's references to its history and public proclamations on its willingness to accept delay could be better packaged, so that they are seen for what they generally are: caution in a bureaucratic culture rather than a malicious desire to disrupt negotiations.

Second, the framing variable continues to be an important one in India's negotiations, much as it was in India's recent, distant, and also mythical past. As Chapter 3 pointed out, the appeal to morality often goes beyond being a framing device and actually comes to condition the content of the negotiation. Indian negotiators here would be well served to identify which particular principles of global order—possibly alternative to existing Western ones— underlie their normative frames, and how they might be translated into a negotiating advantage of greater agenda-setting power. They would have to meet a feasibility and applicability test (so, for example, professing a commitment to pluralism or international equality would not suffice on its own, nor would a vision of global order that expects the developed world to make all the concessions and the rising powers and other developing countries none).

Third, when Indian negotiators are blamed for not taking on international responsibilities in keeping with the rising power of their country, they could point easily to the many alternative responsibilities that India has already taken on, historically and today.[16]

Fourth, while culture is a key factor that affects the negotiation process, it is not a static influence. This book has illustrated the continuities in India's bargaining behaviour, but has also pointed to some important changes in recent times. A good example is the increasing turn to strategic and pragmatic framing of arguments (as was argued in Chapter 3). Even though these usually

---

[16] Admittedly, the effect of providing certain club goods, as India does, is mixed. On the one hand, club goods such as the unity of Southern coalitions or conditionality-free aid, detract from the provision of global public goods by rendering multilateral agreement more difficult. On the other hand, however, they are a valuable source of empowerment not just for India but also its allies in the developing world. And they can also improve the legitimacy of the system by offering greater voice to its diverse players.

appear as additional to the moralistic frames rather than as a substitute, and occur more in confrontational relationships and environments, this is a significant development in its own right and also its potential implication. Moralistic framing usually makes it difficult for negotiators to climb down from publicly declared positions; strategic framing, however, does not bind negotiators in the same way. Thus, somewhat paradoxically, even though India may be adopting more strategic framing because it perceives the particular opponent or context to be antagonistic, it may create opportunities for more conciliatory behaviour by India in the long run.

This book has illustrated the important continuities in India's negotiating culture, many of which have persisted in spite of major political, economic, and technological changes, internally and externally. Even in cases where we see some elements of change in India's bargaining behaviour (as illustrated in the last paragraph), the roots of India's negotiating culture provide a useful baseline against which such changes might be assessed. While our book has focused on only one of the country cases that forms a part of the global power transition of today, we believe that similar studies of the ancestry of other negotiating cultures can provide vital complements to this one. If the global power transition continues along its current lines, we are likely to see the emergence of a significantly more pluralistic core of countries across different multilateral regimes. To ensure that diplomats from these diverse states do not repeatedly end up talking at cross purposes with each other and with those representing the established powers, more studies on the negotiating cultures of the non-Western rising powers will have to become essential reading for all those involved in the theory and practice of diplomacy and global governance.

REFERENCES

Blaker, Michael. 1977. *Japanese International Negotiating Style*. New York: Columbia University Press.

Cohen, Raymond. 2004. *Negotiating across Cultures: International Communication* in an Interdependent World. Washington DC: United States Institute of Peace Press (second revised edition).

Cohen, Stephen. 2001. *India: Emerging Power*. Washington DC: Brookings Institution.

Cohen, Stephen. 2006. A Deal too Far? Research Paper, Brookings Insitution, 26 February. Accessed at <http://www.brookings.edu/research/papers/2006/02/28india-cohen> on 3 April 2013.

Dormandy, Xenia. 2007. 'Is India, or Will It Be, A Responsible Stakeholder?' *Washington Quarterly*, 30:3, 2007, 117–30.

Faure, Guy Olivier. 1998. Negotiation: The Chinese Concept. *The Negotiation Journal*, 14:2, April, 137–48.

Faure, Guy Olivier and William Zartman eds. 1993. *Culture and Negotiation: The Resolution of Water Disputes*. Thousand Oaks, CA: Sage Publications.

Ikenberry, John. 2008. The Rise of China and the Future of the West. *Foreign Affairs*, 27:1, January–February, 23–57.

Malone, David. 2011. *Does the Elephant Dance?* Oxford: Oxford University Press.

Mearsheimer, John. 2006. China's Unpeaceful Rise. *Current History*, 105:690, 16–162.

Mohan, C. Raja. 2003. *Crossing the Rubicon: The Shaping of India's Foreign Policy*. Delhi: Viking.

Mohan, C. Raja. 2006. *Impossible Allies: Nuclear India, United States and the Global Order*. New Delhi: India Research Press.

Mohan, C. Raja. 2010. Rising India: Partner in Shaping the Global Commons? *The Washington Quarterly*, 33:3, 133–48.

Narlikar, Amrita. 2006. Peculiar Chauvinism or Strategic Calculation: Explaining the Negotiating Strategy of a Rising India. *International Affairs*, 82:1, January, 59–76.

Narlikar, Amrita. 2011. Is India a Responsible Great Power? *Third World Quarterly*, 32:9, October, 1607–21.

Narlikar, Amrita. 2013. India Rising: Responsible to Whom? *International Affairs*, 89:3, May, 595–614.

Perkovich, George. 2003. Is India a Major Power? *The Washington Quarterly*, 27:1, 129–44.

Pye, Lucien. 1985. *Asian Power and Politics: The Cultural Dimensions of Authority*. Cambridge, MA: Belknap Press.

Salacuse, Jeswald. 2004. The Top Ten Ways in which Culture can affect your Negotiation. *Ivey Business Journal*, September–October, 1–6.

Saran, Shyam. 2012. The Evolving Role of Emerging Economies in Global Governance: An Indian Perspective. 7 June. Accessed at <http://www.ficci.com/EmergingEconomiesPaper-shyam-saran.pdf> on 6 April 2013.

The Story of the Mahabharata in Brief

The core story of the Mahabharata revolves around the rivalry between two sets of royal cousins: the Pandavas and the Kauravas. Both were descendants of the Bharata clan. Their 'grandsire' Bhishma had taken a vow of celibacy out of a sense of filial duty. In the same clan were born two sons, Dhritarashtra and Pandu. Dhritarashtra, though the elder son, was blind, and agreed to pass his right of kingship to his brother Pandu.

Pandu was unable to father children, but, owing to a boon received by his wife, Kunti, had five sons fathered by the gods, each endowed with special blessings and qualities. Yudhishthira the virtuous was the son of Dharma himself. Bhima the strong was the son of the god of wind. Arjuna the brave had Indra, the king of the gods, as his father. The twins, Nakula and Sahadeva, were the sons of the Ashwini Kumar twins, the physicians of the gods. The five brothers came to be known as the Pandavas. They were married to the beautiful and wise princess of Panchala, Draupadi. Unknown to Pandu or his sons, the Pandavas had an elder brother, Karna. He had been born to Kunti out of wedlock, fathered by Surya, the sun god, and had been abandoned immediately after his birth. He was adopted by a humble charioteer, and for much of his life was derided as a sutaputra, and also believed himself to be none other than the son of a charioteer.

Dhritarashtra, the blind king, had a hundred sons; they were known as the Kauravas. The eldest was Duryodhana. Extremely courageous and loyal to his friends, but misguided and headstrong, he was driven by his hatred of the Pandavas.

All the princes grew up together under Bhishma's tutelage, and received the best possible training in martial skills from the Brahmin warrior, Drona. Drona was an extraordinary archer and teacher, and came to be known by the title of Dronacharya (*acharya* meaning teacher). His only child, Ashwatthama, received the same training from Drona as his princely students, and became as distinguished a warrior as the Pandavas and the Kauravas.

The rivalry between the two sets of cousins grew over the years, and took the shape of jealousy and hatred on the part of the Kauravas against their five cousins. This hatred took a vicious turn when the Kaurava brothers tried to poison Bhima, and also attempted to set fire to the dwelling of the Pandavas and their mother in the forest. The Pandavas bore these excesses with much endurance and patience, and they came to enjoy the sympathy and advice of Krishna—a cousin of the Pandavas from their mother's side: a Yadava king, but also an incarnation of Lord Vishnu (the preserver in the Hindu trinity).

To mark the completion of the princes' education, Dronacharya arranged a demonstration of their skills in an open competition. Arjuna's skills appeared to be invincible and he became the popular favourite, much to the chagrin of Duryodhana and his brothers. At this point, Karna—a handsome stranger and unknown to anyone except Kunti to be of royal lineage—arrived on the scene and challenged Arjuna. The Pandavas ridiculed him for his humble birth and refused to fight him on the grounds that he was not Arjuna's social equal. Duryodhana immediately befriended him, and anointed him as the King of Anga. He thereby won Karna's undying loyalty. In fact, even after Karna was told that he was the eldest brother of the Pandavas, he remained Duryodhana's most loyal ally, and died fighting on the side of the Kauravas.

Dhritarashtra initially attempted to avert the inevitable war by sending the Pandavas away from Hastinapur on the pretext that they could build their own kingdom elsewhere. They were granted one of the most desolate and uninhabitable parts of the kingdom. The Pandavas, through their determination and hard work, managed to transform this desolate area into the most beautiful capital city of Indraprastha, which included a remarkable palace of illusions.

Duryodhana was filled with jealousy at the Pandava success, and resolved to cheat them out of all their hard-earned possessions through a rigged dice game. Not unexpectedly, given the rigged dice, Yudhishthira lost not only the Pandava share of the kingdom, but also surrendered his own freedom, and the freedom of his brothers and wife. The Pandavas and Draupadi were subject to terrible humiliation in the royal assembly, prompting many inauspicious omens and the condemnation of all the wisest elders. Even Dhritarashtra began to feel remorse for the treatment that Duryodhana and his brothers had inflicted on the Pandavas. He restored their freedom and their kingdom. But upon Duryodhana's insistence, Yudhishthira was invited back for a rematch. The stake was still high: the losers would spend 12 years in exile in the forest, and another year incognito in an inhabited city or town; if the losers were discovered in the 13th year, they would have to spend another 12 years in exile. Once again, Yudhishthira lost the dice game, and in keeping with the terms of the agreement left with his brothers and wife for the forest. In exile, the Pandavas endured many hardships; but they still used their time judiciously in cultivating allies and acquiring many divine weapons, which would prove indispensable to them during the war.

The Pandavas returned to Hastinapur 13 years later to reclaim their part of the kingdom. Duryodhana, however, had no intention of keeping his side of the bargain. War seemed imminent. Krishna laboured hard to mediate between the two sides and avert the impending war. His mission failed largely because of Duryodhana's firm refusal to give the Pandavas even such a minuscule portion of land on which the point of a needle could stand. Both sides appealed to Krishna for his assistance. Duryodhana chose Krishna's vast and powerful armies, while Arjuna chose the person of Krishna himself. Krishna had vowed not to participate actively in the war but agreed to serve as Arjuna's charioteer. Hostilities broke out, and both sides knew that this war would be massively destructive and costly.

Standing on the battlefield of Kurukshetra, with both armies facing each other, Arjuna was struck with remorse at the thought of killing his brethren and elders in battle, and laid down his arms. To show him the path of righteous action, Krishna delivered the sermon of the Bhagwad Gita. Thus reminded of his duty, and cognizant of the implications of the war for Dharma, Arjuna now entered the fray in full force.

The war lasted for 18 days. Duryodhana had the most illustrious warriors and distinguished elders fighting at his side (including Bhishma, Drona, Karna, and Ashwatthama). The Pandavas also had brave warriors on their side, and the blessing of Krishna. The sides were well matched, and fought with great courage. Although the rules of war were clearly laid out by Bhishma, neither side could resist resorting to deceit and foul play to gain an upper hand. Thus were some of the mightiest warriors of the Bharata race destroyed. The Kauravas incurred massive losses, and were defeated in battle. Duryodhana himself was killed in a duel with Bhishma, who administered a below-the-belt blow to his thigh. Ashwatthama went on a killing spree to avenge the death of his father and friends in the middle of the night, thereby violating the most basic rules of war. Ultimately, there were only three survivors from the Kaurava side—Ashwatthama (who was cursed to roam the earth for 3,000 years, afflicted with disease and wounds), Kripacharya, and Kritavarma. On the winning Pandava side too, the losses were heavy; survivors included the brothers themselves, Krishna, and Satyaki.

Yudhishthira ruled the kingdom for 36 years. Duryodhana's mother, grief struck, blamed Krishna for his failure to avert the war, and laid a curse that his entire clan would be similarly destroyed in internecine strife. Krishna himself was mistaken for a wild animal and killed by a huntsman. The powers of the Pandavas gradually drifted away, and they decided to make their final journey to heaven. All the Pandavas gradually fell by the wayside on this journey, except for Yudhishthira, who was accompanied by a dog throughout the journey. On his arrival at the gates of heaven, Yudhishthira was welcomed, but the dog was refused entry. The son of Dharma willingly turned down heaven for himself on the grounds that it was being denied to his faithful companion. This turned out to be a test, which Yudhishthira passed admirably. Ultimately, Yudhishthira was united with his kinsmen in heaven.

A Note of Explanation about the Sanskrit References

For those new to the Mahabharata, a brief explanation of the Sanskrit references in this book might be useful.

In each of the ten episodes per chapter that we have recounted in Chapters 2–5, we have also offered some relevant Sanskrit verses to help convey a more holistic sense of the story. In general, for the original Sanskrit verses, we have referred to the Critical Edition from the Bhandarkar Institute's Critical Edition (commonly regarded as the most authoritative version of the Mahabharata). On occasion, where we have used an alternative edition by the Gita Press (which includes stories that were excluded from the Critical Edition as later additions to the original, but remain valuable for our purposes for several reasons, including their hold on the popular imagination). But the Critical Edition presents the default in our references; we specify whenever we use the Gita Press edition. In both instances, we have used our own translations from the original Sanskrit.

We have deliberately avoided using diacritical marks in English transliterations of Sanksrit names and words to facilitate accessibility of the account.

The references to the original verses appear in the following form: I.1.1. The Roman numeral refers to one of the 18 volumes of the Mahabharata, the first Arabic numeral refers to the chapter number, and the second Arabic numeral refers to the specific verse within the chapter.

For ease of reference, we provide a list below of the 18 volumes in accordance with their serial numbers.

Volume Number	Title of Volume	Theme of Volume
I	Adi Parva	Background including stories of the ancestors of the Kauravas and Pandavas
II	Sabha Parva	The Politics of the Royal Assembly
III	Vana Parva (also known as Aranyaka Parva)	The 12 years of exile
IV	Virata Parva	13th year spent incognito
V	Udyog Parva	Effort to avert war
VI	Bhishma Parva	First 10 days of the 18-day war with the Kaurava army under the command of Bhishma
VII	Drona Parva	Day 11 to Day 15 of the war with the Kaurava army under the command of Dronacharya
VIII	Karna Parva	Days 16 and 17 of the war with the Kaurava army under the command of Karna

IX	Shalya Parva	Day 18 of the war with the Kaurava army under the command of Shalya
X	Sauptika Parva	Immediate aftermath of the war, with Ashwatthama's attack on the sleeping Pandava camp
XI	Stree Parva	The mourning of the war dead by the women
XII	Shanti Parva	The establishment of peace and Bhishma's philosophical discourse to a victorious but dejected Yudhishthira
XIII	Anushasana Parva	Bhishma's discourse on the duties of kingship to Yudhishthira
XIV	Ashwamedhik Parva	The horse sacrifice by the Pandavas
XV	Ashramavasik Parva	The departure of the elders into the forest for Vanaprastha stage
XVI	Mausala Parva	Internecine war in Krishna's clan
XVII	Mahaprasthanika Parva	The final journey by the Pandavas
XVIII	Swargarohana Parva	The ascent to heaven by the Pandavas

Index